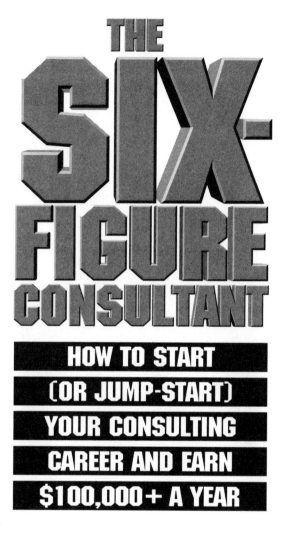

THE SIX-FIGURE CONSULTANT

HOW TO START (OR JUMP-START) YOUR CONSULTING CAREER AND EARN $100,000+ A YEAR

ROBERT W. BLY

Upstart
Publishing Company®
Specializing in Small Business Publishing
a division of Dearborn Publishing Group, Inc.

Acquisitions Editor: Danielle Egan-Miller
Managing Editor: Jack Kiburz
Interior Design: Lucy Jenkins
Cover Design: DePinto Studios
Typesetting: Debra Lenyoun

Published by Upstart Publishing Company®,
a division of Dearborn Publishing Group, Inc.

Printed in the United States of America

98 99 00 10 9 8 7 6 5 4 3 2 1

Library of Congress Cataloging-in-Publication Data

Bly, Robert W.
    The six-figure consultant : how to start (or jump-start) your
consulting career and earn $100,000+ a year / Robert W. Bly.
        p. cm.
    Includes index.
    ISBN 1-57410-120-X
    1. Business consultants—Vocational guidance—United States.
I. Title.
HD69.C6B574   1998   98-28295
001'.023'73—dc21   CIP

Dedication

To Rob Gilbert

Dedication

To Rob Gilbert

Contents

Acknowledgments

Thanks to my agent Bonita Nelson, for finding the right publisher for this book. And to my editor, Danielle Egan-Miller, for making the book you're reading much better than it was when the manuscript first crossed her desk.

Days when I have seen my vision are glorious beads on the chain of my life; the others are drab unbrightened stones.
—Sigurd Olson

Where the needs of the world and your talents cross, there lies your vocation.
—Aristotle

I believe that all people have a spiritual reason for being and that our world is incomplete until each one of us discovers it.
—Richard J. Leider, *The Purpose of Power*

Introduction

Today is the best time to be a consultant—and the most challenging.

It's the best because the demand for consultants in all fields is booming, with organizations throughout the world paying more than $50 billion a year for consulting services.

Consulting is a growth industry. According to an article in *Business Week* (July 25, 1994, page 61), AT&T spent $347.1 million on consulting services in 1993. Arthur Andersen, one of the largest consulting firms, employs 22,500 consultants.

Many successful consultants in solo and small practices now earn $100,000 to $300,000 or more annually. There are approximately 70,000 consulting firms in the United States employing more than 230,000 consultants.

It's the most challenging time to be a consultant because, in this era of corporate downsizing and high white-collar unemployment, more and more people are getting into consulting, flooding the market and making the consulting business more competitive than ever before. According to a survey conducted by Philip G. Ryan, a New York–based outplacement firm, 86 percent of dismissed executives are "seriously considering" going the entrepreneurial route.

Small businesses now employ about half the workforce and generate about half of the gross domestic product. And one-third of new businesses today are run out of homes.

The Six-Figure Consultant: How to Start (or Jump-Start) Your Consulting Career and Earn $100,000+ a Year presents proven strategies—based on real-life experience—that can "jump-start" any consultant's career, whether he or she is just getting started or is an old pro. It presents step-by-step, specific instructions that can mean the difference between being a consultant who earns $100,000 a year or more and being a consultant who is just getting by, wondering where the next assignment is coming from.

The Six-Figure Consultant is a practical guide to consulting. You will learn how to investigate the consulting profession, decide whether to become a consultant, get started, set up your practice, market and sell your services, get clients, render services, keep clients satisfied, run your office, maximize your productivity, computerize your operation, and expand into new profit centers.

The book is richly illustrated with visuals showing actual materials used by successful consultants in their practices including: sample contracts, letters of agreement, sales letters, brochures and fliers, inquiry tracking forms, needs assessment forms, press announcements, ads, correspondence, proposals, and more.

I do have one favor to ask. If you have a management or marketing tactic that has worked particularly well for your consulting practice, why not send it to me so I can share it with readers of the next edition? You will receive full credit, of course. You can reach me at:

Bob Bly
The Center for Technical Communication
22 E. Quackenbush Avenue
Dumont, NJ 07628
phone: 201-385-1220
fax: 201-385-1138
e-mail: rwbly@bly.com
Web site: www.bly.com

1

What Is "Consulting" and
What Do Consultants Do?

What Is "Consulting"?

The American Heritage dictionary defines *consultant* as "a person who gives expert or professional advice." More cynically, Dilbert creator Scott Adams writes in his book *The Dilbert Principle* (HarperBusiness, 1996, page 151), "A consultant is a person who takes your money and annoys your employees while tirelessly searching for the best way to extend the consulting contract."

Others are even more critical of the consulting profession. Alan Farnham, writing in *Fortune* (October 14, 1996, page 119), says: "Quietly, without fanfare, the advice business has been hijacked. New gurus armed with nothing more than pens, podiums, and a tremendous shamelessness have co-opted what used to be a nice, wholesome calling: dishing out sound advice to business men and women."

Yet thousands of consultants practice their trade daily, which wouldn't be the case if they were not satisfying some clients at least some of the time. Consultant Andrew S. Linick says, "Having a consultant who will take you through the business minefields safely will greatly increase your chances of a supersuccessful landing with your business intact."

Consulting in the Information Age

Today we live in an age of specialization. More information has been created in the last 30 years than the previous 5,000, notes Richard Saul Wurman in his book *Information Anxiety* (Doubleday, page 35). As a result, no one can know everything—or even most things—so we naturally seek outside help and expertise to supplement our own.

Consultants exist to guide people through areas in which they have little experience. An engaged couple, overwhelmed by the details of planning a lavish wedding for 200 guests, hire a bridal consultant. The owner of a small trucking business, knowledgeable about trucking but computer-phobic, hires a computer consultant to create a billing, accounting, and fleet management system. The CEO of a corporation, seeking to improve efficiency and streamline operations, hires a "re-engineering" consultant to advise her on managing the change process. I knew what I wanted on my Web site but had neither the time nor the inclination to learn Java or HTML. And so I hired a freelance Web programmer to construct my site for me.

In today's information explosion and rapidly changing marketplace, more organizations and individuals are hiring consultants to provide guidance, answer questions, give "second opinions," train employees, and serve as sounding boards against which executives, managers, and entrepreneurs can bounce ideas, plans, strategies, and thoughts. As a result, the consulting profession is booming.

In an article titled "Seven Great Businesses for You to Start in 1998," published in *Money* magazine (Forecast 1998, page 138), four of the seven "great" businesses listed were consulting businesses. Estimates vary, but worldwide, businesses spend at least $50 billion annually buying consultant services.

We often hear today about how *knowledge* has become one of the most valuable business assets. To the consultant, knowledge is perhaps the single most valuable asset. Because most knowledge can be gained through experience and study, virtually anyone can acquire specialized knowledge that can be sold as consulting services.

Combined with low start-up costs, this makes consulting an ideal business for self- employment. Many consulting firms consist of one or two people and can be run from home. In an interview with *Money* magazine (Forecast 1998, page 27), Gerald Celente says that by the year 2000, nearly

50 million people will work out of their homes, up from about 11 million in 1985.

Why More People Are Becoming Consultants Today

Making the transition from corporate employment to self-employment as a consultant can be scary. It is a little less intimidating for young people who don't have heavy financial burdens, and older workers who can afford to retire but want to keep working. It can be more nerve-wracking for people in the middle of their careers who have to continue to earn a living after leaving the security of their corporate jobs.

Many of us feel the pull of entrepreneurism, and the lure of doing something other than the usual nine-to-five routine can be strong. In a *U.S. News & World Report* poll (October 28, 1996, page 68), 62 percent of those surveyed who were under 30 said they wanted to be their own boss, while 38 percent of those surveyed who were over 30 said they desired to become self-employed.

Entrepreneurism is on the rise. More than 7 million adults in the United States are currently working on starting a business, according to a study from the Entrepreneurial Research Consortium. And the trend is not confined to America. In Taiwan, 17 percent of the workforce works independently in small or home offices, reports an article in *The Futurist* (July 1998, page 7).

One powerful reason to consider consulting as a career is to do work you like. According to an article in *Publishers Weekly* (August 4, 1997, page 73), author William Styron has said that only 17 percent of people in the world have lives worth living. That's an exaggeration, but life can sure seem better when you look forward to going to work every morning. Sales trainer Paul Karasik observes, "What motivates people is doing what they love." When you're a consultant, you can make money by practicing the skill or dealing with the subject that interests you most.

A book review published in the Spring 1992 issue of *National Home Business Report* quotes best-selling author Richard N. Bolles as saying, "What the world needs is more people who feel true enthusiasm for their work. People who have taken the time to think out what they uniquely can do and have to offer the world."

In the December 1997 issue of *Words from Woody,* David Wood quotes Michael Korda as saying, "Your chances of success are directly proportional to the degree of pleasure you derive from what you do. If you are in a job you hate, face the fact squarely and get out." Timothy Butler, a director of career development at Harvard Business School, says, "Vocation has to do with your calling. It's what you're doing in life that makes a difference for you, that builds meaning for you" (as quoted in *Fast Company,* March 1998, page 110).

For those of us not destined to climb the highest rungs of the corporate ladder and become CEO, entrepreneurism offers an opportunity to make more money than we might as an employee. Jerry Buchanan, writing in *Soap Box Journal* (Winter 1992, page 3), advises: "In a free enterprise society, the best chance you have of gaining independence and financial security is in starting and operating your own small business. Find a need and a way to fill that need."

As an independent consultant working from home or a small rented office, you have the potential to make $100,000 to $300,000 a year or more, while keeping your business relatively simple and small. Most consultants I know say they make at least twice as much money as they did when they had a regular job. Some make much more.

For some people, being downsized or laid off is the impetus to take a closer look at consulting as an employment alternative—when you work for yourself, you can't be fired. Consultant Ilise Benun explains how and why she got into the consulting trade:

> I was fired from the second (and last) real job I ever had. I had been working for a year and a half in the New York office of a family-owned, Kenyan safari company. I was hired thanks to my best friend, but ours had always been a rocky friendship and working together, I know now, wasn't a great idea.
>
> One Friday in April 1988, I was called into the conference room by the Big Boss—in reality, a small, silent type not given to emotional outbursts. He sat down at the table, handed me an envelope and said, "Thank you very much." At first I didn't understand what was happening. He couldn't possibly be firing me, but he was, and when I finally got it through my head, I was livid! "I will never work for anyone again," I vowed to anyone who'd listen.

Indeed I had no plan, so I got busy trying to figure out what to do. In terms of my skills and talents, my degree in Spanish seemed useless because I didn't want to work for the U.N. However, I was the most organized person I knew (still am), and all of my artsy friends were completely and utterly disorganized (though they aren't so much anymore). So I came up with the fancy and (I thought) original title of Professional Organizer and got busy telling everyone what I did. (In other words, I started networking!) Before long, I had a few clients willing to pay $15 an hour to have me sit with them and pick through their mountains of clutter, one piece at a time.

It was strangely therapeutic, though very slow going, and little by little, I began to notice a pattern: buried under each person's pile, there was inevitably one piece of paper representing some little self promotion task they were neglecting. Once we'd unearthed that phone message or note from someone asking for information, I'd say, "Let's write them a letter describing your work," or "Why don't we send them those slides?" I didn't know from marketing, but to me, it seemed like nothing more than common sense. It didn't take me long to realize that the clutter was not the problem, but merely the obstacle people used to protect themselves from the responsibility of self-promotion.

Over the course of the next few years, I evolved from Professional Organizer to Self-Promotion Specialist, learning from my own mistakes and those of my clients, practicing what I preached and preaching, running my little self-promotion empire out here in Hoboken, N.J.

Many women are joining Ilise in satisfying their desire to control their destinies through self-employment. According to the *New York Times* (July 20, 1995, page 10), American women started twice as many businesses as men in 1994, for a total of 7.7 million women running their own businesses. An article in *CIO* (January 1, 1998, page 26) reports that by the year 2000, 30 percent of consultants in Information Systems (IS) will be women.

While money and autonomy motivate many of us to start consulting businesses, others do it because they like the lifestyle it offers. According to an article in *The Winner's Circle,* 77 percent of Americans have a goal to spend time with family and friends, and 74 percent want to improve themselves intellectually or otherwise.

For many people, corporate life does not offer the rewards they seek. One survey shows that only 6 percent of employees enjoy corporate life. They may enjoy performing their jobs, but they dislike office politics and the bureaucracy inherent in large organizations.

As a consultant, I can spend my time on things that stimulate me intellectually and are deeply rewarding to me. When I was a corporate manager, by comparison, I spent most of my time doing things I didn't enjoy: meetings, paperwork, budgets, plans, forecasts, project management, and administrative tasks. Writing in *Story* magazine (Summer 1997, page 50), Brian Fleming notes: "Labor for no important purpose dulls the human spirit and lays waste to the soul."

For others, the urge to escape corporate life is even stronger. They feel uncomfortable in the corporate environment, don't fit in, and feel another setting is their real calling. In *The Moon and Sixpence,* W. Somerset Maugham writes: "Sometimes a man hits upon a place to which he mysteriously feels that he belongs. Here is the home he sought, and he will settle amid scenes he has never seen before, among men he has never known, as they were familiar to him from his birth. Here at last he finds rest." This describes the comfort and contentment many people experience when they make the transition from corporate employment to self-employment.

When asked what they *miss* most about the corporate world, 68 percent of entrepreneurs interviewed cited office socializing. Other things missed include pension plans, company-paid health insurance, weekly paychecks, and access to resources.

According to an article in the *Daily News* (March 31, 1997), a poll of 202 small business owners showed that while they enjoy the freedom of being their own bosses and setting their own hours, they also feel pressure to work long hours and are anxious about making ends meet.

David Wood writes in *Words from Woody* (Fall 1992, page 3): "An entrepreneur is the kind of person who will work 16 hours a day just to avoid having to work 8 hours a day for someone else."

Why Consulting Is More Competitive Today Than Ever Before

Although the market for consulting services seems to be expanding, many consultants say it's tougher than ever to get and keep good clients. These consultants say that while they're busy and making good money, the business environment is more competitive and demanding than five or ten years ago.

One reason is the economy. The recession of the late 1980s and early 1990s transformed many service industries, including the majority of consulting specialties, from a seller's market to a buyer's market. Fees stagnated during those years, or even dropped. Clients learned that they had a choice and became more particular. Even though the economy has recovered, this buyer's-market mind-set has and will continue.

Clients are not afraid to ask for what they want or shop around. Even on smaller projects, clients who in the past would have simply called with an assignment are getting quotes from several firms before selecting a consultant for the job. Consultants find more of their time taken up with prospecting, quoting, preparing proposals, following up, and maintaining good relationships with clients.

Clients are choosier and more demanding than ever. It's no longer enough to be technically competent or solve client problems. Your interpersonal and customer service skills must be excellent. Clients have their choice of consultants to work with, and most people prefer to work with those they like or at least feel comfortable with. If you have been a consultant for several years, you may find yourself spending more time on building and nurturing client relationships than in the past. Lord Chesterfield advised, "Cause the other fellow to like himself a little bit better, and I promise you he will like you very well indeed."

Money is tighter than it was in the early and mid 1980s. Since the recession hit, budgets have gotten smaller, clients spend more cautiously and wisely, and buyers shop around more to get a good price.

At the same time, the buying authority of clients in large organizations has been reduced. Most purchases above $1,000 are made by increasingly larger and slower-moving committees. Some corporations have approved-vendor lists or long-term contractual relationships with large vendors that make it difficult for them to purchase services from smaller, independent consulting firms.

According to a news report on New York City's WPLJ radio, the population increases by 214,000 people per day. This means more potential clients for your services, but also more people entering the job market, including consulting. Many people see consulting as desirable and even glamorous, and so are drawn to the profession in greater numbers. Downsizing has left tens of thousands skilled white-collar workers without employment and with uncertain job prospects. For many, hanging a shingle as an independent consultant is a convenient and attractive solution.

The Five Key Consulting Activities

Although there are many variations possible on these categories, most of the work done by most of the consultants today falls into one or more of the following five areas.

1. Advisory Services

In the cartoon strip *Family Circus* by Bill Keane, a mother tells her son: "You misunderstand. I'm a homework consultant, not a homework subcontractor." She means she'll advise him on how to do his homework, but she won't do it for him.

Most consultants act as advisers. They give recommendations and suggestions. But they don't implement their ideas, and they aren't the ones who decide which recommendations will be put into action.

The client makes the decision, and a lot of what you recommend won't be done. That's typical, and no reflection on the soundness of your ideas. There are many reasons clients won't try a good idea. Maybe they tried it already and it didn't work. Perhaps it's against corporate policy. Maybe they just don't have the resources to implement it. Or it is too risky for their tastes.

Don't be put off when clients thank you, pay you, but don't do a lot of what you suggested. It happens all the time.

2. Implementation Services

Some consultants implement the solutions they (or others) come up with. An accountant, for example, not only shows you ways to get a tax refund, but also completes your return. A computer consultant, in addition to recommending a computing solution, may assemble the components, install and integrate them at the customer's site, do the custom programming, train the client to use the system, and even provide ongoing maintenance and support.

It's an odd fact, but giving advice often pays better than implementation. Those who tell others what to do frequently get paid more than those who actually do the work. An information systems consultant, for example, might get $2,000 a day or more to advise CIOs (Chief Information Officers) on high-level computing issues. But a freelance programmer writing a new application or doing code conversion may earn a far more modest rate of $400 to $500 per day.

3. Training and Development

Many consultants specialize in training the employees of client organizations in various job-related skills. About half of the nation's annual training budget goes toward basic and "soft" skills (business writing, customer service, teamwork, leadership, management, time management), while the other half is spent training employees in technical and "hard" skills (local area network troubleshooting, Microsoft Exchange, sales forecasting, compensation management, regulatory compliance).

"Feed a man a fish, you feed him for a day," goes the old saying, "but teach him to fish, and you feed him for life." In theory, the skills a trainer teaches can last throughout a career and increase the productivity of every employee who takes the course for decades to come. For this reason, trainers are well paid, earning $1,000 to $4,000 a day or sometimes even more for classes presented in-house to an organization's employees.

4. Publishing and Product Development

The late consultant Howard Shenson said, "Publishing is every consultant's second job."

One-on-one consulting pays well and can be effective, but it has its limitations. One-on-one consulting is the most expensive form of information delivery, and the amount of such services most organizations can afford is limited. It also requires the consultant's individual attention, and with only so many hours in a week, there's only so much one-on-one consulting you can do.

Much of the information disseminated through consulting can be packaged and sold as "information products" including books, audio and video tapes, workbooks, software, forms, checklists, phone support lines, Internet support, newsletters, and reference guides. So there is an opportunity for almost every consultant to package part of his or her expertise as information products.

Howard Shenson observed that consultants have limited income potential from rendering one-on-one service, because of the limited number of hours you can work each week. He likened the independent consultant to the independent dentist, who continually has to "drill and fill" before he can bill.

Becoming a producer of information products frees you from the limitations of rendering service on an hourly basis. If you bill $1,000 a day for market research, the most you can make for a day of research work is $1,000. But what if you packaged your market research and sold it as a $1,000 report? You can just as easily sell ten reports in a day as you can one report. Or even 20 or 30! The "drill, fill, and bill" limitations on your income fall away.

Many consultants produce information products to generate revenue beyond their daily consulting service. These products can range from a $1 tip sheet to a $100,000 software package. Having a series of products, especially in the $10 to $1,000 range, enables you to package and sell your expertise to clients who cannot afford or do not want custom one-on-one consultation, further expanding your revenues.

5. Contract and Temporary Consulting

An article in *The Record* (November 16, 1997) reports that, according to the National Association of Part Time and Temporary Employment, there are 2.5 million temps nationwide, representing 2 percent of the workforce. From 1982 to 1994, the number of temps rose 361 percent.

Contractors and temps usually operate somewhat differently than traditional independent consultants. Contractors or temps typically work full-time on the client's premises, devoting all or most of their week to that client for the duration of the assignment. They perform a variety of tasks rather than just giving advice, often working as part of a team comprised of both consultants and staff workers.

When accepting contract or temp work, be sure to consult your accountant. Often contractors and temps are treated, from a payroll point of view, like staff employees rather than freelancers or vendors. They get a W-2 or W-4 instead of a 1099 and may be subject to withholding.

Consulting Specialties

Consultants are specialists. They have specific knowledge of a process, task, body of data, discipline, subject, industry, or business.

Consultants typically specialize by discipline, industry, or both. One of my colleagues, for instance, is a consultant specializing in direct marketing. Another is a consultant specializing in direct marketing for political campaign and nonprofit fundraising only. A third focuses on direct marketing of PC software and other technology products.

Appendix I lists many of the better-known consulting specialties by discipline and industry. But the list isn't all-inclusive. Wherever there's a need, consultants will spring up to fill the gap. Things are changing all the time, and these changes create new consulting needs. A decade ago, who ever heard of an Internet consultant? Now, Web site design and development is one of the fastest-growing consulting specialties, with many relatively new consultants grossing $100,000 a year or more.

Should You Become a Consultant?

According to an article in *Business Week* (December 9, 1996, page 32), the sons of self-employed men show a strong tendency to become self-employed.

Aside from heritage, what makes a person a good candidate for self-employment as an independent professional?

In an article in *SAP Connection,* Terri Lonier, author of *Working Solo,* says that successful solo entrepreneurs are self-starters, outgoing, life-long learners, and optimistic. Don't worry if you don't have these characteristics in abundance. Exceptions are plentiful. Again, if you have specialized knowledge, can communicate it clearly to other people, and are willing to do what it takes to succeed, you will.

An essay sent to me via fax by motivational speaker Dr. Rob Gilbert gives this advice, which is extremely applicable to independent consultants: "What you achieve in your lifetime is directly related to what you do. You can choose your own direction. Everyone has problems and obstacles to overcome, but you can change anything in your life if you want to badly enough. Compete. If you aren't willing to work for your goals, don't expect others to."

An article in the newsletter *Creative Business* (Vol. 8, No.3, page 5) notes that solo and small-firm practitioners:

- Enjoy working at home alone
- Are somewhat motivated by money
- Are not that interested in business details
- Do not want to supervise others

That last characteristic describes Don Hauptman, a highly successful freelance direct mail writer. Don says he chooses self-employment over corporate employment because he does not like to be told what to do, and has no staff or assistants because he dislikes telling other people what to do.

Keep in mind that consultants seldom fit all of Terri's characteristic entrepreneurial traits. Some consultants are not outgoing. Many are downright introverted. Most people who become consultants do like to learn. As for being a self-starter, that's helpful but not critical. As an independent consultant, you'll be doing projects clients assign to you with specific deadlines, so your day will be somewhere between that of a classic entrepreneur and a nine-to-fiver—a mixture of work scheduled and on deadline, with a great deal of flexibility concerning what you do when, plus many hours of time to use as you choose.

My feeling is, if you want to become a consultant strongly enough, you will. Everyone knows—or can learn—a skill or information others would pay for on a consulting basis. The other skills needed to run a successful consulting practice—customer service, interpersonal communication, sales, marketing, self-promotion—can also be learned as you go along.

An article in *Money Making Opportunities* (January 1998, page 72) advises aspiring entrepreneurs: "Think big. Dare to dream your dreams and focus on your visions. Develop a vision of the future . . . then plan how to make it a reality." Don't let negative thinking or the negative attitudes of others dissuade you from pursuing your consulting career. As Dr. Benjamin Spock says, "Trust yourself. You know more than you think you do."

Is Consulting Right for You? A Self-Assessment Test

Answer the following questions. The more "yes" answers you score, the stronger your aptitude and desire to become an independent consultant:

1. Do you like solving problems?
2. Do you enjoy research, study, and learning?
3. Are you a reader?
4. Are you an "information junkie"—subscribing to newsletters, clipping articles, browsing the Web, and collecting tidbits and facts on subjects that interest you?
5. Can you work independently without the constant interaction you get in an office environment?
6. Do you have specialized skills, knowledge, or experience that's in demand?
7. Do businesses or individuals regularly hire consultants in your area of specialty?
8. Would businesses or individuals profit or otherwise come out ahead by engaging your services?
9. Can the positive results you can achieve for consulting clients be measured, documented, and proven?
10. Is the service you can offer unique, different, or better than similar services being offered?
11. If not, is there another compelling reason why clients should hire you instead of your competitors?
12. Can you charge an hourly rate that is equivalent to at least twice your current salary as a corporate employee?
13. Can you get along with people well enough to sell your services and deal with clients?
14. If you are not comfortable with people, can you find someone who can handle sales and client relations for you, allowing you to concentrate on the technical side of your business?

15. Are you a self-starter? Can you work productively without having a boss tell you what to do?

16. Do you have the fortitude to handle crises and other business problems?

17. Do you have money in the bank you can live on for a few months if business gets lean?

18. Are you flexible and accommodating, and willing to listen to the requirements and opinions of other people—specifically, your customers?

19. Are you results oriented?

20. Can you commit to and meet deadlines without procrastination or excuses?

21. Does the idea of being self-employed appeal to you?

22. Would you enjoy working at home or alone in a small office?

23. Do you have good computer skills and, if not, are you willing to learn?

Starting a Successful

Consulting Practice

Okay. You want to pursue a career as an independent consultant. This chapter shows you what you need to do to get started.

Determining What Consulting Services You Will Offer

The first step is to determine the consulting services you will offer.

Your area of expertise, by itself, does not define a service. If you said to me, "I will specialize in AS/400 computers," my response would be, "What *about* AS/400 computers will you help clients with?" Will you connect them in a local area network? Create new applications? Recode old software for Year 2000 compliance? Advise IS managers on how to migrate from AS/400 to other platforms?

As noted in Chapter 1, the successful consultant "finds a need and fills it." Consultants are problem solvers. What problems do organizations and individuals have that you can help solve? For business clients, some of the problems you might help them cope with include:

- Accumulating capital for a business venture
- Launching a new product
- Entering a new market

- Expanding share in an existing market
- Computerizing business processes
- Reorganizing the corporation
- Planning employee compensation and benefits
- Implementing or upgrading computer systems
- Opening a new office, branch, or division
- Mergers and acquisitions
- Increasing productivity
- Reducing costs
- Improving quality control

Individuals might hire you to address different needs, such as:

- Writing a resume
- Finding a job
- Selecting a career
- Learning new software
- Learning foreign languages and cultures
- Getting motivated
- Improving workplace skills
- Enjoying better relationships
- Feeling better about themselves
- Becoming more fit and healthy

Pinpointing Your Market

Who will buy your consulting services? You can find the answer by determining who is hiring your competition (other consultants offering similar services). If your competition is successfully selling a particular service to a given market, that means you can too.

For instance, say you want to offer business writing seminars to corporations. Who do you contact about getting hired? the president or CEO? the training director? the manager of the department whose employees need training?

You can test promotions aimed at each group and see which generates the greatest response. But first, ask potential customers who in their organizations would buy writing seminars. Their answers can guide you to the potential buyers most likely to respond to your offer.

Some consulting services, such as upgrading legacy computing systems for Year 2000 compliance, are clearly oriented to and purchased by businesses. Others, such as a tax preparation service like H&R Block, target individuals. Many consultants, however, can target both business and consumer markets.

A fitness instructor, for example, can offer personal training to clients at home. But another market might be local businesses that want to keep employees fit and healthy. I always thought of our local flower shop as a consumer business. But one day, chatting with the owner, I found a significant source of their income was corporate work—providing plants and flowers for meetings, trade shows, gifts, lobbies, and conference rooms.

Most consultants prefer selling to businesses. The budgets are larger, the clients are more sophisticated and accustomed to buying consulting services, and the diverse range of needs provides opportunities for profitable repeat consulting engagements.

Consumers, on the other hand, are unused to hiring consultants, have limited budgets, smaller projects, and are tight with a dollar, because the money is coming out of their own pockets. And, they are often the most difficult clients to deal with. You might think the client who spends less requires the least service, but the opposite is often true: The clients who spend the least are frequently the most demanding.

For some consulting services, the market is obvious. If you are a copywriter, for example, and you target advertising agencies, you focus your marketing efforts on the creative director. Not the media planner, art director, or bookkeeper. If you build Web sites, you may have several target markets: corporate Web masters, local small businesses, associations, state and local government agencies.

For other consulting services, there may be multiple markets and multiple buying influences. Consultant Gary Blake and I developed a seminar on interpersonal skills for technical professionals. The primary market turned out to be information technology (IT) managers, who would hire us to teach active listening, customer service, teamwork, and communication to systems professionals. Vice presidents of engineering turned out to be a secondary market, needing training for chemical, mechanical, and electrical engineers.

The more precisely you can identify your potential client—by size of company, industry, and job title and function—the greater the response will be to your sales and marketing efforts. A promotion for a consulting service that fails to excite one group of buyers can be a smash success with a different group. Testing different efforts—telemarketing, direct mail, sales calls—in small quantities can rapidly indicate what's working, and on whom, so you can focus subsequent efforts more tightly for better results, response, and sales.

Determining Your "Niche" or Consulting Specialty

According to an article in *Across the Board* (April 1992, page 2), the number one complaint of clients about consultants is "wasting time to teach consultants our business." Specialization solves this problem.

A question you face early in your consulting career is "Should I be a generalist, a jack of all trades, taking whatever assignments come my way, or should I specialize in a specific type of assignment, client, or industry?"

My experience is that specialists almost always get paid better and are more in demand than generalists. The reason has to do with the nature of the consulting business.

When companies need a consultant, it's for *one specific project.* They don't want to have to train the consultant or waste time "bringing him up to speed" in their businesses. They want a consultant who can immediately step in, take over, and do the job alone, without supervision—quickly, correctly, and competently. They are looking for a consultant whose background and expertise match the job at hand as closely as possible. They want specific skills. They want to hire a specialist—not a generalist.

For this reason, specialists are more in demand, and they can charge more. Time and time again, I've seen clients who, when faced with the decision about which consultant to hire, will choose the specialist with experience in their type of project over the generalist—seven times out of ten.

Think about it. If you needed a marketing plan for your new software product, which consultant would you choose: the one who does general consumer products, like soaps and shampoos, or the specialist who has worked for Microsoft, IBM, Computer Associates, and other major software firms? If you said the generalist, you're the exception, not the rule. Most people want to go with a proven resource.

What are the specialties for consultants? Some consultants specialize by type of industry—automotive, metalworking, plastics, pulp and paper.

You can also specialize by area of skill or knowledge. There are specialists in transportation, safety, quality, productivity, communications, sales, direct marketing, process control, local area networking, the Internet, and teamwork.

In many cases, consultants seem to drift toward a specialty by accident or circumstance rather than by deliberately choosing a specialty. In my case, I had an engineering background, so industrial and high-tech marketing was a natural for me. I didn't set out to specialize in this area. I would have been happy to handle any work that came along. But industrial clients were eager to hire me because of my technical background, while consumer products companies were afraid that I was too much of a "techie." (Also, all my projects done for my full-time jobs were technical.)

My wife, who freelanced before we had kids, had a similar experience. When she became a freelance editor, the first few clients who hired her were trade associations. This wasn't deliberate; it just happened that way. As a result, she developed a specialty in publicizing and promoting trade associations.

You may find the same thing happening to you. Perhaps your first client is a bank, and your first project is to write a booklet explaining a new IRA. Other financial institutions see your work, or maybe you mail copies of the booklet along with a cover letter to advertising managers at local banks. Before you know it, you're known as a banking specialist! It isn't what you planned originally. But you'll enjoy the extra prestige and income. And you'll like having clients knocking at your door, instead of the other way around.

What's more, there's no reason why you can't have more than one specialty—or handle both special *and* general assignments. Copywriter Richard Armstrong has several specialties: He's known as a speech consultant, a publicity consultant, and a specialist in direct mail for both fund raising and political clients. Although I'm primarily a business-to-business and direct mail consultant, I'm also known as a software copywriter. And I have developed another "sub-specialty" in promoting subscriptions to business and financial newsletters.

The key to having multiple specialties is simply to present yourself as a specialist in a particular field when pitching to clients in that area. You might have three or four different resumes or bios, each with a different cover letter highlighting your specific experience in a particular specialty.

The idea of having different promotional materials aimed at different segments of the market is known as "target marketing," and it is practiced all the time by big corporations. A client of mine in the software business has one ad campaign aimed at the hospital market and another completely different campaign aimed at manufacturers. By targeting a specific service at a specific type of customer, you have a much better chance of making the sale and getting the assignment.

"Your prospects need to pigeonhole you," writes Ilise Benun in her quarterly newsletter, *The Art of Self Promotion* (No. 19). "Although you hate it, let them do it; in fact, help them. Give them a box to put you in, and a label to put on your box. Your prospect needs you to be a specialist. There's plenty of time to tell them more later about your full range of services."

Does this mean you have to have a specialty right from the start of your freelance consulting career? Not at all. If you do not have specialized education or experience that would incline you toward a particular specialty, spend your first year or so in the business as a generalist.

At the end of your first year in business, do an analysis of your assignments. Although you took projects one at a time from a variety of clients, you'll probably find that you've done groups of similar projects. Maybe you've done training for three different banks. Based on this, you can begin to position yourself as a banking specialist. To be a specialist, you don't need heavy credentials—experience with two or three good clients and a handful of projects under your belt will be enough to get you started. As you get additional clients in the specialty, your client list, project list, skill, knowledge, and market value grow, and you find it easier to get clients and projects and charge higher fees.

Just because you're a specialist doesn't mean you have to turn down an assignment outside of your specialty. If one is offered to you—and it will be—and you want to take it, go ahead. Not every client is looking for specialists. So generalists can still get work.

"Diversification helps keep you creatively fresh," writes Cameron Foote in his monthly newsletter for consultants, *Creative Business* (December, 1996, page 12). "What you learn in one situation often helps clients in another. Only you can determine just how much or little specialization is appropriate for you."

In certain situations, being a specialist can work against you, but this is rare. Recently, an engineering society asked several consultants to bid on writing a direct mail package to acquire new members. I sent them a package of engineering samples and highlighted the fact that I am an engineer. I didn't get the job. When I asked why, I was told they wanted the "nonengineering perspective" (which seems an odd thing to want when your audience is 100 percent engineers) and hired a consultant with a general consumer background. (The direct mail package, incidentally, was not successful.)

In most cases, however, having expertise or experience in a specific form of writing, technology, or industry will cause the client to prefer you to other consultants being considered for the job. Last month, the marketing manager of a service firm asked me to send samples, and specifically requested samples of work I did in their industry, if any. I had some, and sent them. Today she called to let me know I had been selected to do the projects, and told me that seeing I had handled projects for another service firm in her industry was an important factor in my getting the contract.

"Specialize," advises an article in *The Successful Practice,* (Issue 4, page 8). "Have great experience and expertise in a certain area." Internet consultant Wally Bock comments: "Have a primary market niche. I define a niche as the junction of a topic [area of specialization] and audience [industry or type of company]."

Computerizing Your Consulting Business

Get the best computer system and software money can buy. If you can't afford to buy, lease; the low monthly payments make computers affordable, and you can lease software as well as hardware. If your local computer seller does not offer financing in-house, have them arrange it for you by calling Studebaker-Worthington Leasing Corporation, 800-645-7242.

Ask the computer salesperson to recommend a system configuration in terms of processor, memory, and hard disk storage. Then get twice that— or at least as much above the recommendation as you can afford.

Reason? Whatever you buy today will cease being state of the art as soon as you learn to use it, so you can never have too much computer.

Example: When I bought my previous system, I was thrilled to be buying "top of the line"—a 486 machine. The instant it was delivered I read about Pentium in the newspaper and realized I was already a generation behind. I'm sure a new chip will soon render Pentium obsolete! As of this writing, I recommend a Pentium II processor running at 300 MHz or faster.

Equip your computer system with as many productivity-boosting tools as possible. Hardware should include a high-speed fax/modem, 100 MB zip drive, 24X or better CD-ROM drive, plenty of hard disk storage, tape backup, and laser printer. You'll love the speed with which laser printers print manuscript. No more wasting time waiting for your dot matrix or daisy-wheel clunker to crank out pages.

As for hard disk storage, my rule of thumb is: A work-at-home professional can never have too many megabytes. Get at least a gigabyte or more. Our new Pentium at home, which my wife writes on, has 1.2 GB. I just upgraded my office computer to 8 GB, which should hold me for a year or so.

Modems are cheap, so get the fastest one you can afford. As of this writing, 56 Kbps is considered a fast modem for a personal computer. But next year the speed of the top of the line model may be even faster. Fast modems speed e-mail transmissions, saving you time.

As for the IBM compatible vs. Macintosh question, do what works for you. Most ad agencies and graphic design firms use Macintosh but are capable of converting your IBM files to the Macintosh format. In corporations, the majority of my clients seem to use IBM compatible equipment and don't know how to convert a Mac file to Windows.

As far as software, I recommend Windows; Word or WordPerfect for word processing; and a contact management program such as ACT! or TeleMagic for maintaining a database of editorial contents and generating personalized query letters. My preference for Word or WordPerfect is based on the observation that many clients like getting documents on disk in these formats. And, these are good programs—lots of features and easy to learn.

Learn to use a spreadsheet. I have Excel and it meets my needs. It's also compatible with Word as part of Microsoft Office, as is PowerPoint. Spreadsheets are a standard tool for marketing, sales, and financial analysis.

An increasing number of corporations are adapting Microsoft Office PowerPoint to do presentations—overhead, slide, hard copy, and screen-based. If your corporate clients haven't asked you to write in PowerPoint for them yet, they probably will soon. It pays to get and learn this program—you'll be able to say "yes" to some nice assignments you would otherwise have to turn away.

Protect yourself and your clients against computer viruses by installing Norton AntiVirus or another good antivirus program. According to Symantec, makers of Norton AntiVirus, there are 15,000 documented computer viruses today. If clients catch a virus from you and find out your system is unprotected, they will be extremely displeased. New viruses pop up all the time, so make sure the antivirus program you buy offers upgrades that can be downloaded online.

Get Online

Traditionally, clients sent source material—background information for consulting projects—to their consultants via FedEx and express mail. Then, with the introduction of the fax, it became standard practice to fax source materials unless there were too many pages, in which case they'd be sent via overnight delivery.

Today clients may want to send you source documents via e-mail. And many will want you to deliver your reports the same way. You should sign up for one of the two most popular on-line services, CompuServe or America Online (America Online recently bought CompuServe; the latter continues to operate as a separate service). Most of your clients will either have one of these services or be able to communicate through them with you online. Once you're comfortable with CompuServe or AOL, you might want to call a local Internet service provider (ISP) and arrange to have a direct connection to the Internet. Look in the business section of your local paper for ads about "Get on the Internet" for ISPs in your area.

With e-mail, you save time submitting your consulting reports to clients. Instead of having to print and mail a manuscript and transfer files to a floppy disk, you simply hit a button and instantly "download" your report or memo to your client's e-mail address. I submit over 50 percent of my assignments in this fashion, and I love it. You can literally send copy for a 25-page document in less than half a minute. You also save money by eliminating postage: It cost me only 14 cents in transaction charges to e-mail a big brochure today to one of my clients.

An article in *Fast Company* (May 1977, page 44) advises: "Always have two ways of getting online. You never know what AOL's service will be like, so it's best to have a backup Internet services provider." At my office we use AOL, CompuServe, AT&T Mail, and a local ISP, Intercall.

In addition to giving you the ability to send e-mail and files over the Internet, the ISP can register a domain name for you. This is the first step in setting up a Web site for yourself, which is something I recommend you experiment with at some point. It's not necessary, but setting up your own Web site will teach you how to do it for others, and you can charge them for this service. Also, potential clients may look for you on the Web, so it makes sense to have a domain name related to your name or your company name. My Web site is at www.bly.com. Register the domain name you want now before someone else takes it.

Your ISP will supply you with a Web browser such as Netscape or Microsoft Explorer. With this simple software, you can surf the Web, which means you can easily get onto various Web sites. This is important for you to learn. Right now, it's not a mandatory skill, although knowing how to Web surf shows clients you're high-tech and a savvy marketer. But within a few years, instead of sending you source documents as background for consulting assignments, many clients will just say, "Look at my Web site." You'll lose work or at least dampen their enthusiasm about you if you tell them, "I don't know how." Get Internet literate. It's not as hard as you think.

All this computer stuff can be acquired and learned gradually, as time and budget permit. Don't feel you have to load up on a complete set of high-tech gear before you start soliciting business. As long as you have basic word processing or even electronic typing capability in your office, you're ready to go. Upgrading, if necessary, can be done within a few days, as computers and software are readily available for lease, rental, or purchase throughout the United States.

Secretaries and Support Staff

Okay. Let's say you are interested in getting help around your office for filing, typing, and other administrative tasks. A major decision is whether to hire an employee or outsource.

When you hire employees, they generally work on your premises using your office space, equipment, and supplies. You pay them a salary and often provide benefits such as sick days, vacation, and health insurance.

When you outsource, you contract with an individual or small firm that provides the services you need on a fee basis. This fee can be a project fee, but is usually an hourly fee. Independent contractors typically work on their premises, using their office space, equipment, and supplies. You pay their invoices like you would pay a bill for any product or service you buy.

I have had both staff employees and subcontractors, and prefer the latter to the former by a wide margin. Here's why:

1. Subcontractors and other part-time workers can perform as well as full-timers but, on average, earn 40 percent less. Only 12 percent get a pension, and only 15 percent get health care benefits. Therefore, they are cheaper to employ.

2. There is no long-term commitment and no recurring overhead. You pay subcontractors only when you give them work to do. Employees get paid as long as they show up, whether they have work to do or not. When you don't need the subcontractors, they work for their other clients (or take time off), and you don't pay them. This is especially important when you are just starting out and have no idea of what your workflow will be on a weekly basis.

3. Subcontractors are independent and responsible for their own welfare. Employees may depend on you for guidance, career satisfaction, and other needs—a responsibility you may not want to deal with.

4. Using subcontractors is less complex, from an accounting and paperwork point of view, than having employees. Employees require social security tax, FICA, workers' compensation, and other complexities. Independent contractors are paid as vendors. NOTE: The Internal Revenue Service requires that people who are paid as independent contractors work on their premises and have other clients. Consult your accountant or tax attorney.

5. Subcontractors are more motivated because they are sellers and you are the buyer. They have a customer-service orientation which is a welcome change from the attitude of resentment or indifference many employees seem to have toward the boss.

6. Subcontractors provide their own equipment and office space, buy their own furniture, and pay their own utility bills. Often the subcontractor will have better equipment than you do, and as the client, you get the benefits of this equipment without buying it. So subcontracting can actually reduce your overhead and capital costs, while hiring employees increases them, because you have to supply the employee with a fully equipped office.

Start small. Hire a part-time secretary or word processor to work for you one day a week. If you can keep one busy, like having the help, and feel it frees you to increase your output and income, you can always buy more of the person's time or, if he or she is too busy, hire a second helper.

Another source of help is college students, who can be hired as part-time assistants or summer interns. The problem is that after the summer, or when they graduate, they're gone. The value of an assistant increases as he or she learns your procedures and business over time; this advantage does not exist when you hire college students and other transients who don't stick around. A professional word processor or secretary running his or her own services business, on the other hand, wants to make that business grow and is looking for long-term client relationships. That's why I prefer professionals to students.

Obviously, I am a big fan of outsourcing. It works for me, and I recommend you try it.

Becoming the Leading

Authority in Your

Consulting Specialty

Clients prefer to hire consultants perceived as experts in their field. Three ways to become perceived as an expert are to write articles, publish books, and give talks on your consulting topic. This chapter shows how to promote yourself as an expert to potential clients in print and at the podium.

Why You Should Write Articles on Your Consulting Specialty

A "planted" or "placed" feature story is an article written and submitted to a publication by a corporation, entrepreneur, consultant, or business professional—either directly by the business or on its behalf by its PR firm or consultant. Unlike freelance writers, who write articles for pleasure and profit, consultants submitting feature articles seek publicity and exposure for their consulting practice, and its ideas or services.

Placing features with appropriate trade, consumer, or business publications is one of the most powerful and effective of all marketing techniques because

- you can get one, two, or more pages devoted to your product or service without paying for the space. (A paid ad of that length could run $3,000 to $20,000 or more.)

- your message has far more credibility as "editorial" material than as a sponsored advertisement.
- the publication of the article results in prestige for the author and recognition for the company.
- reprints make excellent, low-cost sales literature.

Just one article in a trade journal can bring your consulting practice dozens or even hundreds of leads and thousands of dollars in sales. And with more than 6,000 magazines and trade journals from which to choose, it's a safe bet there's at least one that will be interested in a story from your company.

Getting an article published in a trade journal or local business magazine is not difficult—if you know how. While editors are quick to reject inferior material or "puff" pieces, they are hungry for good, solid news and information to offer their readers. And, unlike newspapers, whose reporters are investigative and frequently antagonistic and adversarial toward business, trade journal editors represent a friendlier audience and are more willing to work with you to get information to their readers.

One key mistake novices make in placing feature articles is giving up too soon. Your article is probably not going to be accepted by the first editor to see it, or even the second. But keep trying. Consultant Jeff Davidson, a widely published author, says that to get 400 articles published, he was rejected 8,000 times.

Every Editor Has Unique Needs

Every magazine is different in some way from its competitors. To increase your chances of getting a placement, you must study tone, style, content, and the quality of a journal's writing and graphics.

Offer an editor the type of article that his or her magazine seems to prefer, and your odds of placing the story increase. If a magazine contains all short articles of one or two pages, don't send a 6,000-word thesis. If it does not run case histories, don't propose one.

Study issues of the magazine to see which topics are covered. The key to success is not to send an idea for an article on something never covered, but to offer an article that presents a new slant or angle on one of the magazine's frequent topics.

Consultants and other firms promoting a service or product can increase their chances for coverage by requesting a magazine's editorial calendar and scanning the list of "special issues" to see if there is possible tie-in between their products and services and any articles to be featured in these issues. Call the magazine's advertising department, say you are a potential advertiser, request a free media kit, and ask for an editorial calendar of special issues along with a sample issue. These items will be sent without charge to potential advertisers.

"If people respond to our editorial calendar with ideas for specific issues, great!" says Rick Dunn, editor of *Plant Engineering.* "Or if they can provide background for a story we want to do, they'll have an edge in getting into the magazine."

You may even want to suggest feature story ideas for the next year's calendar. The trick is to do that tactfully. "Don't come across as pushy or demanding," warns Dunn. "Stay away from saying things like 'This is important to your readers' or 'You should run this story.' If someone knows our business better than we do, we'll hire him or we'll go back to school."

However, if you spot a new trend in, say, packaging food in recyclable cardboard containers instead of plastic, and you can provide statistics and information to back up your claim that this trend is important, contact the editors at the appropriate packaging magazines. They will probably appreciate your interest and effort.

Which Magazine?

Aside from *Bacon's Publicity Checker* (see Appendix A), the best source for learning more about magazines and their editorial requirements is a book called *Writer's Market,* published annually by Writer's Digest Books, 1507 Dana Avenue, Cincinnati, OH 45207, 513-531-2222. *Writer's Market* lists more than 4,000 consumer, general, business, and trade publications that accept articles from outside sources. Listings give detailed descriptions of what editors are looking for, along with names, addresses, phone numbers, and other contact information.

The best magazines to target are the ones you are now getting. This is because you read them, are familiar with their editorial slant and style, and are aware of what articles related to your topic have recently run. However, there may be many magazines in your industry that you don't get and are not familiar with; you can find them in *Bacon*'s *Publicity Checker* or *Writer*'s *Market.* Contact each publication that interests you and ask for a sample issue and editorial guidelines. When the sample issue comes, study it and become familiar with the publication.

Timing is important. For a monthly magazine, an article to appear in a special issue should probably be proposed to the editor three to six months in advance of the publication date.

Should you call or write the editor? Most editors won't object to either method of pitching an idea, but they usually prefer one or the other. It's simply a matter of personal choice and time constraints.

If you don't know how a particular editor feels on the subject, call and ask. An appropriate opening might be: "This is Joe Jones from XYZ Consulting Corporation, and I have a story idea you might be interested in. Do you have time to spend a few minutes over the phone discussing it, or would you prefer that I send you a query?"

Editors who prefer to get it in writing will tell you so. Editors who prefer a quick description over the phone will appreciate your respect for their time, whether they listen to your pitch on the spot or ask you to phone back later.

But even those editors who will listen to your idea over the phone will also want something in writing. "With a phone call, I can tell someone right away whether he's on the right track," says Mark Rosenweig, editor of *Chemical Engineering Progress.* "If I like the idea, I'll then request a detailed outline describing the proposed article," Adds Rick Dunn: "A phone call is all right, but I can't make an editorial decision until I see a query letter."

A query letter is simply a one- or two-page letter proposing to write an article for a particular magazine and editor. A sample query letter is reprinted in Appendix F.

At *Modern Materials Handling,* assistant editor Barbara Spencer suggests writers send in a letter of introduction, followed by a phone call a week or two later. "We look for someone who knows his field and products, and the letter helps us gauge that expertise," she says. "But call the magazine first and find out which editor handles the type of article you have in mind."

All letters should be addressed to a specific editor by name. A letter that begins "Dear Editor" may not reach the right one and also indicates you were too lazy to find out that person's name.

Never state in your query letter "And best of all, you don't have to pay me for this article, because I'm doing it to publicize my consulting practice." Even though editors know this, it's a breach of etiquette for you to come out and say it. (Why this is I have no idea.)

Following Up Your Query

One of three things will happen after you mail your query letter:

1. The editor will accept your article "on spec" (on speculation). This means the editor is interested and wants to see the completed manuscript, but is not making a firm commitment to publish. This is the most positive response you are likely to get, and unless the article you write is terrible, there is a better than 50 percent chance it will get published.
2. The editor will reject your query. The next step is to send the query to the next editor and magazine on your list.
3. The third and most likely alternative is that you will not hear one way or the other. There are several reasons for this. The editor may not have gotten around to your query, or may have read it but not made a decision. Your query also may have been lost or never received.

The follow-up should be a polite note asking the editors (1) if the article proposal was received, and (2) if the proposal was reviewed to determine interest.

If I do not get a reply to my query after four weeks, I send a follow-up letter asking if the editor received the original query (copy of which I enclose), and whether there is interest. If there is no reply to the follow-up letter, I make a phone call. If I do not get through after three or four calls, I move on and submit the proposal to the next magazine on my list.

You may be thinking, "If it takes four to six weeks to get an answer from each publication, it might take many months to get my story into print." The answer is to have multiple query letters in the mail simultaneously. Doing so ensures a steady flow of media pickups and makes the results of any individual query much less critical in terms of your overall public relations (PR) success.

Getting the Go-Ahead

An editor is interested. Hurrah! You've passed the first step. Now you must write and deliver the article, or hire a public relations firm or freelance writer to do so for you.

Once your idea is accepted, you'll need to know the length and deadline requirements. If the editor doesn't volunteer this information, ask. The answers may avoid misunderstanding later on. As a rule, be generous with length. Include everything you think is relevant, and don't skimp on examples. Editors would rather delete material than have to request more. While a few magazines are flexible on length, most give authors specific word lengths to shoot for. Ask how long to make your article.

Deadlines also can vary considerably among journals. Some don't like to impose any deadlines, especially if they work far enough in advance that they are not pressed for material. But if the article is intended for publication in a special issue, the editor will probably want the finished manuscript at least two months before publication date. This allows time for revisions, assembling photos or illustrations, and production.

Rule of thumb: Don't put an editor's patience to the test. Missing a deadline may result in automatic rejection and waste the effort you spent making the placement and writing the article. Hand in every article on the deadline date, or sooner. If you cannot, advise well in advance and request a reasonable extension. Editors dislike late copy, but they hate surprises.

Resource Boxes

In addition to building image, increasing visibility, and serving as low-cost sales literature, you can also turn planted feature stories into direct-response tools. How is this done? With a resource box.

Figure 3.1   Sample Resource Box

Robert Bly is a freelance copywriter specializing in business-to-business and direct response advertising. He writes ads, direct-mail packages, and sales letters for more than 75 clients nationwide including Prentice-Hall, Grumman Corporation, Sony, On-Line Software, Philadelphia National Bank, and Associated Air Freight. He is also the author of 40 books including *The Copywriter's Handbook* (Henry Holt). Mr. Bly can be reached at 22 E. Quackenbush Ave., Dumont, NJ 07628, 201-385-1220.

A resource box—a term invented by Dr. Jeffrey Lant—is a box that appears at the end of your article. Instead of the usual brief author bio ("Bob Bly is a consultant whose articles frequently appear in *Business Marketing*"), the resource box gives complete information on who you are, what your company offers, and how readers of the article can reach you. A sample resource box is shown in Figure 3.1.

"I swap the articles I write in return for resource boxes in those publications," explains Lant. "Publications run the article. I get the resource box. Some of these publications swap for outright ad space—that is, they will *not* let my resource box run along with the article. One publication, with a readership of more than 75,000 financial planners, gives me both the resource box *and* an ad. I therefore have a very good sense of which draws better.

"*The resource box always wins.* There are several reasons for this. First, the article acts as a qualifying device. If you're not interested in copywriting, you probably won't read an article on the subject. If you're interested, you may have a need. And if you have a need, you'll be more receptive to filling it. Second, the article plus the resource box is several times larger than the ad. Third, the article gives the product credibility. The buyer reasons that the publication wouldn't publish the article—and as a result 'recommend' the product—if it wasn't good. The article and the resource box lower the buyer's suspicion.

"Finally, the words resource box are far superior to ad. This helps sales. The resource box looks like a public service, which, of course, it is. For these reasons, the resource box always draws substantially better than the same product or service featured in an ad, no matter how well written and complete the advertisement."

How do you get a resource box printed with your article? Don't ask editors outright. Instead, simply type in the resource box at the end of your manuscript and submit it along with your article, I find that 10 to 20 percent of the time, editors will print it as is without questioning you. Another 10 to 20 percent of editors will object but relent after some discussion.

The remainder will refuse you, because they see the resource box as too blatantly promotional and somehow compromising standards of journalistic integrity. But with my method you will have resource boxes running with at least 10 percent and up to 30 to 40 percent of all feature stories you place—significantly increasing the effectiveness of these articles.

How to Recycle Your Published Articles

Don Hauptman, a New York City–based direct marketing copywriter and consultant, says that just publishing any article once does not take advantage of its full potential as a marketing tool. "Most professionals who write for publication stop at this point," says Hauptman. "But for the aggressive, savvy self-marketer, the first publication of the article is only the beginning."

Why recycle your article? Because, as Hauptman notes, "The lifespan of any magazine, newsletter, or newspaper is limited. You want to get as much mileage as possible out of your effort." Here are Hauptman's suggestions:

- When you sell the article initially, make sure the publication gets one-time publication rights (known as "first rights") only. You, the author, retain all other rights. Ideally, try to have a copyright line printed at the end of your article (©1998 by Jane Doe). Reason: You have plans for the article, and you don't want to have to beg for permission to use your own work.
- Be sure to get several copies of the issue as soon as it's off the press. When you receive them, cut apart one copy and paste it up for duplication.
- For its new incarnation, the article may require some creative rearrangement. You will probably want to delete surrounding ads. Cut the publication's logo from the cover, masthead, or contents page

and place it at the top. This step is important—it gives your words the imprimatur of a known (and presumably respected) medium. At the end, tack on your firm's name, address, and phone number . . . easily obtainable from your letterhead or business card.

- Send the resultant mechanical or paste-up to a quick print shop. Or simply run it through your office copier. Watch out for problems that might make your new publicity piece appear unattractive or unprofessional: dirt, skewed paragraph, or cut marks (stray lines created by the edge of the pasted-up article—they'll disappear with the help of typewriter correction fluid).

- For maximum readability, print the article in black on white or light-colored paper. Your name or your firm's name can be highlighted using a second color ink. Or save the extra expense by circling your name or byline on each printed copy with a contrasting color fiber-tip pen.

- Distribute copies of reprints to current, past, and potential clients. Include the reprints in your literature package or press kit, leave them in your reception area or lobby, hand them out at conferences and speaking engagements, and enclose them in a direct mail package. The possibilities are endless.

- Because you own all rights to the article, you are free to publish it elsewhere. Other publications might want to run the article in its entirety, or excerpt or quote from it. Or an editor may ask you to revise the article for his or her publication. Such adaptation is usually easy; the hard work has been done. You can even use the article as part of a book, either your own or perhaps an anthology by someone else.

Establish Your Expertise by Writing a Book on Your Consulting Specialty

Writing articles isn't difficult, and as a self-promotion for the independent consultant, it works beautifully. The next logical step is to go from writing articles to books. Books take longer to write, naturally. But they are an even more powerful credibility-builder than articles.

The fact that you have written a book and had it published adds permanent prestige to your resume which will last for life. Your being a published author impresses others. Your reputation as expert in the subject matter of your book will grow. Having a book published is a credit you'll always include in your biography.

Because people view authors as experts, writing a book will make you an expert on your topic in the eyes of the public, including potential clients. Many people will call as a result of your book. Some of these will become clients.

I recently heard the definition of an expert as "someone who doesn't have more information than other people, but just has it better organized." If that's true, then writing a book really will make you more of an expert, because it forces you to think and write about your topic in a clear, logical, easy-to-follow fashion. When I write a book on a particular topic, I always learn a lot about that topic— and how to make it accessible to others— during the research, organizing, and writing process. I'm sure you will too.

Edward Uhlan, author of the *Rogue of Publishers Row,* notes that just because a person has written a book, the general public thinks he or she is an authority on the subject matter. You can see proof of this on *Oprah* and the other talk shows. Whenever the producers do a show on a particular topic (e.g., "Men Who Hate Broccoli and the Women Who Force Them to Eat It"), there are usually five guests: two people who are the victims (in this case, men forced to eat broccoli), two people who are the villains (in this case, women forcing the men to eat broccoli), and, inevitably, one person who has written a book on the topic (in this case, the author of *Broccoli and Relationships*).

The late science and science-fiction writer Isaac Asimov, who wrote more than 475 books, tells how during a radio interview, he was unable to answer some of the interviewer's questions about the human brain. The radio interviewer was puzzled at Asimov's inability, and asked, "Didn't you just write a book on the human brain?" Asimov replied, "Yes, but I have written hundreds of books on dozens of subjects, so I can't be an expert in all of them. And I am not an expert in the human brain. But, there is one thing I am an expert in." "What's that?" the frustrated interviewer asked. "I'm an expert on being an expert!" replied Asimov. "Do you want me to talk about that?" The interviewer declined to take Asimov up on his offer.

Because writing and selling a book is more involved than writing an article, I can't cover everything here. But I can hit the highlights of the right steps to getting your book published:

Step 1: Come Up with a Good Idea for Your Book

If you already have a good idea, move on to Step 2. If not, analyze your knowledge base, consulting specialties, client base, and service offerings. Which topic is broad enough that thousands of people will buy a book on the topic?

Some first-time authors are intimidated by this step. They feel they lack the creativity to come up with good ideas.

My experience is that all of us are capable of coming up with good ideas, including ideas for books. The hard work is not coming up with the idea; it's writing the book.

Isaac Asimov said that he would frequently get calls from readers who had ideas for science-fiction stories. Their proposal was that they would supply the idea, he would write the story, and they would split the profits 50-50.

"I have a better idea," Asimov always told these callers. "I'll give *you* an idea for a story, you write it, and when it's published, you send me 50 percent of the profit."

No one ever took him up on his offer.

Step 2: Evaluate Your Book Idea

There are many ideas and titles that *sound* good, but once evaluated with a critical eye, must be rejected because they are not commercially viable and would not appeal to a publisher.

When I ask potential authors why they think a publisher would want to publish their book—and why a reader would want to buy and read it—a lot of them answer, "Because it's a good book" or "The subject is important."

In today's marketplace, that's not enough. Remember: According to a recent Gallup survey, people read nonfiction books either for information or entertainment. Your book has to entertain or inform them. A book that does neither is going to be extremely difficult to sell.

Step 3: Create the Content Outline

Once you decide on a topic for your book, I recommend that you develop a content outline. A content outline is similar to the table of contents you find in any nonfiction book except it's more detailed and fleshed out.

Developing the content outline has three purposes. First, it helps you determine whether you can produce enough text on the subject to fill a book. Second, it is perhaps the single most powerful tool for convincing publishers that your book idea has merit. Third, it will save you an enormous amount of time when you sit down to write your book proposal and the book itself.

I always make my content outlines detailed rather than sketchy. I am convinced this is important in selling the book to a publisher.

Step 4: Write Your Book Proposal

The book proposal is often the most mysterious part of the book publishing process, especially to beginners. The reason: You know what books look like, because you've seen hundreds of them. But chances are, you don't know what a book proposal looks or sounds like, because you have never seen one. A complete book proposal is reprinted in my book, *Getting Your Book Published* (Roblin Press, 1997).

Step 5: Get an Agent

Although it's possible to sell directly to the publishers, I recommend you get a literary agent. *Literary Market Place,* (R. R. Bowker) available in bookstores or the reference room of your local library, lists agents you can contact.

Step 6: Send Your Proposal to Publishers and Get an Offer

If you have an agent, the agent will approach publishers for you. If you choose to go without an agent, you can approach publishers directly.

Step 7: Negotiate Your Contract

If you have an agent, the agent negotiates the contract on your behalf, with your input and approval. If you don't have an agent, you handle the negotiations yourself. Key contract terms include advances, royalties, first and second serial rights, termination, and copyright.

Step 8: Write and Deliver the Manuscript

Follow the outline the publisher bought when accepting your proposal. And be on time.

For complete instructions on writing and selling a nonfiction book, see my book *Getting Your Book Published* (listed in Appendix A).

Public Speaking

Public speaking—giving speeches, lectures, talks, papers, and presentations at public events, industry meetings, conventions, and conferences—is a PR technique that consultants and businesses use widely to promote their products or services.

Why is public speaking so effective as a promotional tool? When you speak, you are perceived as the expert. If your talk is good, you immediately establish your credibility with the audience so that members want you and your company to work with them and solve their problems.

Unlike an article, which is somewhat impersonal, a speech or talk puts you within handshaking distance of your audience. And, because in today's fast paced world more and more activities are taking place remotely via fax, the Internet, and video-conferencing, meeting prospects face to face firmly implants an image of you in their minds. If that meeting takes place in an environment where you are singled out as an expert, as is the case when you speak, the impression is that much more effective and powerful.

Speaking is not ideal for every product or marketing situation. If you are trying to mass market a new brand of floppy disk on a nationwide basis to all computer users, television and print advertising is likely to be more effective than speaking, which limits the number of people you reach per contact. On the other hand, a wedding consultant whose market is Manhattan would probably profit immensely from a talk on wedding preparation given to engaged couples at a local church.

Speaking is also the promotional tool of choice when targeting your PR efforts to a highly specific, narrow vertical market in which many of your best prospects are members of one or more of the major associations or societies in that market. For example, in the widget industry, if you wanted to reach widget buyers, you might run ads or write articles for the large circulation magazines going to all widget people. But if your company specialized in widget polishing, you might be better off getting involved in a variety of ways, including speaking engagements or presentation of papers, at meetings of the Society for Widget Polishers and the National Association for Widget Cleaning and Polishing, if two such organizations existed.

Finding Speaking Opportunities and Selecting a Topic

Unless you are sponsoring your own seminar, you will need to find appropriate forums at which your company personnel can be invited to speak. How do you go about it?

First, check your mail and the trade publications you read for announcements of industry meetings and conventions. For instance, if you design furnaces for steel mills and want to promote a new process, you might want to present a paper on your technique at the annual Iron and Steel Exposition.

Trade journals generally run preview articles and announcements of major shows, expos, and meetings months before the event. Many trade publications also have columns that announce such meetings on both a national and a local level. Make sure you scan these columns in publications aimed at your target market industries.

You should also receive preview announcements in the mail. If you are an advertising manager or the owner of your own small business, professional societies and trade associations will send you direct mail packages inviting your firm to exhibit at their shows. That's fine, but you should also find out whether papers, talks, or seminars are being given at the show, and, if so, how to get your people on the panels or signed up as speakers. If the show mailing promotion doesn't discuss papers or seminars, call up and ask.

Propose some topics with your company personnel as the speakers. Most conference managers welcome such proposals, because they need speakers. The conference manager or another association executive in charge of the " technical sessions" (the usual name for the presentation of papers or talks) will request an abstract or short 100 to 200 word outline of your talk. If others in your consulting firm will be giving the talks, work with them to come up with an outline that is enticing enough to generate maximum attendance but also accurately reflects what the speaker wants to talk about.

Because many advertisers will be pitching speakers and presentations to the conference manager, the earlier you do it, the better. Generally, annual meetings and conventions of major associations begin planning eight to twelve months in advance; local groups or local chapters of national organizations generally book speakers three to four months in advance. The earlier you approach them, the more receptive they'll be to your proposal.

You can "recycle" your talks and give them to different groups in the same year or different years, tailoring them slightly to fit current market conditions, the theme of the meeting, or the group's special interests. When you create a description, outline, or proposal for a talk, keep it on your hard drive. Then, when other speaking opportunities come your way, you can quickly edit the file and produce a customized proposal or abstract you can fax or mail to the person in charge of that meeting.

Because your goal is to sell your consulting product or service, not educate the audience or become a professional speaker, you want to pick a topic that relates to and helps promote your business but is also of great interest to the group's audience. Importantly, the presentation does not sell you directly, but sells you by positioning you and your company as the expert source of information on the problem your product or service addresses. As such, it must be objective and present how-to advice or useful information; it cannot be a sales or product presentation.

For example, if you consult on automated telemarketing systems, your talk cannot be a sales pitch for a particular system. Instead, you could do something like "How to Choose the Right Computer Automated Telemarketing Software" or "Computer Automated vs. Traditional Telemarketing Systems: Which Is Right for Your Business?" Although you want people to choose your system, your talk should be (mostly) objective and not too obviously slanted in favor of your product; otherwise, you will offend and turn off your audience.

I once spoke at a marketing meeting where one of the other presenters, a manufacturer of such computerized telemarketing systems, was giving a talk. Although he was supposed to talk about how to improve telemarketing results with software, he proceeded to haul in his system and give a demonstration. The comments from attendees were openly hostile and negative. I'm sure he didn't get any business, and this did not enhance his reputation either.

One last tip: If you are not on the mailing list to receive advance notification of meetings and conventions of your industry associations, write to request that they place you on such a list. Their names and addresses are listed in *The Encyclopedia of Associations,* published by Gale Research and available in your local library.

Screening Speaking Opportunities

On occasion, meeting planners and conference executives may call you up and ask you (or a representative from your firm) to speak at their event, rather than you having to seek them.

This is flattering, but beware: Not every opportunity to speak is really worthwhile. Meeting planners and committee executives are primarily concerned with getting someone to stand at the podium, and do not care whether your speaker or your firm will benefit in any way from the exposure. So, before you say yes to an opportunity to speak, ask the meeting planner the following questions:

- What is the nature of the group?
- Who are the members? What are their job titles and responsibilities? What companies do they work for?
- What is the average attendance of such meetings? How many people does the meeting planner expect will attend your session?
- Do they pay an honorarium or cover expenses?
- What other speakers have they had recently and what firms do these speakers represent?
- Do they pay those other speakers? If so, why not you too?

If the answers indicate that the meeting is not right or worthwhile for your company, or if the meeting planner seems unable or unwilling to provide answers, thank him or her politely and decline the invitation.

Negotiating Your "Promotional Deal"

Because your goal is not to make money as a speaker but to promote your product or service, you can use the group's lack of payment for your talk as a weapon in negotiating extra concessions that can help maximize the promotional value of your talk.

In addition to the opportunity to address the group, you should try to get all or at least some of the following concessions.

A List of the Association's Members

Tell the meeting chairperson you would be happy to speak at no charge, provided you receive this. You can use the list to promote your company via direct mail before and after your presentation. A pretalk mailing can let people know about your upcoming talk and serve as a personal invitation for them to attend. A posttalk mailing can offer a reprint or audio recording of your presentation to those who missed it.

Inclusion of Your Materials in the Conference Kit

At larger conferences and conventions, the conference manager provides attendees with show kits including a variety of materials such as a seminar schedule, passes to luncheons and dinners, maps, tourist sights of interest to out-of-town visitors, and the like. These kits are either mailed in advance or distributed at the show.

You can tell the conference manager you will give the presentation at no charge if your company literature is included in the conference kits mailed to attendees. If that is possible, you can supply as many copies of your literature as they need. You then get your promo pieces mailed to hundreds, even thousands, of potential clients *at zero mailing cost.*

PR Placement in the Organization's Newsletter or Magazine

Although a speech is an effective way of getting known to a particular audience, making a permanent impression on a market segment requires a series of contacts, not a single communication. You can easily transform a one-shot speaking engagement into an ongoing PR campaign targeted to the membership of this particular group by getting one or more PR placements in the organization's newsletter or magazine. For instance, tell the meeting planner you will supply a series of articles (your current press releases and feature articles—recycled for this particular audience) to run in the organization's newsletter before the talk. This not only makes you known to the audience, which is good PR for your firm, but also helps build interest in attending your program.

After your talk, give the editor of the organization's newsletter the notes or text of your speech, and ask that all or part of it (or a summary) be run as a posttalk article, so those who could not attend can benefit from the information. Additional articles can also be run as follow-ups after the talk to reinforce your message and provide additional detail to those who want to learn more, or to answer questions or cover issues you didn't have time to discuss in your speech.

Free Advertising

If the association editor will not run a resource box with your articles, talk to the meeting planner about getting some free ads for your product or service. For a national organization that actually charges for ads in its magazine, the value of your free ad space should be approximately twice what your fee would be if you were charging for your talk.

Extra Copies of Conference Programs or Mailings

The organization will do a program or mailing (or both) with a nice write-up of you and your talk. Usually, left over copies are thrown away. Mention that you would be glad to take those extra copies off their hands. Inserting those fliers is a nice added touch to your press kits and inquiry fulfillment packages.

A Professional Audiotape or Video of Your Speech

A professional audiotape or video of you giving a seminar can be a great promotional tool and an attention-getting supplement to printed brochures, direct mail, and other sales literature. But producing one can be expensive. One way to get an audio or video produced at low cost is to have someone else foot the bill for the taping. If an organization wants you to speak but cannot pay you, ask them to have it professionally recorded and give you a copy of the master. If they object to the expense, tell them they can copy and distribute the video or audio of your speech to their members, or even sell it to those who attend the meeting.

At many major meetings, it is standard practice for sponsoring organizations to audiotape all presentations and offer the tapes for sale at the conference and for one year thereafter in promotional mailings. If you are being taped, tell the sponsor you normally do not allow it unless you get the master. (Also make clear that, while you will allow the sponsor to sell it and will waive any percentage of the profits, the copyright is to be in your name.)

A List of Other State and Local Chapters

If the group is a local chapter of a national organization, ask the meeting chairperson for a list of the other chapters, along with addresses, phone numbers, and the names of the meeting organizers for each of those chapters. Then contact these chapters and offer to give the talk to their members.

Planning Your Objective and Preparing Your Presentation

Of course, your objective is to sell. But be careful. People attending a luncheon or dinner meeting aren't there to be sold. They want to be entertained. Informed. Educated. Made to laugh or smile. Selling your product, service, or company may be your goal, but in public speaking, it has to be secondary to giving a good presentation, and a "soft sell" approach works best.

The trick to reducing preparation time is to have two or three "canned" (standard) talks that you can offer to various audiences. Even with a canned presentation, you'll need at least several hours to analyze the audience, do some customizing of your talk to better address that particular group, and rehearse once or twice.

A talk has three parts: beginning, middle, and end. All are important. But the beginning and ending are more important than the body. Most people can manage to discuss a topic for fifteen minutes, give a list of facts, or read from a prepared statement. And that's what it takes to deliver the middle part.

The beginning and ending are more difficult. In the beginning, you must immediately engage the audience's attention *and* establish rapport. Not only must members be made to feel that your topic will be interesting, but they must be drawn to you, or at least not find fault with your personality.

To test this theory, a well-known speaker put aside his usual opening and instead spoke for five minutes about how successful he was, how much money he made, how in demand he was as a speaker, and why he was the right choice to address the group. After his talk, he casually asked a member, "What were you thinking when I said that?" The man politely replied, "I was thinking what a blowhard you are."

How do you begin a talk? One easy and proven technique is to get the audience involved by asking questions. For example, if addressing telecommunications engineers, ask: "How many of you manage a T1 network? How many of you are using 56 Kbps but are thinking about T1? And how many of you use fractional T1?"

If you are speaking on a health topic, you might ask, "How many of you exercised today before coming here? How many of you plan to exercise after the meeting tonight? How many of you exercise three or more times a week?"

Asking questions like these has two benefits. First, it provides a quick survey of audience concerns, interests, and levels of involvement, allowing you to tailor your talk on the spot to their needs. Second, it forces the audience to become immediately involved. After all, when you are in the audience and the speaker asks a question, you do one of two things: you either raise your hand or don't raise it. Either way you are responding, thinking, and getting involved.

While the beginning is important, don't neglect a strong closing, especially if you are there not just for the pleasure of speaking but to help promote your company or its products. As Dorothy Leeds observes in her book *PowerSpeak* (Prentice-Hall): "Speakers, as you now know, are also in the selling business, and the conclusion is the time to ask for the order. Nothing will happen if you don't ask. And you ask by telling the audience what you want it to do with the information you've presented and *how* they can take that action. An effective speaker presenting a central idea ends by pointing out to those in his audience exactly what is needed from them to put that idea to work. For example . . . if you've been persuading them to give blood, tell them where. And make it sound easy to get there."

Action doesn't always have to be literal. If you simply want the people in your audience to mull over your ideas, tell them this is what you want them to do.

Although you want a great opening that builds rapport and gets people to listen, and an ending that helps "close the sale," don't neglect the body or middle of your talk. It's the "meat"; it's what your audience came to hear. If your talk is primarily informational, be sure to give inside information on the latest trends, techniques, and product developments. If it's motivational, be enthusiastic and convince your listeners that they can lose weight, make money investing in real estate, or stop smoking.

If your talk is a how-to presentation, make sure you've written it so your audience walks away with lots of practical ideas and suggestions. As actor and toastmaster George Jessel observes, "Above all, the successful speaker is sincerely interested in telling his audience something they want to know."

When speaking to technical audiences, tailor the content to listeners' expertise. Being too complex can bore a lot of people. But being too simplistic or basic can be even more offensive to an audience of knowledgeable industry experts.

Using Handouts

The "leave-behind" or handout can take one of several formats: hard copy of the slides or overheads, brochures, article reprints, or reprints of the narration (with visuals incorporated, if possible). It can be the full text of your talk, an outline, just the visuals, or a report or article on a topic that is either related to the presentation topic or that expands on one of the subtopics you touched on briefly in the talk. Every handout should contain your company name, address, phone and fax numbers, and if possible a full resource box with a brief summary of who you are and what you do—as should *every* marketing document you produce.

If the handout is the full text of your talk or a set of fairly comprehensive notes, tell the audience before you start: "There's no need to take notes. We have hard copies of this presentation for you to take home." This relieves listeners of the burden of note taking, freeing them to concentrate on your talk. Handouts such as transcripts of a speech, articles, reports, or other materials with lots of copy should be handed out *after* the talk, not before. If you hand them out before you step up to the podium, the audience will read the printed materials and ignore you. You can hand out reproductions of visuals or pages with just a few bullet points in advance, so attendees can write notes directly on them.

Why do you need handouts? They enhance learning. But the main reason to give handouts is to ensure that every attendee (most of whom are potential customers) walks away with a piece of paper containing information on what you offer and how to contact you. That way, when the person goes to work the next morning and thinks, "That was an interesting talk. Maybe I should contact them to talk about how they can help us," he or she has your phone number in hand. Without it, response to your talk will be zero or near zero. Most people are too busy, lazy, or indifferent to start tracking you down if they don't have immediate access to your contact information. It is most important to give a useful, interesting, information-packed talk that convinces prospects you know what you are talking about and makes them want to talk with you about doing work for them. But without the contact information immediately in hand, the prospect's interest and curiosity will quickly evaporate.

Because you cannot tell in advance who in the audience will want to follow up with you, your goal is to get as many people as possible to pick up and take home your handout material.

There are several ways to distribute handouts at your talk. The most common is to leave the materials on a table, either in the back of the room or at the registration table where people sign in for the meeting or your session. But this is not effective. Most people will walk right by the table without picking up the material. Many won't even notice the table or stack of handouts. Even if you point out the table and say that reprints are available, many won't take one. And you might feel embarrassed at the silence that follows your announcement—it makes you seem less authoritative, more of a promoter.

Another technique is to put a copy of your handout on each seat in the room about a half hour before the start of your presentation. Most people will pick it up, look at it; about 25 to 50 percent will take it with them when they leave and half or more will leave it on the chair. Disadvantages? People may read the handout and not pay attention to your presentation. Also, some people resent this approach, seeing it as being too pushy.

The most effective method of distributing handouts is the "green sheet" method. It maximizes the number of attendees who take handouts, increases their desire to have the material, and importantly, eliminates any hint of self-promotion or salesmanship. Here's how it works. Prepare a handout that expands on one of the points in your talk, covering it in more detail than you can in a short presentation. Or make the handout a supplement, covering additional points not discussed but related to the topic.

Another option is to do a handout that's a resource guide. For example, a bibliography of reference books on your topic, tables of technical data, a glossary of key terms, a series of equations or examples of calculations, and the like. The important point is that the handout relates to *but does not merely repeat* information covered in your talk; instead, it *expands* on it.

When you get to that topic in your speech, which should be about halfway or three-quarters through the talk, discuss the point, then say something like, "I really can't cover in this short talk all of the techniques related to this, so I've prepared a checklist of twenty-five points to consider when planning this type of project, and reprinted it on this green sheet." Pause, hold up the sheet for everyone to see, then continue, "I have plenty of copies, so if you want one, come up to me after the talk and I'll give you a copy."

After your talk, you will be surrounded at the podium by a large crowd of people with their hands out to get the free green sheet. Try it—it works. Oh, and why a "green sheet" rather than copying it on plain white paper? Doing it on colored paper and calling it a green sheet just seems to make it more special. Also, instead of having to remember what's actually on the sheet, people can just come up and say, "May I have a green sheet please?"

If the conference organizer will not release a list of attendees or those who go to your specific session, but you want to capture as many of those names as possible for marketing follow-up, offer your handout as a bait piece rather than giving it out at the session At the conclusion of your talk, discuss your handout and what it covers, and say: "So if you would like a free copy of our telecom security checklist, just write 'TSC' on the back of your business card and hand it to me. I'll mail a free copy of the checklist to you as soon as I get back to the office." The more enticing and relevant your bait piece, the more business cards you will collect. A really strong bait piece offer can get you the business cards of 25 to 75 percent of attendees or more.

How to Generate More

Sales Leads Than You

Can Handle

One of the most essential capabilities of the independent consultant is the ability to generate a sufficient quantity of leads that will provide a steady stream of lucrative consulting assignments and clients. Yet this is the aspect of being an independent consultant with which many of us are least comfortable. We are happiest practicing our consulting specialty, but less comfortable selling ourselves to others.

"You were probably never taught how to market," observes Murray Singerman, a tax attorney in Maryland. "Consequently, you are most likely very uncomfortable with the idea of actively pursuing clients and referral sources."

Ilise Benun writes: "In the service business, the hard sell doesn't work. It's a waste of everyone's time to try to convince someone who has no interest or need for your services that they do in fact need your services. The purpose of marketing is to find people who know they need your services, either currently or at some future point, introduce yourself to them, allow a relationship to develop, and then be there when they're ready to work for you."

This chapter shows how to generate leads that identify people who know they need your services, so you can get them to hire you, now or later. Solo and small-firm consultants have limited resources to spend on marketing activities. With rising postage and printing costs, and shrinking budgets, even larger organizations are looking to make their lead-generating activities as cost-effective and result-getting as possible.

Concentrating marketing efforts on one or more key marketing segments is the basis of target marketing. The four major ways to segment a market are:

1. *Geographic segmentation.* People located close to your place of business are more likely to become customers than those who are far away. If you can fulfill inquiries and product orders by freight or mail, you can also target markets in geographic areas not near you. For example, a water treatment company might target prospects in another state where the water is especially hard or polluted. A manufacturer of solar energy panels might concentrate efforts in areas that are sunny; Seattle would probably not be at the top of the list.

2. *Demographic segmentation.* You may choose to market to groups of prospects based on age, race, sex, social class, marital status, or income.

3. *Type-of-business segmentation.* Your market may be specific types of businesses (car dealers, hotels, steelmakers, restaurants, computer companies) and organizations (hospitals, universities, federal agencies).

4. *Product segmentation.* The market for your products may be determined by how customers will use your product, and what benefits they derive from it. For example, beer brewers know that there are " heavy" beer drinkers who purchase 90 percent of all beer, and light (not "Lite") drinkers who buy an occasional six-pack. The heavy beer drinkers drink for taste and develop loyalty to a brand; light beer drinkers are likely to buy the low-priced brand.

Lead Generation Specifics

Within your business and marketing plan, you must determine exactly how many leads you need and what promotional activities you must do to achieve your goal.

Let's take a look at how to create a simple but totally effective lead plan. To keep the model plan simple, we'll assume that you have chosen direct mail as your primary lead-generation tool. The elements of the plan include:

- Income objective
- Average unit of sale
- Conversion rate
- Lead rate
- Mailing activity level (pieces mailed per week or per month)

This plan is so brief and simple you can literally write it on the back of an envelope (but use a clean sheet of paper anyway), and you can do it in about 10 minutes. (Have a calculator handy.)

To begin, you need to have a sales goal. If you don't know how much money you want to generate, how do you know whether you're on track? How much money do you want to gross this year from the leads you produce? Write down the amount on a piece of paper. Now divide by 12 to determine the amount of money you want your business to be grossing every month. Gross annual sales of $100,000, for example, translates into sales of $8,334 per month.

What is the gross amount of your average unit of sale? $100? $1,000? $10,000? Write down this number on your paper. Divide your total sales goal for the year by the dollar amount of the average unit of sale. This will show you how many sales you have to close to reach your stated objective. For example, if your income objective is $100,000 in sales and your average sale is $5,000, you have to close 20 sales this year to reach your goal.

Obviously, your mailings will generate inquiries. But not everyone who makes an inquiry will become a customer. In fact, most won't. The conversion rate is the percentage of leads that will become customers after repeat follow-up efforts are made. If for every ten inquiries, you make one sale, your conversion rate is 1/10, or 10 percent. If you convert one out of every four inquiries to a sale, your conversion rate is 1/4, or 25 percent.

Calculate your conversion rate now and write it down on your paper, preferably as a fraction—1/2, 1/3, 1/15 . . . you get the idea. If you haven't done much lead generating and don't know what your conversion rate is, make

an educated guess. Anywhere from ⅒ to ¼ is typical. As a rule of thumb, the more costly your product, the lower your conversion rate will be.

Now, flip the fraction. If your conversion rate was 25 percent, or ¼, flipping the fraction gives you ⁴⁄₁, or 4. If your conversion rate was 10 percent, or ⅒, flipping the fraction gives you ¹⁰⁄₁, or 10. Flip your fraction and write down the new number. Multiply this number times your required sales volume. If your number was 10, and your required sales volume was 20 sales, you multiply 10 by 20 and get 200. This is the number of leads you must generate to meet your sales goal.

This makes sense. If you generate 20 inquiries, and close 10 percent, you get two sales. If you generate 200 leads, and close 10 percent, you will get the 20 sales you need.

Okay. We know you have to get 200 leads to make your sales quota of $100,000 or 20 deals closed. But most of the mailing pieces you send out will not generate a lead. If your response rate is two percent, for example, 98 out of every 100 people receiving your mailing will not respond. As a result, we have to mail many letters or self-mailers to get one lead. How many pieces must we mail to get the required number of leads to achieve our sales quota?

First, determine how many mailing pieces you have to mail to get one inquiry. If you get a 2 percent response rate, you must mail 50 pieces to get one lead. So your number for this calculation would be 50. Now take this number and multiply it by the number of leads you require to meet your sales goal. In our example, we have already determined you need 200 leads to make the 20 sales that will result in $100,000 in income. If you must mail 50 pieces to get one sales lead, then multiply 200 leads required by the number 50, and you find you must mail 10,000 pieces this year to achieve your objective.

Dividing 10,000 pieces by 12 months a year, you see you must mail 834 pieces every month to generate the required number of leads, sales, and dollars to meet your planned objective. It's that simple.

Having gone through this planning process, you now have written down on your piece of paper the following information: income objective, average unit of sales, number of sales to make, conversion rate, lead rate, yearly mail volume, and number of mailings per month.

For our example, the plan should look something like this:

Annual income objective:	$100,000
Average unit of sale:	$5,000
Number of sales required to meet annual income objective:	20
Conversion rate (percentage of leads that convert into sales):	10%
Number of leads required (based on conversion rate) to meet goal:	200
Prospecting rate (number of prospects you must mail to produce one good lead):	50
Total number of pieces to mail this year:	10,000
Direct mail volume per month:	834

The bottom line of the plan is the last number. You now know what your goal is and, to achieve it, exactly what you must do each month: mail your letter to 834 prospects. What could be simpler?

How Can You Reach Your Customer?

Try to outline realistic methods of reaching your customer. Each business reaches its audience in a variety of ways. For some businesses, a sign over the door is the only way in which they let their potential customers know of their existence. However, considering the unlimited ways in which to use advertising, press releases, articles, flyers, brochures, radio, TV, newspapers, and magazines to help us communicate our message to the public, it seems foolish not to at least explore many possible avenues for exposure.

In the case of a fledgling photographer, he may choose to stimulate interest in his work by circulating a press release focusing on one aspect of his work. In his press release (Figure 4.1), photographer Tom Okada used his past associations as well as the opening of his new studio as "pegs" upon which to construct the release. By circulating the press release to local newspapers and magazines involved with photography, advertising, and the media, Okada was able to create interest in his work and gain some lead-generating publicity.

Figure 4.1   Sample Press Release

Client: **Contact:**

Tom Okada   THE COMMUNICATION WORKSHOP
45 West 18th Street   207 East 85th Street
New York, NY 10011   New York, NY 10028
                                      212-794-1144

For Immediate Release:

FORMER APPRENTICE TO MASTER PHOTOGRAPHERS
W. EUGENE SMITH AND ARNOLD NEWMAN
OPENS MANHATTAN STUDIO

NEW YORK, NY—"When you work with a good photographer, you get a lot
of good information; when you work with a great one, you receive inspiration." So
says Tom Okada, who gained not only inspiration but earned the respect and affection
of top photographers Arnold Newman and W. Eugene Smith.

Now, with a versatility and experience few photographers achieve, Okada, 29,
has just opened his own photographic studio at 45 West 18th Street in New York.

Because a Newman or a Smith can have his pick of eager photographic
assistants, Okada had to prove himself in a number of areas. His portfolio established
him as an expert in a number of photographic formats. He's at ease with tungsten as
well as strobe lighting; in studio as well as location settings. Okada is also a fine
carpenter, and is as exacting building sets as he is in photographing them.

Specializing in "fine-image" still-life photography, Okada hopes to broaden his
experience in candid photography, catalog work, and general advertising. Says
Okada, "A photographer is one artist who can't afford to be a prima donna. . . ."

This excerpt from a three-page release shows how a press release arranges thematic
material. The central idea (the studio opening) is blended with the photographer's
background to give importance to the event.

After writing the release, Tom must choose where to send it. If his
goals are purely to gain recognition in artistic circles, he might send it only
to photographic "arts" magazines. But if he is interested in stimulating
business, he will select magazines that reach people who have the power to
make a decision to hire him for an assignment, such as fashion or women's
magazines.

In the same way, a gourmet store owner has a variety of promotional
options, and must choose his goals for a particular promotion. A great deal
of care must go into a promotional decision, because the goals sometimes

conflict with each other. For example, it would be easy to print 10,000 flyers announcing the store's opening and hire high school students to distribute the flyers throughout the neighborhood. That would certainly get the word out, and it might bring in customers. But an inexpensively produced flyer might tacitly label the store as "cheap" or, worse, as just another "takeout place." So, although you might gain customers, you wouldn't be gaining the "right" customers—people who are motivated to buy good food, not just curiosity seekers.

A gourmet store owner may have to take a long-range view. The owner may want to throw a grand-opening party for the press or try to line up corporate catering business, reasoning that these methods will build a continuing market for his store's food. The critics, once they know of the store, may review the food; if the reviews are good, customers will follow. In the same way, a promotion aimed at food service managers and meeting planners of corporations might result in the catering of several business luncheons or office parties. After that, word of mouth might take over.

A stenography service that has determined its four prime customers are (1) local business people, (2) out-of-town business people staying at local hotels, (3) screenwriters or playwrights, and (4) job seekers who wish to dictate cover letters to accompany resumes, has taken the first step toward reaching these people.

In the same way, a dating service segments its market by recognizing that there are a number of subgroups within its market, and by approaching each subgroup with a unique angle. For example, a dating service might wish to send one type of message to young singles and a completely different one to senior citizens. Another message could be fashioned for middle-aged singles or recently divorced or widowed singles, assuming that you can segment these people and address them separately. Mailing lists of people who fit each category may be available from mailing list brokers, specialty magazines, or associations. By addressing the particular needs of each group separately, you give the impression that your organization specializes in that group's needs. That will go a long way toward making families with young children, senior citizens, or the recently divorced respond to your message.

Direct mail and sales promotion worked for the dating service; a press release worked for Tom Okada; a grand-opening press party helped gain attention for the gourmet store. Other businesses might make use of late-night radio advertising, or phone calls to prospects. In any case, you should consider the risks, costs, and time demands of all types of promotions before deciding which ones to pursue.

A Few Direct Mail Tips

When doing a promotional mailing to generate leads for your consulting practice, the following strategies may be useful.

Develop a Primary Offer

The main reason direct mail for consulting services fails is the lack of a specific offer. Ending a letter weakly with "Looking forward to working with you" or "I will call in a week or two" is certain to depress response to almost zero. If you tell people you will call them, they then have no incentive to call you first.

Far better is to identify the next step in the sales process and then tell the reader to take it. Many consultants want the mailing to result in an initial meeting with the prospective client. Therefore, the letter might offer a "free, no-obligation initial consultation." Being more specific about the nature of this exploratory session and attaching a benefit to it will increase response. For example: "We will analyze your current insurance coverage at no cost *and* make suggestions that will reduce your annual premiums by 10 percent—or more."

Develop a Secondary Offer

The primary offer will attract those prospects who are most eager to do business today or in the near future. However, this represents only a small fraction of the potential market. Therefore, a secondary offer is needed to attract those prospects who are not ready to meet right now but may have a need in 3 or 6 or 12 months.

This secondary offer is usually a free booklet, special report, brochure, fact sheet, or other printed information the reader can send for by calling or mailing back a postpaid business reply card. I usually stress the primary offer in the body copy of my letter and the *secondary* offer in the postscript. For example: "P.S. To receive a free report explaining our four-step Market Planning Process, complete and mail the reply card today."

Typically, from 50 to 90 percent of those who respond request the free information (secondary offer) rather than a face-to-face meeting (primary offer). Calling those who request the free booklet only and " selling" them on the benefits of a free consultation will reveal that 10 percent to 25 percent of the booklet requesters have genuine interest and can be talked into a meeting.

Encourage Both Phone and Mail Response

Always include a business reply card or fax-back reply form in mailings. Its absence can depress response to almost zero. Some consultants feel that using a business reply card in a personalized mailing aimed at executive prospects is somehow unprofessional. This is nonsense.

Stress that the reader can respond either by mailing the reply card or calling. To encourage telephone response, mention the phone number in the letter copy, even if it appears on the letterhead. Omitting either one of these two basic response options (mail or telephone), will depress response.

Establish Credibility

Prospects want to deal with consultants who are experts in their fields. Here are some techniques that can build this sense of credibility into the direct mail package.

- Enclose an article you have written that deals with the topic of the consulting service being sold. This will help convince the prospect of your expertise.
- Enclose a recent article written *about* you. This establishes that you are a recognized authority.
- Mention some of your clients—especially well-known names in the prospect's industry. If this would cause the prospect to worry about confidentiality, mention that you have obtained permission to list the names.
- Enclose copies of written letters for you by your clients. Testimonials are extremely effective; they make prospects feel comfortable and confident in your ability to serve them successfully.
- Create a separate brochure that lists your credentials and answers any questions the prospect might have about your service. This kind

of "full disclosure" alleviates anxiety and creates the impression that you are reliable and professional in your dealings.

- Include your photo on the brochure, unless you think your appearance is a negative (e.g., you are extremely young-looking or odd in grooming or dress). A photo gives prospects the feeling that they know you before they even meet or talk with you.

What Do You Want to Say to Your Audience?

The answer: Anything that might stimulate them to buy your product or service! You are arranging your product or service's "sales points" in a clear, careful manner. You hope that your customer will seize upon one or more of them and keep them in mind when it is time to make a purchase.

A dating service that stressed its empathy with being alone and aging might well be remembered by a single senior citizen. On the other hand, a food store might have to work hard to truly separate itself from the crowd. Perhaps the chef is famous, or the store has a new concept in takeout food. It might be that the store has a dazzlingly beautiful interior or that it specializes in salads or cheesecakes or baby back ribs. To entice the media into writing about the store, the owner must keep in mind that his is one of many similar stores, all craving media attention. Attention will be paid, therefore, to the store that presents itself in the most newsworthy light.

It's not hard to gain publicity for an odd business such as a love-letter-writing service or a breakfast-in-bed catering service that features a strolling violinist, but it is often difficult to gain ongoing publicity for more mundane businesses—beauty parlors, accountants, or plumbers. Therefore, you should consider not just the uniqueness or "sexiness" of the concept of your business, but its ability to grow, gain new customers, and entice ongoing media coverage or consumer interest.

For many businesses, a sale, new item, or new location provides the spark for a new promotion. Perhaps a personnel change—a new chef, decorator, or administrator—is noteworthy. The thrust of your promotion, though, remains steady: You are selling quality or service or low cost or all three, and you need to keep reminding the public that you, above your competitors, are best equipped to handle its business. It also helps to just say "thank you" to past customers. A Christmas card is one of the easiest and nicest ways of keeping your name in front of your customers without making a blatant sales pitch.

Subtlety doesn't work for everyone. A new pizza place doesn't want subtle promotion; it wants to tell people that its prices are reasonable, the mozzarella is fresh, and the crust is crusty. A flyer dropped strategically near the mailboxes at a few hundred large apartment buildings in the neighborhood can do the trick. So can posting the flyer at nearby coin laundries, supermarkets, and community bulletin boards. Because anyone might crave a pizza, there need not be any targeting of the market, except that the flyers will pull best if they are delivered within walking distance of the pizza place. It would be absurd to spread the flyer to other neighborhoods, because they are likely to have their own pizza parlors.

However, a business selling an expensive service must take great care to hone its promotional messages, and even greater care to target them to decision makers. For example, a consultant who sells training seminars in writing or presentation skills must make sure that his promotions are especially well written, concise, and clear. He, above all others, must avoid redundancy, antiquated phrases, clichés, and self-serving statements. When preparing his promotional message, the consultant must tailor his ideas to fit the interests of his audience.

And who is the audience? They may be training directors who purchase training seminars from outside vendors. Or people with similar titles or corporate functions: manager of management development, vice president of human resources, or vice president of personnel planning. These people receive numerous sales messages every day, and a consultant must catch attention before he can present his full message. An example of a consultant's sales letter is shown in Figure 4.2.

How Do You Want Your Customers to Respond?

When a pizza parlor delivers flyers to an apartment house, the pizza purveyor hopes that the flyer will stimulate the reader's appetite, and that the message will translate into the sale of a pizza or at least a meatball hero.

But sometimes sales are not that simple. It would be unreasonable for the writing consultant to expect a person receiving his mailing to pick up a phone and, without gaining more information, order one writing seminar "to go." The writing consultant's package brochure, cover letter, and return

Figure 4.2   Sample Sales Letter

This year, my business writing seminars will save a large insurance company $50,000. Next year, they'll save the company even more.

Here's how:

Recently, I designed and implemented a writing program for twelve supervisors at Mutual of New York. Among the many skills they learned was how to edit the "fat" out of their letters, memos, and reports.

We figured out that if each of the twelve trainees cut just one paragraph out of each of their communications, MONY would save 2,400 paragraphs per year. Because each paragraph takes an average of 20 minutes to write, edit, type, read, and understand, MONY would save 800 work hours a year.

As corporate time costs about $60 per hour, the savings could amount to as much as $50,000 in the first year. And that's a conservative figure.

Why? Because extra dividends are paid in an employee's greater confidence, improved productivity, and sharper communication skills, as well as in a better corporate image.

Next year, these same twelve people will again save their company $50,000 in wasted words, effort, and time and it won't cost MONY another penny. And, if MONY trains another twelve people, they'd probably save an additional $50,000 a year . . . every year.

Insurance companies such as MONY and The American Re-Insurance Company, for whom I designed a similar program, must feel I'm doing something right—they've invited me back to help train new groups of employees.

Please take a moment to review the enclosed brochure. If you'd like more information about how improved writing can make your company more productive, just fill out the enclosed card and mail it.

Gary Blake, Ph.D.
Director, The Communication Workshop

---

postcard aims at stimulating a request for additional information—an inquiry. There's no expectation of an immediate sale.

If the training manager returns the postcard, he is taking the first step in what may be many steps between the first contact and the final sale. Considering that the price of a seminar is several thousand dollars, it would be unrealistic to expect a purchase to take place before the prospect calls references, sees the consultant in action at another organization, or asks for a proposal. The true value of a return postcard is its help in building a reliable mailing list of qualified prospects.

When a mail or TV solicitation is used solely to generate immediate sales, we call that "mail order" advertising. In this type of advertising, products such as subscriptions, records, books, and cutlery are sold directly to a consumer who, upon hearing or reading the solicitation, writes a check. Perhaps he'll be induced to act quickly because he's been promised a "premium" or gift for speedy action. Keep in mind that the more money your product or service costs, the more sophisticated the promotion must be, and the more times you'll have to contact your prospect before completing the sale.

5

Your Promo Kit—Selling Your

Consulting Service with

Printed Material

Does Your Consulting Practice Need a Brochure?

Many potential clients you talk with will not be at the stage where they are ready to hire you or even meet with you. Prospects who seem somewhat interested in your services will often say, "Can you send me some information?"

Your brochure, literature package, or whatever materials you produce about your services is the information you mail to these prospects. You should have standard descriptive and promotional materials prepared and ready to send. To reply to a request, "No, I can't send you any information," is unprofessional and a turn-off.

What Size Brochure Is Best?

A full size brochure has pages that measure 8½ by 11 inches, or 7 by 10 inches. Most consulting brochures of this size are four pages, possibly six pages. A four-pager would be made by printing on both sides of an 11 × 17 inch sheet and folding it once vertically.

The advantage of the larger size is greater impact; more space for photos, diagrams, tables, charts, and other visuals; and the fact that the material doesn't get lost at the bottom of a file folder if the prospect decides to file it for future reference.

Most small consulting firms use a smaller size, called a *slim jim.* These brochures are made by folding a letter size (8½ × 11 inch) or legal size (8½ × 14 inch) sheet two or three times vertically to fit in a standard #10 business envelope.

The advantage of slim jim brochures is they fit regular business envelopes, making them easy to include with correspondence or send as part of a direct mail effort. The smaller format allows you to use less-sophisticated graphic design, saving money. In fact, many consultants desktop publish their slim jim brochures using their laser printers. Several companies sell fine papers specifically designed to be used for laser-printing slim jims. The largest of these is Paper Direct (800-A-PAPERS).

How to Write an Effective Capabilities Brochure

Start Selling on the Cover

Whether someone receives your literature in the mail or plucks it off a rack, it is the cover that makes your prospect either read further, set it aside, or throw it out. Yet the majority of advertisers waste the front cover. They decorate it with the product name, a fancy graphic, or the company logo, and hope that will be sufficient to prod the reader to go on. It's not.

The cover should display a strong selling message, ideally in headline form. This message can identify the audience for the product or service, stress the usefulness of the product, or highlight other potential benefits.

A well thought-out cover headline increases the selling power of the piece. Take, for example, the headline on a pamphlet promoting a bank's Christmas club:

IMAGINE HAVING AN EXTRA
$520 FOR THE HOLIDAYS

It's easy.
It's painless.
It's automatic.
It's just $10 a week.

This headline is more likely to grab a depositor's attention than is a pamphlet labeled, "Christmas Club Account."

Here are some other effective headlines taken from actual brochures:

- Now there's an easy way to implement interactive multimedia in your broadband network products
- Boosting melting productivity and efficiency with oxy-fuel combustion techniques
- Seamlessly integrating telephony and computer technology

A headline isn't the only way to begin selling on the cover. Telling a story illustrated with dramatic photographs is another option. A booklet used in a fundraising mailing for an animal welfare society might feature heart-breaking photos of mistreated animals. Usually, though, words and pictures are stronger than images alone.

Make Your Story Flow

A brochure is in many ways like a miniature book and, like a book, a good brochure tells a story. That story should have a beginning, a middle, and an end, and flow smoothly from one point to the next.

Once you've written the first draft, sit back and read it as you would an article or short story. Does it progress logically? Or are there points where the transitions are awkward, where you are jarred by a phrase or sentence that doesn't seem to belong?

If the transitions aren't smooth, perhaps the material needs to be rearranged a bit. Maybe adding a subhead, headline, or introductory paragraph will take care of the problem. Or perhaps a transitional phrase can bridge the gap between one sentence and the next. Here are some of the transitional words and phrases that copywriters use to make a sensible connection between copy points:

- *Additionally*
- *Also*
- *And*
- *Another reason is*
- *As a result*
- *As well as*

- *As we've discussed*
- *At the same time*
- *Best of all*
- *But*
- *But wait, there's more*
- *By comparison*
- *Chances are*
- *Even better*
- *Even worse*
- *First*
- *For example*
- *For instance*
- *Here's how*
- *Here's why*
- *However*
- *If (   ), then*
- *Imagine*
- *Most important*
- *Importantly*
- *In addition*
- *In other words*
- *In this way*
- *Moreover*
- *Most important*
- *Obviously*
- *Of course*
- *On the other hand*
- *Or*
- *Perhaps*
- *Plus*
- *The reason*
- *Remember*
- *Similarly*
- *Since*
- *Still*
- *That's where (product or service) can help*
- *Then again*
- *The results*

- *Therefore*
- *There's more*
- *Thus*
- *To be sure*
- *What's more*
- *Why? Because*
- *Yet*

Strive for a Personal Tone

Write your brochure copy in a natural, relaxed, friendly style. Strive for the easy, conversational tone of spoken language—the short words, the short sentences, the personal touch. If what you've written sounds stiff, unnatural, or dull, it's not conversational and you need to revise it. Your copy should make people want to do business with your organization.

Some examples from recent brochures:

Today we live in the Age of Now—the nanosecond nineties. When customers order a product, they want it right away. You must deliver—fast. Or your customer might find someone else who can.

An oxygen supplier who knows only oxygen is of limited value. But an oxygen supplier who knows oxygen and EAF steel-making—like BOC Gases—can be the strategic partner who gives you a sustainable competitive advantage in today's metals market-place.

Losing your hair? It happens to millions of men. Yet unlike the millions of men who are actually walking around with bald heads, you have the power to do something about it. Now. Before it's too late.

Stress Benefits, Not Features

Too many promotional brochures stress the *features* of the product or service—the bare facts about how it works, what it looks like, how it is made, where it is made, who designed it, and so on.

Effective copy translates features into benefits—reasons why customers should buy the product. A benefit explains what the product can do for customers.

After you identify the key features of your product, make a corresponding list of benefits. Here is a partial list for a familiar item—a clock-radio:

Feature:	Benefit:
Large illuminated digital display	Time easy to see at a glance—even at night.
Snooze alarm switch	Tired? Just hit a button for 10 more minutes of sleep.
Digital alarm	Alarm wakes you at precisely the right time.
Wood veneer finish	Handsome design will complement your bedroom decor.
Felt pads on bottom	Won't scratch or smudge furniture.
Alarm/radio option	Wake to the sound that suits you—gentle strings, hard rock, or the buzz of an alarm.
AM/FM	Clear reception guaranteed. Gets all your favorite stations.

Be Specific

People read brochures because they want information. And they are quickly turned off by brochures that are long on fluff and short on content. So be specific. Don't write, "saves you money" when you can say "reduces fuel consumption up to 50 percent." Don't say "we're reliable" if you can tell the customer, "service technician arrives within 24 hours or we fix it free of charge." Don't be content to talk about "a lot of energy saved" if you know your insulation "reduces heating bills by 30 to 50 percent a month." Remember, specifics sell.

Another tactic that can work is to give the prospect a reason to call now, rather than later. If you can only take on a limited number of assignments, and you take on new clients on a first come/first serve basis, say so.

Graphic artist Ted Kikoler writes in his self-promotion piece, "With my track record, you can understand that I'm busy and find it difficult to take on new assignments." Consultant Somers White formats his brochure in question and answer format. The first question is, "Why should I hire Somers White?" The unexpected—and challenging—answer is, "Perhaps you should not." He then tells what makes his services exclusive and expensive, positioning himself as a top resource in his field.

Support Your Claims

Even if you stress benefits instead of features and make specific claims, the customer still may not believe you. In his book *Direct Mail Copy That Sells,* (Prentice Hall) copywriter Herschell Gordon Lewis describes modern times as an Age of Skepticism:

> This is the Age in which nobody believes anybody, in which claims of superiority are challenged just because they're claims, in which consumers express surprise when something they buy actually performs the way it was advertised to perform.

How can you overcome skepticism and get people to believe you? Here are some things to include in your brochure:

- *Track record.* The most powerful copy for promoting a consulting practice is to say what you have done for other clients and the specific positive results. Ted Kikoler's promotion piece is packed with examples of how his direct mail graphic design service increased response for numerous clients.
- *Guarantees.* Offer a guarantee: money back, free replacement, free revisions and reworks, unlimited service, work redone at no cost. Guarantees allow the customer to try your service at no risk and ensure satisfaction.
- *Testimonials.* A testimonial is a statement of praise or endorsement from a satisfied client (or, in some cases, a celebrity). The testimonial is written in the customer's own words, appears in quotation marks, and is usually attributed to a specific person.
- *Client list.* Include a list of your most prestigious, well-known clients. This impresses prospects by association: They figure if you are good enough for American Express or Lever Brothers, you're good enough for them too.

- *Case histories.* Case histories are success stories. They tell how a particular customer benefited by selecting, buying, and using your services or methods. They present the reasons why the customer selected your service over competitive offers, and the results achieved through its application.
- *FAQs (frequently asked questions).* If what you say in the copy is likely to raise questions in the consumer's mind, put this reader at ease by answering these questions in that same piece of copy.
- *Demonstrations of your reputation and stability.* Prove your stability and reputation by talking about your track record and past successes. Cite number of years in the business, number of employees, the size of your operation, number of offices, annual sales, and reputation.
- *Illustrations.* Help customers visualize how your service works or is put together and why this makes it better. For example, a flier claims a new four-step dental procedure to be quicker and easier than the conventional method. The flier shows a series of photos and captions to demonstrate the new procedure, step by step.
- *Examples.* Don't just say your product or service saves money or improves life. Show that it does. Say you're selling an energy-efficient air flow management system to building owners. Instead of just talking in a general sense about energy savings, provide sample calculations that show *exactly* how much money buyers can save based on their utility rates, building size, and thermostat setting. Make it easy for readers to follow the calculation and come up with money saved based on specific situations.
- *Comparisons.* If your product or service clearly beats the competition, you can include comparisons, as long as they can be supported by documentation (e.g., specifications taken from competitors' brochures).

Lively Copy

Most copywriting texts tell you to keep sentences short, because short sentences are easier to read. But writing gets monotonous when all sentences are the same length. So vary sentence length. Every so often, put in a fairly long sentence. Also use an occasional very short sentence or sentence fragment. Like this one.

Lively writing is personal, not impersonal. Personal pronouns (*we, they, us, you*) make the copy sound less lawyerlike, more like person-to-person conversation. Addressing the reader directly as *you* in the copy adds warmth and creates the illusion in the reader's mind that the copy was specifically written just for her or him.

Human beings have been telling and recording stories since the first cave dwellers drew a crude picture of his latest hunting experience on the cave wall. Storytelling is an inherently powerful technique for getting your message across, much more so than a dry recitation of mere facts.

You can use storytelling to liven up your promotional copy. For example, instead of just stating that your bottle-coating process is superior, tell how one of your customers actually doubled his bottling business because of your better coating, got rich, and retired to Florida at age 51. People have a great interest in other people.

Separate and highlight key information. If you need to include a detailed methodology outline, for example, put it in a separate table or sidebar, and keep your body copy lively. (A sidebar is a short article or section of copy separated from the main text and enclosed in a box or other graphic device.)

Make Sure the Information Is Relevant

All copy should be interesting to read, but not everything that's interesting to read belongs in your copy.

Copy should be relevant to the message you're trying to communicate and to the people you want to reach—those who are most likely to buy your product, join your club, take your course, or donate to your cause.

If a brochure selling your Web site design services begins with an intellectual essay on the impact of the Internet, that may interest Web enthusiasts or techies. But the business owner looking for specific information on how to create a profitable Web site may not be willing to wade through this nonessential stuff to get to the part about how you help them save time and make money.

Check for Accuracy

Then check it again. Then have three or four other people in your organization check it, too. A single mistake can result in having to reprint the entire brochure. And that's expensive. So even though proofreading is boring, it's well worth the time and effort.

In addition to accuracy, you should also check for consistency. Make sure you've used the same style of grammar, punctuation, capitalization, spelling, numerals, abbreviations, titles, and product names throughout the copy. If you're inconsistent—if you write "GAF" in some places and "G.A.F." in others—you're automatically wrong part of the time.

Remember the Details

One manufacturer spent $2,400 revising and reprinting its product sheets only to discover that the location of the company's new $20,000 Web site had been omitted on the new sheets!

We devote so much time and energy to the promotional aspect of our literature that we sometimes shortchange the details. But these details can be just as important as your sales pitch and graphic images.

Review your copy before it goes to the printer. Make sure you have included:

- Company name
- Logo
- Address
- Phone numbers and extensions, including toll-free numbers
- Fax number
- E-mail address
- Web site
- Hours
- Credit cards accepted
- Branch offices
- Guarantee
- Disclaimers
- Other required legal wording
- Brochure date and code number
- Permissions and acknowledgments
- Trademarks and registration marks
- Copyright notice
- Product codes and other official emblems (e.g., Good Housekeeping Seal, Underwriters Laboratory)

The lack of this so-called fine print can kill the effectiveness of an otherwise fine promotion. For example, one restaurant handed out hundreds of promotional fliers offering a substantial savings on a fine dinner at their grand opening. The flier was widely distributed but brought in little business. Why? Because the restaurant was in a hard-to-find location, and although the flier contained the address, it didn't give directions, and potential customers couldn't find the place.

Additional Promotional Materials

In addition to a capabilities brochure, consultants use a variety of other printed materials to promote their services to clients. These can include the following:

- Reprints of articles by and about you
- Reprints of speeches and presentations you've given
- Samples of your work (e.g., employee benefits manuals you've produced if you are a human resources consultant)
- Lists of clients
- Client testimonials
- Rate card or other pricing information
- Recommended vendors—allied consulting firms and other suppliers you regularly work with in solving client problems or refer clients to for services you do not personally provide
- Mailers or color reprints of jackets of books you have written
- A cover letter tying the whole package of materials together and encouraging the prospect to discuss a potential project with you

Packaging Your Fulfillment Kit

If you are using multiple promotional pieces, not just a slim jim, you may want to mail the pieces in a pocket folder. Double-pocket colored folders can be purchased in a stationery or office supply store. You can also use custom-imprinted folders with your logo, name, contact information, and even some promotional copy. One source for folders is Clients First (listed in Appendix E).

What should you send? I recommend sending different materials to different prospects. A "hot" lead, for example, might get a very detailed package, including samples and articles customized to its particular need or industry. Consider overnight delivery of the package. A qualified lead who does not have the same urgency can get a similarly customized, detailed package, but it can be sent via priority mail rather than overnight express. Those prospects who are less qualified can be sent a minimum of material—perhaps just your slim jim, or your slim jim and an article reprint.

Post Your Marketing Materials on Your Own Web Site for Easier Access

My practice, when fulfilling inquiries, is to ask prospects whether they want the information sent via Federal Express, fax, or priority mail. If they are in a hurry, I overnight or fax the material according to their preferences.

I also ask "Do you have access to the Web?" If they do, I tell them they can get an advance look at what I'm sending them by going to my Web site, www.bly.com.

You should put your promotional pieces—brochure pages, fact sheets, client list, testimonials, article reprints, case histories, samples of your work—on a Web site organized in a clear, logical fashion that makes everything easy to find.

Increasingly, potential clients are Web-enabled. Many are in a hurry and want to learn more about you instantly. Having your promotional kit posted as a Web site gives them access to instant information. I advise you to have print and electronic versions of your promotional materials, and to maintain current electronic documents on a Web site.

Select a domain name that ties in with your business name or consulting specialty. Edith Roman, a firm offering database and Internet marketing consulting services, is at www.edithroman.com. Even if you are not ready to put up a Web site, register and reserve your unique domain name now; otherwise, someone may take it.

As soon as you have a domain name registered, put up a brief one-page description of your company and services on your Web site, with a banner on top that says "Web site under construction." This way, people going to your site will at least get some basic information (including your phone number) until your full Web site is completed.

People who visit Web sites—both prospects and nonprospects—like to find free how-to information. Therefore, I recommend you post articles you've written under the category "articles" or "article reprints." Let visitors access, read, print, and download any of the articles as they wish. Don't force the visitor to fill out a guest page to get articles. Reserve the guest page for a higher level of qualification, such as receiving customized information via mail or e-mail.

Give people browsing your Web site multiple options for getting in touch with you in addition to filling out a guest page, which is the online equivalent of a business reply card or fax-back form. Put your name and phone number on every page in the site. The visitor should also be able to instantly e-mail you by clicking on a line or button that says "Click here to send an e-mail message to Joe Consultant."

Unlike brochures, which cannot be changed once printed, a Web site is easily modified or expanded. Don't feel you have to put up a perfect Web site. Concentrate on getting your basic information up on the Web site. You can always add more sophisticated "bells and whistles" later.

For example, since its inception, my Web site has listed the books I've written. Now it includes scans of the front covers. By clicking on the book description, the Web surfer can order the book online. (I don't take or fulfill the orders; these buttons on my site are linked directly to www.amazon.com, an online bookstore, which pays me 15 percent for every book they sell through their link to my site.)

Following Up with

Interested Prospects

You drop everything to do an estimate, you begin to clear your schedule to make room for a new project, you submit the quote, and then you wait. And you wait. Don't you hate it when this happens after you talk with a prospect who seems to have an urgent need for your consulting services?

When you don't hear back, you call to follow up and the prospect says he hasn't had time to look at your proposal yet. You wait some more and, though you dread it, you call again. Or maybe you don't. In any case, you never hear from him or her again.

This happens all the time—not just to you—and there's little you can do about it. Here's what it may look like from your prospect's perspective:

On the day you spoke with the prospect, this project was at the top of his list. But the next day, something else came along which took priority and kept pushing the project further and further away, until it was on a permanent back burner. He never bothered to let you know, probably because he didn't have time. Or, more likely, he got caught up in his own world.

The reality is you can't control your prospects, and it's almost impossible to know in advance if a lead is a good one or if the project you're quoting will go anywhere. On first impression, you can't always tell the literature collectors from the bona fide prospects. Sometimes you may

want to say, "Tell me either yes or no, but don't keep me hanging on like this." But they can't. Only time will tell.

What you can control is how you spend your time. And you decide how vigorously you want to pursue each project and how much time you can afford to devote to each prospect. In order to do that, you have to rate your prospects and prioritize your efforts toward them.

Fast Response Prevents Lost Sales

To satisfy anyone's urgent need, have the basic information about your consulting services ready and faxable (three pages maximum). Then, if necessary, take your time to put together a more tailored package and mail it. Even better, register a domain name on the Internet for your consulting business, then post this literature on your Web site. That way, prospects can access it at any time of the day or night.

When you promise to send information, be sure to send it promptly. Sloppy lead handling looks really bad and, as marketing consultant David Wood writes: "Failure to fulfill your first commitment to a client establishes you as unreliable and undependable. In addition, the sooner your material gets there, the fresher your conversation is in his or her mind and the more quickly your relationship can be continued."

Follow-Up Strategies That Work

These days, people rarely return phone calls. It's unprofessional, but it's a reality. So now, more than ever, it's up to you to follow up.

For qualified leads (e.g., hot prospects—especially those who've contacted you) follow-up calls make sense. The call should be made approximately a week after the information is sent out, on any day but Monday.

For cold prospects (e.g., people who don't know you), follow-up calls can only help. It's unrealistic to think that you could do follow-up calls to everyone on your calling list, but you could certainly make calls to the top 10 percent of potential customers on the list.

Chances are they got your mail and it's in a pile somewhere. Your phone call will resurrect your piece of paper from that pile and, because timing is everything in marketing, that follow-up call could provide the final push needed to get the project on track. A prospect might surprise you with, "You know, I've been meaning to call you."

From the time you make your first contact with the prospects, until the time they are ready to buy from you, these follow-up activities are all effective:

- Make a follow-up phone call.
- Send an e-mail.
- Fax a note.
- Send a birthday or holiday card.
- Send articles of interest.
- Send any publicity you get.
- Send a short note or postcard inviting them to check out a new item or function on your Web site.
- Jot down any ideas relating to their project.

When making follow-up contacts, these phrases can help warm up the prospect and set the right tone:

- Thanks for speaking to me (or meeting with me).
- I know your time is valuable.
- As we discussed.
- I look forward to continuing our conversation.
- Call me with any questions.
- Call me to continue the conversation.
- Let me know if I can be of any help.

For subsequent follow-up phone calls, the following phrases may also be helpful:

- We haven't spoken in a while and I wanted to check in and see if anything has changed.
- Perhaps you are in a better position to use our services than when we first spoke.
- I was wondering if you are still planning to buy these services?

Here are some additional tips and thoughts about following up:

- Following up is marketing to the same group over and over.
- Don't forget to follow up with your former clients.
- Make follow-up letters brief. Use a Post-It note. They're just reminders, to jog memories.
- Always call to make sure your information was received.
- Capture their e-mail addresses. Send periodic short items of interest to them over the Internet.

Understanding Prospect Response

Many consultants read too much into prospects' responses, worry unduly, or spend too much time trying to decipher what the prospects really mean, when most of the time, what they mean is pretty much what they said. The following guidelines may be helpful in dealing with prospects in sales situations:

WHAT THEY SAY: I have a project. Could you send your information?

WHAT YOU HEAR: They want me.

WHAT THEY MEAN: They're gathering information on potential candidates.

WHAT TO DO: Mail or fax your info. Follow up in a week.

WHAT THEY SAY: Your info is here somewhere but I haven't looked at it yet.

WHAT YOU HEAR: They chose someone else.

WHAT THEY MEAN: Other things have come up and the project isn't as urgent.

WHAT TO DO: Ask when to call back and keep in touch.

WHAT THEY SAY: I've looked over your materials and they look interesting, but we haven't decided what direction to take. We'll be in touch.

WHAT YOU HEAR: They chose someone else.

WHAT THEY MEAN: Things have changed and the project isn't as important anymore.

WHAT TO DO: Keep in touch quarterly for other possible projects.

WHAT THEY SAY: Nothing. No call back.

WHAT YOU HEAR: They chose someone else.

WHAT THEY MEAN: They're busy with other things. Maybe they did choose someone else. It's not the end of the world.

WHAT TO DO: Keep in touch every few months by fax, mail, and phone.

Which Prospects Should Be Followed Up?

You can't follow up with everyone and the good news is, you don't have to. But in order to decide whom to pursue and whom to let go, you have to determine their value to you—qualify them, in marketing lingo.

The big question: Is there a fit? Don't be so eager to get a project that you fail to consider a prospect's fitness for you. Figure 6.1 presents a checklist of questions to consider about each prospect to help you assign a rating: A, B, C or Hot, Warm, Cold, whatever labels work for you.

Measuring Results

"I don't like to assess success simply by measuring response," says Ilise Benun, publisher of *The Art of Self Promotion* quarterly newsletter. "There are too many unknowns that figure into the ultimate results. This is a lesson I've learned many times, but I'll never forget one time several years ago.

"I spoke at a conference that was very poorly publicized and, thus, poorly attended. My workshop had five people. I spontaneously changed the format of my presentation, put us into an intimate circle and gave a highly interactive self-promotion workshop (which I wouldn't have been

Figure 6.1   Follow-Up Checklist

Business Potential

1. Why aren't they still working with their previous vendor?
2. Do they have future needs? Immediate needs?
3. Is there potential for ongoing business?

The Decision-Making Process

1. Is your contact the decision maker?
2. Are there several layers of bureaucracy to deal with?
3. Can they afford you?
4. Can they pay a percentage of your fee up front?

Personality/Working Style

1. Does your contact respect your time and labor?
2. Do they require a lot of hand-holding?
3. Do they understand that you have other clients?
4. Do they buy based on price? Quality? Both?
5. Do they respect your professional boundaries?
6. Do they do business honestly and with integrity?
7. Do you feel comfortable with them?

Your Fitness for Them

1. Does this project fit into your specialty?
2. Could you refer someone who would be a better fit?
3. Do they require more time, service, or technical expertise than you have available?

Once you've given each prospect a rating, determine your strategy. Here's a sample rating system and strategy.

HOT —Has an immediate need. Follow up right away.
WARM—Will have a need soon. Ask how they want you to follow up.
COOL—May have future needs. Keep on the mailing list and contact quarterly.
COLD—Worth one call to see that they received information. Otherwise, let them come to you.

The key point: Not every prospect should be followed up. And not all prospects should be given an equal follow-up effort. Spend the most time and effort following up with your hot prospects. Give others only occasional reminders of your existence.

able to do with a big group). It turned out to be extremely productive and everyone left feeling great, myself included. If asked the next day how many people showed up, the number five would have drawn a groan from anyone. But more is not always better—and it wasn't that day. A year later, one of those five became an important client for me."

Of course, response is important. But, while response is indeed significant, it's not everything. It's difficult to imagine that those who receive phone calls but don't respond are affected in a positive way. But don't assume they're not.

There are too many unknowns. People's needs and interests are constantly changing. You'll never know, for example, how many people put your brochure in that infamous "in-basket," which they really do plan to go through just as soon as they get a free minute. You'll never know how many people file your material for future use, or bookmark your Web site for future reference. You'll never know how many people pass your catalog along to a colleague who may be calling soon. You'll never know how many people are presenting the idea of working with you to their bosses but haven't yet received approval.

Yes, they're intangible and unquantifiable but all of these events can have an impact on the results of your promotional efforts and you'll never be able to trace them back to any one mailing.

But you have to measure something. You need some way to know if what you're doing is working—a gauge by which to judge. If you need some hard facts, go ahead and measure response. Make 500 calls. Count how many people respond positively, and keep track of how many jobs result from that one phone effort. Just keep in mind that it's not the whole picture.

Give each marketing effort six months, minimum. More often than not, it's not just one communication that brings a client; it's the succession of messages. It can take four to nine calls to make a sale.

When you do make a judgment, take a wide view and go with your gut. You will know if what you're doing is worth the time and energy involved. You will know if you enjoy the process. You will know if people like it, remember it, notice it. You will know if, over the course of a year of consistent marketing, your business has grown.

You'll know if it works. It will show at your bottom line.

Timing

How often should you follow up? There's no set formula, only some guidelines.

A good starting point is the "Rule of Seven," formulated by marketing expert Dr. Jeffrey Lant. It states that to penetrate the buyer's consciousness and make significant penetration in a given market, you have to contact those people a minimum of seven times within an 18-month period. This is slightly more than once every quarter. Although your frequency may be less or more, seven contacts within 18 months—or four to five contacts within a year—is a good starting point for a follow-up plan.

You can modify this plan to suit your preferences. It's really up to you. Do what works. Don't get locked into a formula. If you get better results contacting warm prospects monthly, do so . . . as long as you keep below a frequency they will find annoying or offensive.

How do you know if you are following up too frequently? If only one or two prospects complain or seem annoyed, just modify your schedule to accommodate them. But if 5 percent or more respond negatively to your frequency of follow up, scale back on follow up for that entire group of prospects. Use prospects' feedback to guide you in your efforts.

What is the best time of day and days of the week to make follow-up calls? Opinions differ. For business prospects, Tuesday, Wednesday, and Thursday are the best follow-up days. Monday people are too cranky, and Friday they are too eager to get to the weekend. Mornings are usually better than the afternoons, because most people have more energy.

Follow-Up Scripts for Typical Situations

When you follow up, you will often encounter prospects with an attitude. That attitude may be positive and friendly. But more often, it is reserved, guarded, or adversarial. Here are some ideas for handling these different situations.

Calling and Finding the Prospect Friendly or Receptive

Here's a rare thrill: You call and the prospect actually seems happy to hear from you again! Don't get excited or interpret levels of commitment and enthusiasm that may not be there. Some people are naturally effervescent and outgoing, yet may not have the slightest interest in dealing with you. Others who are stony and silent may surprise you with an order.

When the prospects are friendly or receptive, match their enthusiasm, but don't exceed it. Prospects resent it when salespeople misinterpret friendliness as interest or commitment. They resent being pushed to a place they are not ready to go. Mirror the prospects' levels of energy, but let their responses guide you. Don't push to close a sale or set an appointment until you get signals they're ready to do so.

If you are not certain whether the prospects are ready to take action, during a lull in the conversation or toward the end, ask, "What's the next step?" or "What do you want to happen next?" If the prospects want to buy, they'll tell you what they need next from you to make a buying decision. Provide it.

Certainly you should always seek to get to the next step in the buying process. Push the prospect, but do it gently. Don't rush prospects, because it doesn't work, and often backfires.

Many salespeople try to achieve a different next step than the prospect seeks. It's okay to try to do what you want as well as what they want. But don't ignore or refuse prospects' requests. One sales training institution teaches its students, "Never send literature, even if the prospect asks for it." This is ridiculous. Can you imagine calling up a company, asking for a brochure, and being told, "No, we can't send one." Can you imagine your prospects' reaction if you said this to them? It's absurd.

Calling and Finding the Prospect Neutral or Reserved

More often, the prospects will be slightly cool to you when you call to follow up. This doesn't mean they are not interested. But obviously, if they were ready to buy at that second, they probably would have called you versus you calling them. You are interrupting their activities to try and sell something. So why be surprised if you receive a reception that's lukewarm at best?

You can do several things to warm up the call. Of course, ask, "Am I catching you at a bad time?" If the prospects seem busy or say they are busy, say, "I understand how busy you are. Do you have three minutes now?" When you tell prospects the entire call will take less than three minutes, they become more comfortable, because they realize you aren't going to try to keep them tied up.

A short conversational exchange on a slightly personal note can help here, too. Comment on the weather, or the World Series, or some other fairly neutral topic. If the prospect makes such a comment, pick up the thread and go with it for half a minute or so.

With contact management software (discussed later in this chapter and in Appendix B), you gain the advantage of having all data about the prospects in front of you on a computer screen as you talk. If a prospect mentioned she was going to Hawaii last time you talked, ask her how it was. If she was playing in a golf tournament, ask her how it went. You get the idea.

How long you continue the call depends on whether the prospects warm up. If they get in a chatty mood, keep the conversation going, while steering it toward your objective. If they remain distant or cool, or seem pressed for time, respect that, and keep the call brief. Use your own judgment.

Calling and Finding the Prospect Negative or Unreceptive

"Am I catching you at a bad time?" works well here too. It either gets them to drop the stuffed shirt act and behave in a friendlier fashion, or prompts them to share with you that they are busy, in which case, you set a time for a call back.

Do not assume there is something wrong if a prospect seems distant or cold. He may be busy, under pressure, working against a deadline. Maybe his wife is divorcing him, his sales are lousy, his child is ill, or he has lost his biggest customer. A poor reception doesn't mean there is an objection to you or your call. It just means now is not the best time. If that's the case, the best move is to find out when is the best time . . . and call back then.

Calling and Getting Blocked by the Secretary or Receptionist

The last two times you called you reached the prospects, no problem. But now you can't reach them. Instead, you always get a secretary or receptionist.

Again, this doesn't mean the prospects are deliberately ducking your calls—although if they are busy or not ready to buy, that may be the case.

It usually means they have someone else picking up the phone because they are too busy to talk to anyone—they're not singling you out for special treatment because you're a salesperson.

One of the most common screening questions is, "Is he expecting your call?" If the callback is scheduled, the answer is easy—"Yes, we had an appointment to talk today at this time"—and will often bypass the secretarial blockade.

We have an even better technique at my office: We include each secretary's name in our sales database. And we consider them as a first contact rather than a barrier to overcome. Therefore, instead of trying to fool secretaries or bully our way past them, we talk to them, and make them our allies in reaching their bosses. Some even like us so much, they do some of the selling for us, urging their bosses to buy from us instead of the other suppliers who treat secretaries like second-class citizens.

Calling and Being Told "We're Looking at Other Suppliers"

The critical issue is not whether they are interviewing other people, but whether they have made a decision to choose someone else and have made a commitment to do business with that supplier.

If they have, you're probably sunk—for now. But keep in touch. The vendor they've chosen may not work out. Or the prospect may have additional needs. Use follow-ups to remind them you are available.

When prospects choose someone else, don't sulk. Don't tell prospects they made a mistake or try to hunt for weakness in the other suppliers' credentials. The decision is already made. If you say they made a bad one—even if you believe it—they'll get angry. No one likes hearing that.

People want to believe they made the right choice. Once a choice is made, they want it praised. Not damned. So when your prospects choose a competitor, congratulate them. Say they made a good choice and should be happy. This creates a favorable impression. Then gently remind them you're available if additional needs arise. This leaves the door open to future business. Never criticize or degrade the prospects' decisions. Why burn bridges?

If the prospects haven't made a decision yet, say: "Will you do me a favor? Before you make your final selection, call me, and let's talk briefly . . . whether we're the firm you select or not." The purpose? To give you a chance to talk with the prospects one last time before the decisions are made. If you reach the prospects before they have committed to someone else, there's still a chance of getting the business. On the other hand, if the next time you talk with the prospects, the choices have already been made, there's little to zero chance of changing the prospects' minds—at least for the time being.

Calling and Being Told, "We've Looked It Over and We're Not Interested"

Again, this isn't necessarily a rejection of you. It's possible your service doesn't meet their needs, or the needs have changed or vanished.

Still, you want to find out more. Maybe another one of your services would meet the requirements—but your prospects don't even know you sell it. Or maybe your service still fits their new needs, but you have to help them see it.

How do you find out the reason why they're not interested? One way is to be direct: "When we last spoke, you seemed very interested. I'm curious. What happened?"

Another way is to act as if the selling part of the conversation is over—because they told you they're not buying—and get them to confide in you. Say, "I understand I'm not going to sell you anything today. And I'm going to take your name out of our prospect database so we don't bother you any more. But now that it's over, let me ask: What did we do wrong? What could we have done differently to get you to say yes?" Often the prospects will reveal the real objections, which, once in the open, can sometimes be overcome.

Strategies for Getting Unanswered Calls Returned

As we noted earlier, there is an unfortunate tendency in business today to not return calls. What can you do?

One method is to send a short fax. It tells the prospect, "I've been trying to reach you without success. Please indicate your preference below." Then have a series of boxes the prospect can check and fax back to you. They may read something like:

❏ I've just been very busy. Try me on (date) _____

❏ Now is not the right time. Try me on (date) _____

❏ I'm no longer interested because (please give reason) _____.

Many prospects will respond. If they check one of the first two boxes, call back on the date specified. If they check the last box, and the reasons they are no longer interested are objections you can overcome, call or fax a reply.

Keeping Track of Prospects (When They're Not Ready)

If none of your prospects fell through the cracks, isn't it just possible that you'd have enough business? Fewer people would be so frantic about getting new business if they were on top of all the leads that came their way, responded promptly to requests for information, and followed them all the way through.

Call it apathy or just plain disorganization (it sometimes looks to me like sabotage), but without proper management, leads and referrals fall through the cracks and, alas, much business is lost.

Often it's the details that prevent you from following up. To do it properly, you must have everything in one place: phone numbers, notes from previous conversations, price quotes. You can use a manual system, such as a hanging file or a three-ring binder, but that will only work if you remember to open them. Other manual systems include appointment books, wall schedulers, calendars, three-ring notebooks, hanging files organized by month and day, and index cards in recipe file boxes.

In theory, these systems are simple. You note all relevant information about the prospect on their index card or a piece of paper. Each prospect is on a separate card or sheet. Cards and sheets are filed not alphabetically, but according to when the next follow-up call is to take place.

This works. But there are drawbacks. As the number of prospects and customers in your sales database grows, paper systems become cumbersome: there are too many cards, too many sheets, too many files to deal with. Also, the paper files can only be retrieved according to the way they are organized, which is by call-back date. If you want to look up information on a prospect, you won't be able to find his file unless you are lucky enough to remember the call-back date.

The computer solves these problems. Put your sales database on your computer. You can use software to schedule follow-up calls. But at the same time, you can instantly retrieve any file by customer name, company name, state, or whatever other criteria you choose. So prospect files don't get lost, and vital information is always just a click of the mouse away.

Now, of course, there are loads of software packages to help you do what is called contact management. My intention here is not to review software programs but merely to tell you how easy ACT! and TeleMagic for Windows can make follow up. These and other programs are listed in Appendix B. I can't compare them to other packages because they are the only ones we've ever used in my office, except for LeasePower 5, which I discuss below.

I can tell you that when we turn on the computer in the morning (because I've already scheduled the tasks), the information is all right there and all we have to do is make the calls. Nothing falls through the cracks. The program tells us: who we have to call that day, what we discussed last time, the date we last spoke with them, the topic of today's conversation, even what time to call them! It all comes up on your screen automatically, so you don't miss follow-ups you promised to make.

Another good contact management program is LeasePower 5, but this is designed specifically for—and available only to—resellers. If you are a computer consultant who is also a reseller, and want more information on LeasePower, contact Studebaker-Worthington Leasing Corp., phone 800-645-7242.

You don't have to buy contact management software to track prospects and sales on your computer. You can buy a database program and design your own custom system. But with so many good contact management programs on the market at prices ranging from $95 to $600, I'd recommend investing in one and learning how to use it.

Whether you are shopping for a contact management program (they are sometimes called "sales database programs" or "personal information managers") or planning to design your own, the software should be able to capture the following information for each prospect:

- Name
- Title
- Company
- Business phone number

- Home phone number
- E-mail address
- Web site
- Fax number
- Street address
- City
- State
- Zip code
- Country
- Source of inquiry (how they found out about you)
- Date of inquiry
- Description of their product or service requirements
- A record of follow-ups (dates and discussion summaries)
- The date for the next follow-up call

The software should have the following capabilities:

- Retrieve any prospect file by company name.
- Retrieve any prospect file by prospect name.
- Automatically schedule follow-up calls.
- Keep track of prospect contacts.
- Print a complete list of prospects with company names, addresses, phone numbers.
- Sort and print prospect lists by alphabetical order, city, state, zip code, or other criteria you specify.

Additional capabilities that are nice to have but not a necessity include:

- Form and custom sales letters
- Generation of quotes and proposals
- Online product literature or fact sheets
- Mail-merge for sending out direct mailings
- Automatic dial-up of prospects' phone numbers
- Compatibility with other software applications

What If They Still Won't Call You Back?

There may be times when you call prospects repeatedly and don't get through, despite the fact that they asked you to call, requested information, or were referred by a business associate. Let's say you've called numerous times and a prospect so far has not returned your call. Should you call again?

That's really up to you and how far you want to pursue the lead. Some salespeople might say, "Persist until you get through." I think there's probably a limit after which you give up—perhaps two, three, or four callbacks, but certainly no more.

Here's a strategy you can use with the secretary on the final call.

SECRETARY: Joe Smith's office.

YOU: This is [your name] calling again. Is he in?

SECRETARY: He's not in. Would you care to leave a message?

YOU: Yes, but . . . excuse me, what is your name?

SECRETARY: Mary.

YOU: Well, Mary, maybe you can help me. Joe requested information on our Danglemaster-2000 Processor, and I've called four times and left four messages, but he hasn't returned my calls. If he's interested in my service then I still want to help him and will keep trying, but if he's not interested, I don't want to keep bothering you or waste your time. Could you do me a favor and ask him if he's still interested in the service and if so, when would be a good time to talk about his particular needs?

SECRETARY: Yes, I can do that.

YOU: Thanks, Mary, I appreciate it. Today is Monday. Would it be okay if you could ask him today or tomorrow, and I'll call you back on Wednesday to find out where we stand?

SECRETARY: That would be okay.

YOU: Okay, Mary, I'll call you Wednesday. And thanks.

If you still get the same old brush-off Wednesday, forget about the lead.

But more likely, Mary will give you the information you asked for—either a time to call Joe to discuss his needs or the message that Joe got your material, but he'll call you if he needs you, don't call him.

If that's the case, you might ask Mary if you can at least put Joe on your mailing list. When she says yes—and she probably will—you can at least follow up in the future by mail a couple times.

Not all contacts have to be formal direct mail promotions. You can send a relevant article, a short handwritten note, or even a birthday card. The idea is not to close a sale, but to remind the prospect of your existence.

"The mailing of Christmas cards, congratulatory cards on promotions, and best wishes cards on corporate transfers increases visibility and reminds your constituency of the existence of your consulting business," David Armbruster, a consultant in the chemical engineering field, correctly observes.

Making Sales Presentations That Win Consulting Assignments

Following up persistently will eventually produce prospects who are considering using your services for a current or upcoming project. You will need to present your capabilities to these prospects to convince them that hiring you is better than doing it themselves or hiring one of your competitors. This convincing is usually done in a conversation, either over the phone or face to face, depending on your proximity to the prospect's office.

This chapter provides guidance on how to handle the initial sales meeting with your prospect so that you walk away with what you want: either a signed contract or a fairly firm commitment that the prospect will engage your services.

Learn to Listen

Most people who sell do it absolutely wrong. They follow their own agenda, reciting a memorized list of features and benefits to prospects. But what prospects care about, as copywriter Sig Rosenblum points out, are their needs, problems, concerns, fears, desires, goals, and dreams. Successful salespeople tailor their presentations to show how the features of their product or service can satisfy the prospects' needs and solve their problems.

But how do you find out what prospects want or desire? First and foremost, you listen. Prospects who do not hear what they want to hear from you will tell you so. Usually these statements are in the form of objections.

You may think, "I always listen to prospects and clients." But do you? Be honest. Aren't there times when the prospect is talking and you're not really listening, but instead planning what you want to say next? And when a prospect says something that you don't agree with or don't want to hear, aren't you immediately planning your rebuttal rather than sitting back and listening to see whether the complaint or statement has merit?

Here are some tips for more effective listening.

Focus • When you are listening and doing something else at the same time, you aren't really listening. When prospects speak, give them 100 percent of your concentration. If, for instance, you're talking with a prospect over the phone, don't go through your mail at the same time. Follow the advice of poet May Sarton, who said, "Do each thing with absolute concentration." Listening is an active process, not a passive one, and it requires your full attention.

Take notes • Bring a pad and pen to the meeting. As the prospect talks, take notes.

There are several benefits to this. First, you can jot questions as they occur to you, so you don't forget to ask them later on.

Second, you can quickly and easily prepare a good proposal or follow-up letter based on the notes. When you take notes, your follow-up documents will be full of good, specific material prospects want to see, because you recorded their requests and preferences.

Third, the act of note taking is reassuring, visible proof to prospects that you are indeed paying attention to what is being said.

Bring a tape recorder • Ask prospects, "Do you mind if I tape- record our conversation? I like to make sure I have an accurate record of the information you give me." Most people will readily agree to this. If not, put the recorder away and use a pad and pen to take notes.

I prefer the minicassette recorders because they fit easily in a jacket pocket or briefcase, and their smaller size seems less intimidating to prospects. Be sure to bring several extra tapes and spare batteries; I have had batteries die in the middle of a meeting! Also bring a note pad and pen as backup. Some people like to take notes even when recording. They let the recorder capture the conversation, using the pad to jot questions and key points.

Respond verbally • Say things that indicate to prospects you are listening and have empathy for what they are saying. One simple, effective communication technique for demonstrating your understanding is simply to say "I understand."

> PROSPECT: We're looking for a contractor who can handle the job from start to finish. I don't want to have to coordinate and deal with half a dozen or more different vendors. We want one firm to do the whole job.
>
> YOU: I understand.

Another technique is to rephrase the prospect's statement and repeat it back

> PROSPECT: We're looking for a contractor who can handle the job from start to finish. I don't want to have to coordinate and deal with half a dozen or more different vendors. We want one firm to do the whole job.
>
> YOU: So what you're saying is you want a contractor who can provide all the pieces and provide single source responsibility for getting your system designed and installed.
>
> PROSPECT: Yes, that's correct.

Equally effective is to rephrase the prospect's statement and repeat it as a question to which he or she will answer affirmatively. This gets the prospect agreeing to things you say, which eventually leads to a close.

> PROSPECT: We really need an ad campaign that will penetrate the under-thirty market for this product.

YOU: So would you be interested specifically in dealing with an ad agency with a proven track record in selling to the under-thirty market?

PROSPECT: Yes, that's what we're looking for.

Some salespeople are more aggressive, phrasing their question so that the answer indicates a tentative (if small) commitment on the part of the prospect.

PROSPECT: We would need seminars to train one hundred staff members no later than February 1.

YOU: So if we could train your total staff of one hundred by the first of February, you'd be interested in going ahead, wouldn't you?

Respond physically • "Body language" lets prospects know you are interested and actively involved in the conversation. I like to lean forward slightly, look a prospect in the eyes directly, and nod my head slightly to indicate I am listening and understanding. If you sit back with your arms folded, or stare into space vacantly, the prospect will assume you are not being receptive or attentive.

Listening is such a broad topic that entire books and seminars have been devoted to it, and I can't repeat all that information here. The key is to remember that you are not in the meeting to "give a pitch," as so many salespeople and consultants mistakenly believe, but to help the prospect solve a problem or achieve an objective. You cannot help solve the problem or achieve the objective until you know what it is. And you can't find out what the problem or objective is unless you listen to the prospect.

Also be aware that if you're talking too much, you're listening too little. According to consultant Howard Shenson, when selling your services you should be speaking 40 percent of the time or less which means you should be listening during at least 60 percent of the conversation.

Ask Questions

Questions are the single most powerful technique for successfully selling your services to prospects. Questions

- demonstrate your concern for the prospect's problems;
- put the focus where it should be—on the prospect's needs, not your services or background; and
- enable you to determine the prospect's requirements so you can tailor your services to address those requirements.

"In the first meeting with the prospective client, focus on what they really need to make their problem go away," says Howard Shenson. "Don't waste the prospect's time providing a verbal resume. If prospects need information on your skills, abilities, and experience, they will certainly ask."

Often in meetings you go into far more detail about your qualifications, company, industry, methods, or service than prospects care to hear. Many will sit politely because they think it's rude to interrupt; but they are not really listening. Instead, they are eager to get to their agenda. You want to shift the focus to their agenda, not yours, almost immediately. Questions help you do that.

When sitting down with prospects after greetings have been made and pleasantries exchanged, I like to get directly to the reason I'm there. I typically open with a question or request for information, such as "Tell me a little bit about your situation and how I can help you," or "What problem do you have that you'd like me to help you with?" Believe me, this gets them talking.

Here are some other questions I find helpful in getting prospects to open up and tell me how I can help them:

- "Why did you want to get together with me today?"
- "How can I help you?"
- "Tell me a little bit about your current situation."
- "What specifically do you need me to do for you?"
- "What are you looking to accomplish in [name their specific area of interest]?"
- "That's interesting. Can you tell me more?"

- "What did you have in mind?"
- "What do you want to happen next?"

At times, prospects are unable to articulate their requirements and instead go on and on without getting to the point. I help them get back on track by interrupting and saying "I understand. But what exactly is it that you would like me to do for you?" This usually helps them focus on why they called me in the first place.

If a prospect and I are having a conversation, and I decide to interject a question, I don't jump in and immediately ask it. I pause for a second, then say, "May I ask you a question?" This interruption forces prospects to stop talking, prepares them to listen, and puts them in a receptive, thoughtful state, ensuring that they will hear my question and provide an answer to it. It also says, "I think this is so important that I want us to stop and question what we're talking about so we can proceed on an accurate basis." Use "May I ask you a question?" It works!

Of course, the point of the sales meeting is not to ask endless questions or gather infinite information. Each question is designed to clarify and diagnose the prospect's requirements, so that you get, as quickly as possible, to the point where you can outline the prospect's project requirements, your proposed plan of action, and your fee.

Show That You Can Solve Their Problem—But Don't Solve It for Free

In the 1980s, sales trainers and authors introduced the concept of consultative selling. Essentially, clients and customers want you to solve problems for them, not "sell" them. Good salespeople aren't peddlers or hucksters; they're sales "consultants" who work closely with clients, helping them fulfill their needs.

Suddenly salespeople in all fields stopped referring to themselves as salespeople and began calling themselves consultants. People who sold financial services, for example, began putting such impressive-sounding titles as "financial planner" or "financial counselor" on their business cards. The consultative salespeople even developed a slogan—"Solve, don't sell"—to push their approach to sales.

Much of the consultative approach to selling is valid and can be applied effectively to the selling of consulting and professional services. However, in one respect, the consultative selling gurus and disciples went overboard. Some did so much free "consulting" before they were retained by the prospect that they ended up giving away their services, removing the need for the prospect to hire them.

The successful consultant today practices what I call "modified consultative selling." That is, we selectively consult with prospects on their problems during the initial meeting. We give enough information to convince prospects that we are experts who can help them, without giving away so much that they can solve the problem themselves and without our help.

For instance, let's say you run a graphic design studio. A prospect asks, "Is there any way to design a brochure that features all six products but could be easily updated if one of the products changes?" Because you know the answer, your tendency might be to dash off a sketch or fold together a dummy out of scrap paper to show how it's done. Have you sold effectively? No, because the prospect now knows the answer and can take your solution to his or her current graphic designer or staff artist—or, if the prospect is cheap, directly to a printer.

Instead, you should say, "Yes, that's a requirement we've handled in the past for other clients, and when we're further into the design process, we'll present some options that would work with your particular product." This answer indicates that you are the designer who understands and can solve the problem, but makes it necessary for the prospect to hire you (and not someone else) to get this solution.

And that's the essence of modified consultative selling. Under consultative selling you act like the problem-solving genius at the initial meeting, do everything you can for prospects, and they will hire you out of gratitude and because you're so impressive.

With a modified consultative selling approach on the other hand, you act like the knowledgeable problem solver at the initial meeting, do and say things that convince clients you indeed know the answers, but you don't give the answers away right there. Instead, you disclose just enough information so that clients perceive the need to hire you to get the solution or results they desire.

Be a consultant, by all means, but don't give away the store. Say and do things that demonstrate your abilities and create (rather than eliminate) the need for your services.

Come Prepared

Why do so many consultants stumble painfully through sales presentations? Because they haven't planned what they are going to say in advance. Planning means not only having a well-practiced presentation, but also knowing what to say in reply to prospect comments, questions, and objections.

The key to being polished and smooth is to anticipate what prospects will say and prepare, in advance, sensible answers. This way, when prospects say, "But I can get it cheaper from the printer around the corner," instead of saying, "Uhh . . . well . . . ummm," you launch immediately into a confident, clear explanation of why *you* should print the brochure even though you cost a bit more.

When you are prepared, you feel confident speaking with prospects and clients. When you are not prepared, you are nervous, because you're afraid they'll state an objection or ask a question to which you have no answer. The more prepared you are, the less likely this will occur.

One executive told me, "I am ill at ease meeting potential clients for the first time, because I don't know what to say to get the conversation going." My advice: Visit their Web sites and check their press releases for recent news. Then use this information as a starting point. For example: "I heard you just got ISO 14000 certification at your Michigan plant. How's that working out for you?"

Be Flexible

Being prepared is not a synonym for being inflexible. Yes, your presentation should be planned. But be willing and able to change course midstream if the prospect takes the conversation in a direction you didn't intend to go.

Recently we had Mike, a general contractor, come to our home to give an estimate on adding a family room. Mike, a creative and talented professional, had his vision of what a family room should be. Unfortunately, it conflicted with the family room I had dreamed of having.

Mike insisted that at the rear of the room, there should be sliding glass doors leading onto a deck. I, however, do not like sliding glass doors. I don't like the temptation and easy entry they offer burglars, nor do I like the heat loss in winter.

I explained this to Mike. He countered with an explanation of what a wonderful view the doors would give me. I told him a window would do just as nicely. He countered with an explanation of how a rear door adds value to the home. After going back and forth a few times, it should have been clear to Mike that I didn't want sliding glass doors.

At that point, he should have rearranged his presentation to meet my needs. For instance, he might have suggested a fireplace or a wood-burning stove or wall-to-wall built-in bookcases for the kind of cozy family room I envisioned. But he was inflexible. He wanted to design a family room with sliding glass doors and one of his famous decks, and nothing else would do for me.

After fifteen minutes I became impatient, quickly ended the conversation, and showed Mike the door. It's possible I may still give him the job—I like him and his work—but his sales presentation actually decreased the probability of this happening.

And that's the risk of being inflexible. If you refuse to listen to prospects, to acknowledge their ideas and wishes, and to tailor your presentation to show that you understand and want to meet their needs—in short, if you insist on doing it your way and your way only—your sales presentation not only won't get you a go-ahead but may actually make prospects less inclined to hire you. Yes, an ineffective meeting with a prospect can actually unsell you and your services!

Don't Overpromise

How honest should you be about your abilities and the results you expect to achieve for the prospects? The position I advise you to take is: Present yourself and your services in the most favorable light possible without misrepresenting yourself.

Financial services marketing expert Denny LeBarron advises consultants, "Don't make any commitments or claims you can't live up to."

I agree. But at the same time, remember that your competitors are puffing their own abilities and making themselves look good. They stretch the truth, exaggerate. Some even just plain lie.

You should not lie, but in the face of all this hype, it doesn't pay to be overly modest either. Management consultant Gary Blake gives this advice: "Present yourself as about 10 percent better than you really are." My feeling is that you shouldn't lie or exaggerate, but you should present yourself as the very best you can be and have been.

As the song says, "Accentuate the positive." Tell all the good things about your service. Highlight your successes. Don't go out of your way to tell prospects about your weaknesses and failures. Your competitors will gladly do that for you. Present yourself in the most favorable light possible while maintaining complete honesty and integrity. Prospects want to hire people who are successful, not mediocre. Position yourself as such.

Give the Prospect Some Choices, But Don't Overwhelm Her with Options

"Don't give your client too many choices," advises direct marketing consultant Joan Harris. "This either confuses her, if she's the decision maker, or slows down the process if lots of people have to see it."

This is an old trick of clothing salespeople that can easily be applied to selling services. The clothes sales clerk knows that if a customer is confronted with rack after rack of ties to choose from, he or she will become overwhelmed and unable to make a decision. And so the customer does the easy thing, which is to make no decision and walk away.

Instead, the sales clerk begins narrowing the choices: "Do you want silk or polyester?" You say silk. The polyester ties are removed from the counter. "Do you want plain or patterns?" You say patterns. Solid color ties are removed from the counter. "Stripes or polka dots?" You say stripes. Polka dot ties are taken away. "Do you prefer bright colors or pastels?" This continues until two or three ties remain. Then the close: "Do you want this one, this one, this one, or all three?"

The point is to not overwhelm prospects with lots of choices. Remember, they are looking to you for guidance. If they seem unsure, say "We could do it this way or this way. Which do you prefer?" By all means, give prospects choices. Prospects resent being told what to do and like to think it was their decision. But in reality, you control the presentation, presenting enough options to enable choice without causing confusion.

Deal with Prospects Person to Person, Not Just Business to Business

Like it or not, personal chemistry is a major factor determining whether prospects hire you. It's really quite simple: People hire people whom they like and feel comfortable with. They avoid hiring people whom they dislike, are afraid of, or who make them uncomfortable.

In certain instances, there will be a strong reaction between two personalities that cannot be avoided or controlled. One person will, for a number of reasons, take an instant and overwhelming liking or disliking to another person.

But in most cases, you can create good chemistry—or at least create behavior that allows good chemistry to grow and flourish. For instance, if you have a big ego, be aware that most people don't like braggarts and egomaniacs. No matter how smart, right, or good you are, many people won't hire you because they can't stand the way you behave.

Suzanne Ramos, a manager at American Express, says she occasionally sees consultants who violate what she considers the unwritten rule that "the client is always right." They talk too much or come across as overconfident, argumentative, even mildly disdainful or arrogant. She is also alert to people who might be difficult to work with. "Life is too short," she says.

In general, people like others who

- are friendly.
- are warm.
- are courteous.
- are polite.
- are on time.
- are respectful.
- like them.
- share their interests.
- listen to them.
- show an interest in them.

- ask them about themselves.
- treat them well.
- help them.

"I make a big effort to have prospects comfortable with me," says freelancer Mary Beth Lareau. "Businesspeople need to be reassured that you are normal and dependable."

Be Their Cordial Colleague, Not the "Great Guru"

In meeting with prospects, you should not come across as superior, nor should you allow them to put you in a subservient position. The encounter should be treated as a meeting of equals. The prospect is an important person with a need to be fulfilled or a problem to be solved. You are important because you are the expert who can fill that need or solve that problem.

You will feel most comfortable with prospects if you establish with them what Robert Ringer, author of *Looking Out for #1* (Fawcett Crest, 1978), calls a "value-for-value relationship." That is, for a relationship to work, both parties must exchange value for value. In the selling of services, the client exchanges money for your time, expertise, labor, and the benefits or results you provide. In such a relationship, there is no superior or subordinate, merely two equals exchanging equal values.

There is no need to feel that, because they are the buyers and you are the seller, clients are the superior, you the inferior. Indeed, they need you as much as you need them. And in some cases, they need you more than you need them, such as when they have problems no one else can solve, and you have more work than you can handle.

But don't rub that in their faces. Establish yourself as their peer, not their subordinate or superior. When this is accomplished, both parties can proceed happily and with dignity intact.

Be Enthusiastic

Enthusiasm is a key ingredient in any sales situation. "Develop the habit of enthusiasm," advises *The Book of Powerful Secrets* (American

Publishing Corporation, 1994). "Enthusiasm works like a magnet—it draws people and success. It's a pleasing personality trait that people like to be part of. It seems to be contagious—the people around you become enthusiastic too and become more cooperative. Enthusiasm sparks initiative and singleness of purpose."

You must be genuinely enthusiastic about your service and about the prospect's proposed project or assignment. If you're indifferent, disdainful, or just plain bored, you are unlikely to get the job. And if you do get it, you'll probably do it poorly.

How do you show enthusiasm? For once, there's no technique for you to learn, because if you are enthusiastic, it will naturally show through in your voice, attitude, manner, and presentation. By the same token, any lack of enthusiasm will also become apparent to the prospect. So to be successful, only provide services, accept projects, and deal with clients that you can be enthusiastic about. Life is too short to do otherwise!

Sell a Result or "Package," Not Merely Your Time

"The consultants who consistently are in the $200,000+ range in income develop whatever they're selling into a 'system,'" says Stephen J. Lanning, editor of *Consulting Opportunities Journal.* "Clients like to buy systems or 'total packages' rather than consulting time."

Consulting can be billed in two ways: by time or by the project. In some cases, the only option is to bill by the day or by the hour—for example, freelance technical writers frequently subcontract to large corporations to work on the premises writing manuals on a weekly or monthly basis, with the fee set per hour.

But whenever possible, it's best to offer a complete package price: so much for writing the manual, or so much for designing the system. There are several reasons for this.

First, clients generally prefer to buy a package or project for a fixed fee that is known in advance. They can budget for it, and there are no surprises. Billing them at a high hourly rate makes them uncomfortable, because they don't know what size bill to expect and are afraid you will "pad" the bill with extra hours to increase your revenue.

Think about it. Let's say the plumbing in your house was old and had to be replaced. Which would be more acceptable to you: the plumber saying "We'll put in an all new copper plumbing system for $8,000" or "Our hourly rate is $65 but I have no idea of how long it will take"? Most people would opt for the security of the package price.

Second, a package makes clear to prospective clients what you will do and what they will get. Hourly service is more nebulous. As a marketing consultant, I tell prospects that I can give them a complete marketing plan for one of their products or services for a package price of X dollars, and the plan will include the specific information and recommendations. Although the package price is high, this is a fairly easy sell to those who know they need marketing help.

I have far more difficulty saying to prospects "My consulting fee is X dollars per hour," because their immediate thought is "What exactly do I get when I buy 'consulting'?" It seems less tangible, and therefore less valuable. Even though an hour or two of time is far less expensive than my project fee for a full-blown marketing plan, many prospects perceive it as more costly.

A former client of mine, Dennis Ryan, was one of the innovators of this packaging concept. He once told me, "I want to package my firm's computer consulting services and sell them like products." He gives each package a name, describes the problem it will solve, and explains exactly what he will do for the client and what this service will cost. This approach has been successful for him and many other consultants.

Ten Additional Tips on Selling Consulting Services

From freelance copywriter Judy Brewerton comes this list of ten more helpful ideas on how to present yourself at the initial client meeting to secure the assignment or job:

1. *Silence is golden.* Nervousness or excitement can make you babble. Instead, sit back, ask one or two short questions, look friendly and expectant, and let prospects tell you all about their problems. When you do want to speak, force yourself to speak slowly, and be brief.
2. *Behave as if you already have the job.* Prospects often forget they called you in (or allowed you to visit) to have a look at your samples or resume. As a result, you can often sidestep the whole

"audition" mode completely. You can start right in with questions about what the prospect needs—and go home with an assignment.

3. *Once you have heard their needs, you now know what to tell them about yourself.* Make sure they hear all the bits that will identify you as the person they want. Find low-key ways to work them into the discussion. Don't include your whole work history (especially the unfortunate parts). Use only the things that relate to the prospect's business or problem.

4. *Don't show your samples, resumes, job photos, or brochures unless you're asked.* Remember, you want to be out of the "job applicant" mode and into the "consultant on the job" mode as fast as possible.

5. *Don't tell the prospect your sad stories.* Stress only the positive.

6. *Prospects only want to associate with success.* Make sure you come across as a success. Hiring a difficult or inept supplier will make prospects look bad to their bosses or clients. No matter how successful they look, your prospects all have defeats in their pasts. They're looking to hook up with someone who can improve their track records—not with a war-torn fellow victim.

7. *Remember who you are—the expert source who helps clients.* Instead of stating, "I recently did a big job for Pepsi Cola," say "I recently helped one of my large clients deal with a problem similar to yours." Remember to protect past clients' anonymity if you're speaking of their problems. The fact that you're discreet might impress this prospect too.

8. *Don't be a name dropper.* Name dropping frequently fails to impress prospects. Many prospects are turned off or bored by it. Besides, why run the risk of fondly dropping the name of someone they despise or dislike?

9. *Develop ways to end the meeting profitably.* In other words, ask for the order. If this has been an exploratory meeting about a major project, and you feel you haven't yet been able to seize the inside track, try mentioning a smaller part of the project, and ask to do it independently. Say, "Why not let me do that for you right now? Then you'll have that taken care of, and you can see how I work firsthand."

10. *Don't hang around.* You're an enthusiastic, friendly consultant who'd love to do business with them. (Be sure to say so.) But

because you're so capable, you're also busy, so don't hang around. Hanging around gives the impression that your time, which you're trying to sell to this prospect for a hefty price, is not valuable.

Closing the Sale

How to Accurately Assess the Prospect's Needs and Requirements

You will have gathered a lot of preliminary information in your meeting with the client by asking the right questions, as discussed in Chapter 7.

Ask whatever additional questions will help you make an estimate of the scope of the project, time frame, work involved, and your fee. If the prospect has done similar projects in the past, ask what the budgets were for those projects. A winning bid for the current project will probably be somewhere in that range.

If most of your projects require prospects to answer basically the same set of questions you've asked previous clients, consider creating a questionnaire the prospects can fill out and return to you (a sample questionnaire appears in Appendix F). If the selling process stalls because you and the prospect aren't sure what should happen next, you can say that the next step is to complete and mail the form. Another way to move forward is to ask the prospect, "What do you want to happen next?" then do what is asked of you.

Do You Need to Write a Proposal?

It depends. If the client issues an official Request for Proposal (RFP), it's probably necessary to answer with a formal proposal if you want to win the contract.

The leading authority on proposals is my fellow Dearborn author Herman Holtz, and his book, *Proven Proposal Strategies to Win More Business* (Dearborn, 1997), is in my view the authoritative guide to the topic of proposal writing for consultants.

If a client doesn't ask for a formal proposal, don't write one. Proposals are time consuming. "Proposals should not be a sailing expedition to see if the prospect will agree with a course," writes consultant Alan Weiss. "Send a proposal as a confirmation, not an exploration."

Not doing proposals is actually a sales strategy some consultants use to position themselves as busy and in demand. The rationale being that writing a proposal gives away a lot of my time and information for free, which is something I don't do, because there is a large and continual demand for my services.

Some potential clients have told me, "There are other consultants we are interviewing, and they are willing to write a proposal and give us ideas for free." My reply is, "If they have time to give away their advice and expertise for free, how good could they be? The advice is probably worth what you are paying for it—nothing."

If the client needs some sort of written summary of the work scope and your cost estimate, use a short letter of agreement, even a memo, rather than a formal proposal. Sample letters of agreement and cost estimates are included in Appendix F.

I don't like the term proposal, since it positions me as someone hoping to get business. If I send a letter or memo serving as a proposal, I label it "Preliminary Recommendations." This implies that (a) the client is getting useful advice, not a sales pitch and (b) the advice is preliminary, and the real solution will be provided only when I am retained.

If I am presenting a price to a client, I usually label the document as a "cost estimate" rather than a quotation or bid. An article in the newsletter *Overcoming Objections* states that a quote implies a fixed amount that the customer expects you not to exceed. An estimate, by comparison, refers to an educated guess that customers know may vary as work commences.

How to Set and Present Your Fees

Consulting fees vary widely depending on specialty, competition, market, demand, reputation, experience, track record, services offered, credentials, and how well you market and sell.

According to an article in *Parade* magazine (March 23, 1997), partners in law firms billed clients a median hourly rate of $183 in 1996.

And *Creative Business* (December 1994, page 5) reports that the average self-employment income of creative advertising professionals in 1994 was $50,000 after expenses and before income taxes.

As direct marketing specialist Sig Rosenblum points out, "Fees are all over the lot." A novice consultant in direct marketing could get $50 an hour, where a veteran consultant hired to do training could get $2,000 to $4,000 a day, reports *Business Marketing* magazine (November 1996, page 14).

In information systems, a freelance programmer writing code may make $400 to $500 a day. Web site developers charge anywhere from $50 to $100 an hour or more. A specialist in an area such as Internet security, local area networking, object oriented design, or strategic planning might get $1,000 a day or more.

An article published by the Institute of Management Consultants shows that, according to a survey by Carey Associates, the average hourly fee of consultants in 1997 based on number of years experience was:

2 years: $125
5 years: $140
10 years: $165
15 years: $175
20 years: $205

Find out what other consultants in your field, at your level of experience and expertise, are making. This is a good starting point for setting your own fees. I estimate most readers of this book will bill between $800 and $2,000 a day.

Seven Pricing Pitfalls You Can Avoid

When someone else was your boss, you didn't need to be concerned with pricing. Now you're the one setting prices for your products and services. How do you determine the right price?

Overhead, labor, cost of materials, and profit margin are just a few factors to consider. Then, you must weigh the intangibles: perceived value of your offering, the image you want to project, your experience and knowledge, and the value of your time. How do you make sense of all these variables to come up with a price?

Like most aspects of running your own business, you learn by trial and error, making adjustments along the way until you find a price that will both appeal to customers and bring you sufficient profit.

But imagine! What if you could avoid many of the trials and errors of pricing? How much time, money, and energy do you think you could save? How much more money do you think you could generate?

J. David Harper, Jr., a chartered financial consultant and president of Harper Financial Group LLC in Atlanta, lists the following seven pricing mistakes entrepreneurs often make, and shows you how to avoid each.

1. Minimizing the Value of Your Time

Many employees-turned-entrepreneurs assume their former salary is a good starting point. Say you earned $20 an hour as a public relations writer for an agency. Surely that's a fair rate to charge when you start your own home-based PR consulting firm, right? Not if you expect to stay in business. Your employer took care of overhead, marketing and advertising costs, health insurance benefits, self-employment social security tax, and so forth—all expenses you need to factor in your hourly rate.

To cover the extra expenses and risk, multiply your former rate by at least 2.5: $20 an hour multiplied by 2.5 is $50 an hour. Imagine trying to keep your business afloat if you failed to factor in the extra $30 an hour.

2. Underselling the Competition

Avoid the temptation of entering into price wars. As a small operation, you can't afford to cut your profit margin. If you drop prices to steal customers away from the competition, don't expect to be able to raise prices back up to profitable levels and still keep those customers.

Instead, position your business for success, not by lowering prices, but by increasing the value of your offering. Strive to serve better, perform faster, and do more than your competition.

3. Confusing Profits with Wages

You undoubtedly know the formula: gross sales minus expenses equals profit. What you may not know is that your living expenses would be included in the "expense" column. Many first-time entrepreneurs fail to realize this, thinking they have made a profit when, in fact, they have earned only a wage. If your " profit" is the same cash you need to cover your living expenses, you won't have any capital to grow your business.

Tally your costs, including the money you need to live. What's your break-even point? Now tack on at least 10 to 20 percent. Including a profit margin is the only way to ensure your business will actually produce a profit.

4. Bidding Too Low

Once you quote a price, you won't be able to raise it. Bidding at your break-even point gives you no room to negotiate. You'll either lose the sale or lose money on the sale. In both cases, you lose. Be confident in the value you offer. Start high. You can always negotiate down. When you demonstrate confidence in your business, prospects will more likely trust your product or service is worth the value you give it.

5. Establishing Value According to Price

Focusing on price without considering what value you bring the customers will limit your profit potential. Customers are willing to pay whatever price they think is worth their money. That's why some professional speakers can charge several thousand dollars to conduct seminars. Their preparation and presentation time isn't what justifies the high fee. People see the value of what these speakers have to offer: information on how to make more money, build lasting relationships, or live more fulfilled lives.

What value does your product or service bring to your customers? Do you help people make more money? Do you save them time or give them peace of mind? Even when you establish your break-even point and tack on a 20 percent profit margin you could still be selling yourself short.

6. Being Too Flexible

Being over-anxious to make a sale will invariably downgrade the value of your offering. In the words of the famous deodorant commercial, "Never let them see you sweat." The more eager you appear to lower your fee, the more likely you will lose credibility with that prospect.

After quoting what you feel to be a reasonable price, be willing to walk away from the table. If you are confident your price accurately reflects the value you offer, you will attract people willing to pay it.

7. Overlooking Target Market Expectations

Charging the same fee to a major corporation that you would to a small not-for-profit organization could hurt your business credibility. Suppose you are a personal development consultant. Charging $250 to give a one-hour workshop may be a little steep for a not-for-profit group, but it would position you as an amateur to a major business that may expect to pay $2,000 for those they deem top-flight speakers.

Develop an economic profile of your ideal client. Are your prices consistent with the income level and expectations of your current target market? If not, either adjust your price or target a market segment that fits your fees.

Remember, what you charge can make or break your consulting business. Don't allow pricing mistakes to trip you up. If you know yourself, your business, your customer, and the marketplace (and make adjustments when necessary), you will position your consulting practice for long-range success.

How to Overcome "Your Price Is Too High" and Other Common Objections

Many consultants, especially novices, charge too little at the beginning to get the job, then resent it when they realize they are doing too much work for too little compensation. Yet they are afraid to charge higher prices, for fear the potential client will object, "Your price is too high."

Speaker Linda S. Blackman, writing in *NSA Tri-State Speaker,* says: "Charge more only when you have more business than you can handle." When you only have one client and a couple of prospects, you feel you need to close every deal, and therefore can be negotiated downward in price by clients who sense your softness. The solution is continual, effective marketing to generate more leads and sales than you can handle. When you have more clients than you can handle, with a line around the block of others who want to hire you, it's much easier to tell a particular prospect "no" if they try to negotiate a lower fee.

You should also raise fees to existing clients only when you have more business than you can handle. According to an article in *The Competitive Advantage,* annual price increases to business clients should not exceed 7 to 8 percent.

When faced with a price objection, show how the results you achieve for clients far outweigh the small fee you are charging. According to an article in *Personal Selling Power* (August 1995, page 21), engineer Charles Steinmetz once charged General Electric $10,000 for inspecting a system and marking an "X" on the faulty component with a piece of chalk. When they protested, he sent them an itemized invoice showing $1 for making one chalk mark and $9,999 for knowing where to make it.

An article in *Bottom Line/Business* (November 1997, page 4) gives the following tips for negotiating:

- When told something unacceptable, flinch and grimace—the other side will back off.
- Be reluctant. Once you show enthusiasm or eagerness, the other side has the advantage.
- Use trade-offs. If you give up something, get something else in return.

Keep in mind that not every prospect will agree to your terms, fees, and conditions. When they say "no," it usually has nothing to do with you—and everything to do with their budgets, needs, personalities, and priorities.

Some people will not budge, even when rational proposals and accommodating compromises are presented by the consultant. It's not worth your time trying to convince them to see things more clearly. "It is generally futile to argue with people who are dogmatic in their beliefs," wrote Sydney Harris in *Soap Box Journal* (Winter, 1993, page 2). "They have a deep emotional investment in defending their prior positions, and the more you try to pry them loose, the more stubbornly they think."

Techniques for Closing the Sale and Getting the Assignment

"Closing" means getting the order. For product sellers, this means getting a signed contract or purchase order. For consultants and other service sellers, it means getting the prospect to agree to retain you, or at least make a tentative commitment contingent upon final approval of your fee and contract.

Many businesspeople understandably don't enjoy pressuring prospects and would prefer that potential clients close themselves by saying "Okay, let's go, I'm ready to buy." Others, many of whom work on Wall Street, enjoy closing and pushing for the order.

Unfortunately, fewer and fewer prospects close themselves these days. Consumers are more hesitant to spend money and more likely to examine each purchasing decision more carefully than they did ten years ago. As a result, you are going to have to bring up and negotiate the final details of the deal if you want to get the order.

Closing requires that you come right out and say to the prospect, "I would like to have you as a customer. May we get started?" This makes many professionals uncomfortable. Many of us were taught that asking for the order is inappropriate. It is not.

Ilise Benun has developed a wonderful line that can be used both during intermediate stages of the sales cycle as well as at closing. It's effective in moving the prospect one step closer to a final decision in a way that is not adversarial and does not make you seem desperate or overeager for the order.

When you reach a point where it seems you should move forward, but the prospect doesn't seem to know what to do next and doesn't suggest a course of action, say to the prospect, "What do you want to happen next?" This works beautifully because the prospect tells you what is required to consummate the transaction.

You Might Hate Closing, but You Have to Do It Anyway

Closing is necessary because it overcomes prospect resistance, inertia, and ignorance.

Prospects are *resistant* because, like most people, they hate to part with money. They suffer from *inertia*—the natural tendency of all objects, animate and inanimate, to resist action and movement. Worse, they are also, to a degree, *ignorant,* because even if they want to hire you, they're not quite sure how to go about it. Do they sign a contract? Write you a letter? Phone? Pay some money up front? Try your system for 30 days? Lease, rent, or buy your equipment?

When people are unsure of what to do next, their choice is to do nothing. By closing, you provide prospects with welcome guidance on what the next step is and how to take it. So if you want the prospect's business, you've got to step forward and ask for it. Clearly. Forcefully. Directly. And persuasively.

Proven Closing Techniques You Can Use

Get Prospects to Invest Time and Effort in Your Relationship

The more time and effort prospects invest in making the decision whether to buy from you, the more likely you are to close the sale.

This doesn't mean you should waste prospects' time or make it deliberately difficult for them to communicate with you. Far from it. But it does mean that if you can get prospects to invest their time and effort in a relationship with you before you are officially retained to perform services on a paid basis, you are more likely to get the assignment than someone with whom prospects have not invested a lot of time and effort.

"If a client asks you to sit in on a developmental meeting, whether you are paid for that effort are not, you are the vendor of choice," says business writer Paul D. Davis. "I have never, except once, had a client give an assignment to someone else after I helped with the concept and planning of that project."

Consider this scenario. You have been talking with a prospect on and off for the past six months. She's visited your office two or three times, and you've exchanged lots of letters and information. Now she's ready to hire a consultant to handle her firm's outplacement. Who will she be more likely to hire? You, a person with whom she is already familiar and comfortable, or your competitor, who called her for the first time last week? Unless your competitor offers some tremendous advantage or proprietary method you don't have, you stand the better chance of getting the business.

For this reason, it pays to get prospects involved with you at an early stage, even before any money is exchanged or any contracts are signed.

If you're a professional speaker, for example, send a demo tape or invite prospects to your next talk. The time prospects invest in going to see you or listening to your tape is an investment for which they won't get any return *unless they ultimately hire you.* If they go to your speech or showcase presentation and don't use you, they've wasted their time, and they know it. So prospects naturally tend to want to hire the service provider they have already invested time and effort learning about, investigating, or speaking with.

In my business, instead of just sending prospects my brochure, I'll also ask certain ones to mail to *me* extensive background material on their companies. I tell prospects I need this material to better understand their marketing problems and how I can help them (all true).

This helps me close the sale for two reasons. First, it impresses prospects that I care enough about them to want to read and learn about their company. And second, it requires prospects to spend some time deciding what to send me, making the selection, writing a covering letter, and preparing the package for the post office or Federal Express (some, of course, can avoid this by sending me to their Web sites).

I believe that while making the decision to hire me, many prospects say to themselves, "Well, I already spent all that time sending him our background material, and he's already up to speed on our situation, so the easiest thing is to go with Bly." They pass over my competitor because that person isn't ready to start the job, and because they haven't invested any time briefing him.

In keeping with this strategy, many consultants offer a free initial meeting or consultation, even though their hourly rates may be substantial. Now, in such cases prospects aren't motivated to hire you because they feel guilty about wasting your time. No. Rather, they consider such an initial meeting an investment of *their* time, and they are afraid of wasting their time, not yours.

Think about how you can involve your prospects early. Do you survey their employees? Give them a demonstration? Get them to attend your free seminar? Have them watch a videotape? Install a system in their office for a free 30-day trial? The more time prospects invest, the more eager they will be to make sure that the relationship moves forward on a productive (and for you, a paid) basis.

Incremental Closes

In sales lingo, closes are categorized as "major" or "minor." In a *major close* prospects say, "Yes, we'll take it." Before that occurs, there will typically be a series of *minor* or *incremental closes*. These incremental closes involve getting prospects to agree to different ideas, concepts, and suggestions you propose as you talk your way to the close of the sale.

Basically, this technique involves getting prospects to say yes to a number of mini-proposals. Each mini-proposal covers one of the items or conditions of the sale. Taken together, they are the total package of services you want to sell the prospect.

After getting prospects to say yes to each mini-proposal, you then sum up the total package, noting that they have agreed to each point. Finally, you restate your proposition in its entirety and get prospects to finalize the agreement.

For instance, here's how I used this technique recently with a prospect who wanted me to write a mailing piece promoting his graphic design studio.

ME: So Mr. Green, I understand you are looking for a direct mail piece to generate sales leads that will result in new clients for your design studio.

PROSPECT: Yes.

ME: As we've discussed, the best format would be a sales letter with an illustrated brochure and reply card.

PROSPECT: Yes.

ME: And you would prefer that it be mailed in a personally addressed, standard size business envelope.

PROSPECT: Yes, that's correct.

ME: We've gone over my fee schedule and you understand that it's $1,200 to write the brochure, $950 for a one page letter, and $150 for the reply card.

PROSPECT: Fine. I have no problem with that.

ME: And you would like to have a first draft of the copy in two weeks or sooner, is that right?

PROSPECT: Yes.

ME: And because you're a design firm, you'll handle all the graphics and design of the piece yourself.

PROSPECT: Yes.

ME: Okay. So let me prepare an agreement that spells out I'll be writing for you a lead generating direct mail package, with letter, brochure, and reply card that is due two weeks from today, for a fee of $2,300 total.

PROSPECT: Fine.

See the technique? First I get clients to agree to each point concerning the deal we are making. Once they've done that, how can they say no to my final proposition, as it merely sums up a number of points they've already said yes to?

A series of small or incremental closes, in which you get prospects to say yes to each step of the deal, makes it easy to go for the final close, where it is almost impossible for prospects to refuse you.

Of course, if prospects say no to one of your intermediate closes, then it becomes an objection, and you either must overcome that objection or remove that particular element from the agreement you are trying to finalize.

Act As If You Already Have the Business

This doesn't mean you pour the foundation, write the report, conduct the seminar, do the survey, ship the merchandise, install the equipment, or start the work. That would be premature and foolish.

When I say act as if you already have the job, I mean your tone, mannerisms, and posture should exude confidence. Without being obvious or high handed, you should behave as if getting the project is a foregone conclusion, with fee negotiations, contracts, and purchase orders a mere formality standing in the way of you getting started. As writer Judy Brewerton observes, you want to get out of the "audition" mode and into a working relationship mode as soon as possible.

Most service providers handle the closing phase of the sales process awkwardly. They act as if they don't know what to do, are ashamed and embarrassed to be closing the sale, and want to give prospects sufficient time to contemplate this major decision.

Successful consultants are confident and decisive. They feel sure enough about their abilities to say to prospects: "We are best qualified. Our service can solve your problem and do it well. What are you waiting for? Sign on the dotted line and we'll get started."

Prospects want to hire people who appear to know what they're doing. This means being a man or woman of action. It's time for prospects to move forward, but inertia, laziness, or uncertainty prevents them from doing so. They look to you for guidance. You must take prospects by the hand and gently, but forcefully, get them to commit to action.

False modesty (or maybe genuine lack of confidence) prevents many of us from acting confidently. Our attitude is "Gee, Mr. Prospect, I don't blame you for not wanting to make a decision. There are lots of people who can do what I do. And besides, it's a lot of money and I don't want you to make a rash decision. Take your time; we're in no hurry." Unfortunately, this attitude only feeds prospects' natural inertia. It will not get you the sale you want, which means prospects will not benefit from the services you provide.

Act as if you already have the job, project, or order. Your attitude should be: "Mr. Prospect, I'm happy you called me here today because I've handled many clients with needs like yours, and I know I can help you immensely. The fee is X dollars payable in these installments. I'm really looking forward to working with you!"

This attitude will subtly alter the texture of the conversation between you and prospects. Instead of being in a *selling* mode, you'll be in a *working partnership* mode. Your comments will be directed toward understanding clients' requirements or helping to find the best solution for their problems, not desperately thinking of what you can say to persuade them to give you a retainer check or sign a contract.

And when this happens, you'll perform better and close more sales. Why? Because prospects like to deal with vendors who are genuinely helpful and interested in them. They don't like to deal with vendors who are pushy and only seem interested in getting their money. When you act as if you're already on the job, you will behave as if you're in the former category, not the latter. So prospects will like you better. And you'll close more sales. Always act as if you already have the job, not as if you're auditioning or begging for it.

Avoid Time-Limited, High Pressure Face-to-Face Closings

In direct mail, having a time-limited offer is an extremely effective technique. Phrases like "Offer expires December 15," "Supplies are limited—order today!" and "This is a limited offer, and once it expires, it may never be repeated" give prospects genuine reasons to respond now instead of later, which dramatically increases response rates.

But, while most people are understanding and responsive to such time limited offers in direct mail situations, they resent such pressure in a selling situation. For instance, when buying a car, I resent it when the salesperson tells me, "This price is good today only—if you walk out of the showroom it'll be more costly if you come back later." My response is to walk out and buy the car across the street. True, some prospects will be scared into buying the car on the spot. But this tactic makes them unhappy and resentful.

While the car salesperson can afford to make the prospect uncomfortable by using high-pressure selling—he'll probably never see the customer again, anyway—you cannot. You may be dealing with prospects on a daily or weekly basis if they become customers, so you don't want to start the relationship off on a negative note. And that's exactly what pressure selling does.

Here are a few of my "don'ts" concerning pressure selling.

- *Don't* tell prospects, "I can give you this price, but only if you commit today." This makes you look sleazy and makes prospects extremely uncomfortable.
- *Don't* tell prospects, "I'm getting extremely busy, and unless you sign up with me today, I may not be able to handle your job" unless it's the absolute truth. (If it's true, then you're doing prospects a favor by indicating to them what they must do to ensure they can get you for this project.)
- *Don't* lie or say things that prospects will not believe. If business is scarce, and you're desperate to make the sale, don't try to pressure prospects by saying, "We're very busy and we only have one slot open on our schedule, so you need to sign up this week or we won't be able to take you on." Prospects will know you are lying.
- *Don't* use two-tier pricing—that is, a low price if prospects buy today versus a higher price if prospects want to think about it and get back to you. While this works effectively in direct-mail selling, it can backfire in personal selling. Be careful.

Remove the Risk

The fastest route to overcoming buyer resistance when attempting to close a sale is take the burden of risk off prospects' shoulders and place the risk on the shoulders of you, the seller. For instance, if prospects resist your closing, stress the fact that they can hire you risk-free; that you will make any changes they request at no charge; that you guarantee your product for thirty days, or ninety days, or better still, for one year; that you will warrant the product against defects in materials and labor; that you stand behind clients 100 percent; that you will give more service at no cost or refund all or part of the money if you don't perform as promised.

Obviously, we can't make our guarantee *too* good, or we leave ourselves open to unscrupulous buyers who would take advantage of us. The trick is to appeal to sincere prospects with an offer that makes it as painless, easy, and risk-free as possible for them to try our goods and services. You can do this with either some sort of guarantee, warranty, or promise of performance, or by allowing prospects to buy a demo or sample before committing to a larger contract.

In my consulting business, for example, I charge $200 an hour, as do many consultants in my field (direct marketing and selling). But most of the others have minimums of $2,000 or $3,000 or more. I, on the other hand, will take on a job for as little as $600. I tell prospects, "This allows you to try my service and see if you like it for a minimal investment." This puts prospects at ease. Many are uncomfortable committing thousands of dollars to someone they don't really know or haven't worked with before.

How do you work this into your closing technique? Let's say a prospect resists having you do her ad campaign because she's not sure if the firm really wants to switch ad agencies (despite her claim they *were* ready to switch when they called you in). You could ask, "Do you have any one ad that needs to be done right away?" Then offer to do the single ad on a project basis.

You'll probably close, because it's much less of a commitment for a company to hire you to do one ad than to switch their entire account to your agency. Interestingly, in the advertising business, most ad agencies I know would refuse to do this. Their attitude is "We want the whole account or nothing at all." Competitors who are more flexible and willing to allow the prospect to "sample" their services with a trial project can succeed against them in winning new business.

AFTO—Ask for the Order

Marketing and sales expert Ray Jutkins says the key to success in marketing and selling is AFTO, which stands for "ask for the order." This means if you want a signed contract, you must present a contract ready for signature and preferably, place the pen in the prospect's hand and put his hand over the blank space provided for him to sign. If you want a check, tell the client, "Make out a retainer check for X dollars, and we'll get started."

You have to ask for the order, the assignment, the project, the contract, the agreement, the paperwork, the go ahead, the check, the purchase order, the job. If you don't, you won't get it.

At a meeting of the Wednesday Club, a group of independent PR firms based in and around New York City, owners of small PR agencies were discussing how they closed sales and got clients to put them on retainer. I asked one experienced PR man, "What do you do when the client is ready to go and wants to know what the next step is?" The man reached into his briefcase and pulled out a poster board. On the poster was a pasted-up copy of his agency agreement, with a big arrow and the words "SIGN HERE" (drawn in huge lettering) indicating a blank space at the bottom. "The next step," said this successful consultant, "is to get them to sign on the bottom line."

Act Fast

When prospects indicate they are ready to buy, act fast. Immediately write up a quotation, prepare the contract, or send an agreement. Have it in the prospect's hands within 48 hours. You can send it by first-class mail, Federal Express, or, if it's just a page or two, via fax or e-mail.

Why is prompt response important? Two reasons. First, it makes sense to get prospects to commit right away. If they have too much time to think about it, they may find additional reasons for delaying or deferring. The delay may also give your competitor time to move in.

Second, prospects judge you on first impressions and form their opinion of you largely based on how you perform in the initial phases of any engagement or relationship. If you're tardy or indifferent about preparing the quotation or contract, or getting started on the assignment, this gives prospects cause to think you'll be even less motivated and caring later on. And that's not what they want.

Constantly Closing

When, exactly, can you consider the sale *closed?* When prospects call and say they're tentatively interested? When clients say, "Yes, go ahead?" When the contract is signed? When you get your advance check? Or is it when the check clears in the bank?

In one sense, the sale is never truly closed. We are constantly closing— that is, we're always striving to make sure customers are satisfied and pleased with us. We can't really consider the sale closed when we get the signed contract or purchase order, because clients can always cancel, and it may be difficult to collect all or even a portion of your fee if that happens.

One consultant confided in me, "I consider the sale made when the client's check clears in my bank account." But even that isn't the end of it. You've got to perform as promised, or the client might sue for return of fee based on nonperformance.

Plus, for many businesses, the one-shot customer is the least profitable. The real money is made with repeat buyers and clients who retain us on a periodic or, even better, an ongoing basis. The repeat business is where the profits are made. To get these repeat assignments, our performance on the initial job must be superior.

In a sense, everything we do or say in the course of our relationship with the client determines whether we close that next sale. We are constantly closing this sale and the next. Selling does not end with the signed contract but is ongoing throughout the life of the consultant/client relationship.

Let Prospects Help You Close

According to veteran salesman Tim Connor, as reported in *In Business* magazine, your prospects will tell you what you need to say to them in order to close the sale. This means you have to ask questions, get them talking, and listen to what they really want from you.

For instance, I was trying to get a prospect to retain me as a consultant to help him start up a mail order business for an exciting new product. Although the prospect had been enthusiastic when he called me, and he maintained his enthusiasm for me throughout the meeting, I couldn't quite get him to commit to the next step (a signed contract retaining me for eight hours of service at my rate of $200 per hour).

Finally I said, "What's holding you back?"

The prospect said, almost reluctantly, "I believe you know what you're talking about, but all of this is new to me. I'm afraid that other vendors I need—the designer, manufacturer, printer, mail house, and list broker—will sense my novice status and take advantage of me."

Based on his statement, I understood that the cause of his reluctance was that I was a "hands-off" consultant and would not assist him with the nitty gritty details. When I assured him I could act as project manager (for a separate fee), overseeing the details and coordinating with his vendors, his anxiety disappeared and I won the contract.

Listen to your prospects. Frequently they will tell you, word for word, what they want to hear from you—indeed, what they *need* to hear from you—before they will hire you. A technique that works well is to ask prospects what they want, then repeat it back to them in your own words. When prospects hear their requirements spoken by you, they will be confident that you truly understand what they need.

PROSPECT: I need someone who can meet with our production people next week.

YOU: So if we could prepare an initial briefing for your production team to be presented next week, I take it you'd be interested in proceeding with this project?

PROSPECT: Yes.

Match Closing Tactics to Buyer Mood

Another piece of good advice Tim Connor gives is that you must sell to prospects in the way they are comfortable buying, not the way you are comfortable selling. And this goes especially for the closing—a situation in which the prospect, faced with finally having to make a real decision, has the greatest level of fear and anxiety.

We've all been in situations where we haven't bought a product or service because the salesperson made us uncomfortable. To increase your chances of closing the sale, be in sync with the mood and personality of your prospects, and adjust your presentation accordingly.

For instance, consultants speak at an average rate of 150 words per minute. But they will speed up when calling New York City and slow down when calling Tennessee or Georgia, because they sell more effectively when the pace of their chatter matches that of the person they're calling.

In the same way, training seminars on selling overseas advise international businesspeople to follow the local business customers of the client's country. After all, most people would rather buy from people who are like them rather than from people who are strange and different. Now, this doesn't mean you should be a chameleon, totally changing your stripes and colors to match whatever personality you think would be ideal for selling a particular prospect. This would be phony, and people can spot a phony. However, it does pay to be sensitive to the prospect's personality and mood, and adjust your style within reason to match.

For example, if prospects seem pressed for time, compress your sales pitch to accommodate their busy schedules and get to the close quickly.

On the other hand, if prospects seem relaxed, with plenty of time on their hands, you can slow down and have a more leisurely chat.

I have one client, Shirley, who is a real gabber. She loves to talk and talk and talk. While I can't afford to let her go on indefinitely, I generally settle in for a five- or ten-minute chat. Why not? I genuinely like Shirley. She's interesting and has a lot to say. And with the fees she pays me, I can afford to indulge her a bit—something I might not do with a smaller client.

Another client, Randy, is a brisk, no-nonsense, to the point guy. Many people are turned off by Randy's brusqueness and consider him rude. Not I. We get along great, mainly because my personality is close to his.

Leo, on the other hand, was a child of the sixties and is into touchy feely interpersonal relationships. He frequently tells me how beautiful a human being I am and that he loves me. I'm not fully able to respond to Leo in the same way, because I'm not like that, and we both know it. But that's okay with us, and I am more personal and warmer with Leo than I am with Randy.

Adjust your presentation and style to the prospect's mood and personality, especially during the sensitive closing period, and you will improve your sales results and client relationships.

Become Comfortable with Closing

You may hate closing now. And although many service providers come to love the selling and marketing aspects of their business, some never do. But most people I talk to tell me they become more at ease with selling, more comfortable with the idea of asking for the order, over time.

Here are three suggestions for putting yourself more at ease with the concept of closing.

1. Remember, the worst the prospect can do is say no. And that's really not so terrible. There are plenty of other prospects out there for you. There's always tomorrow.

2. The situation need not be awkward or unpleasant if you maintain professional, cool, detached behavior at all times. If the prospect says no, it doesn't mean loss of dignity or face for you. Your inner mental attitude should be, "I'd like to help you, Mr. Prospect, but if you refuse to see the wisdom of buying from us, the loss is primarily yours, not mine."

3. Most independent consultants take the position that any customer who buys from them is doing them a favor. They aren't. Think of the transaction as (in the words of *Looking Out for #1* author Robert J. Ringer) a "value-for-value" exchange of goods and services for money. Realize that they need you as much as you need them.

How to Go After the Business When the Prospect Is Looking at Several Companies for the Assignment

Here are some tips for winning business when you know the prospect is looking at other consulting firms.

- Find out what clients want and give it to them.
- Ask clients how they will be making the decision. On price? Other factors?
- Only pursue leads you have a reasonable chance of winning. If you are a premium service but you know the prospect is buying on price and also talking to your low-end competitor Joe Low-Ball, why bother even bidding?
- Offer a value or service package or a guarantee your competitors don't. According to an article in *CIO* (January 1, 1998, page 116), Cap Gemini America, an IT consulting firm, guarantees renovation of between 750,000 and 1.5 million lines of COBOL code in four weeks—or your money back. This sets them apart from other Year 2000 consultants.

Achieving Profitable
Relationships with
Your Clients

Today's clients are fussier and more demanding than ever, which makes them a difficult bunch to satisfy. However, it's still possible, even in the "Age of the Customer," to keep clients happy and run a successful consulting business based on *high client retention through continual client satisfaction.*

What's more, the secret to keeping your clients satisfied can be summed up in a single statement: *To keep your clients satisfied, don't just give them their money's worth—give them MORE than their money's worth.*

I certainly didn't invent this principle, and it's been stated in different ways in many different places. Jerry Hardy, publisher of Time-Life Books, made that division fabulously successful by declaring, "Our policy will be to give the client more than he has any right to expect."

What this means is that the consultant who merely fulfills the contract or proposal and does what the client asks is missing an *enormous* opportunity for creating a high level of client satisfaction. The secret to making your clients love you is not to give them their money's worth, it's to give them *more* than their money's worth.

Meeting Clients' Needs: Three Performance Options

When asking a consultant to perform a task, render a service, or supply goods, there can be only one of three outcomes.

1. The consultant performs below expectation, failing to deliver all that was ordered or requested.
2. The consultant performs satisfactorily, delivering a product that meets the specifications or rendering the services called for in the contract.
3. The consultant performs "above and beyond" the call of duty, providing a superior product (or more product than was ordered) or rendering a superior service (or providing more *services* than expected).

Let's look briefly at the client's reaction in all three scenarios.

Scenario 1: The Consultant Performs Below Expectation

In this scenario the consultant's performance is subpar, he fails to deliver all that was ordered or requested or delivers but in an inferior manner.

The client's reaction? Dissatisfaction. In the "Age of the Customer," your buyers are far less tolerant of error than they were in the 1970s or even the 1980s. They demand more and are less forgiving of slipups, mistakes, delays, and defects.

When the consultant fails to perform as delivered in today's competitive marketplace, he is literally inviting his competitors to step in and take the business away from him. Clients are *much* less loyal to consultants today than years ago, so dissatisfied clients will be quicker to shop around and try a new supplier when they get ticked off at you. Worse, that client becomes dissatisfied easier and faster. It takes very little to incur a client's wrath or displeasure or make the client become unhappy with you.

A satisfied client is your most valuable asset, in terms of repeat sales, referrals, and favorable "word-of-mouth" advertising. The quickest way to lose that precious asset is to fail to deliver as promised. Why risk it?

Scenario 2: The Consultant Performs Satisfactorily

This is the level where 80 percent of businesses aim: Do what the client asked. No less, no more.

It sounds logical. The client paid you for product "X" or service "Y." If you deliver product "X" or service "Y" reliably, on time, courteously, and at the price you said you would charge, you've done everything they asked. So there is nothing for them to complain or be unhappy about, and they must, by default, be satisfied.

Unfortunately, the truth is this: When you do merely what was asked of you and nothing more, the client may be satisfied, but they won't be thrilled, delighted, or ecstatic. And the latter is precisely what you want. A transaction in which the client's expectations are met retains business and prevents client dissatisfaction, but a transaction in which the client's expectations are exceeded becomes memorable and "welds" the client to your company in a way ordinary transactions cannot.

Think back to your childhood. As a child, you were yelled at, scolded, and punished when you did not listen to your mother and father—that is, when you failed to do what was asked of you. Misbehavior on your part generated displeasure on theirs.

Doing as your parents asked eliminated this displeasure and may even have generated some praise or rewards. Do the dishes as asked and get the allowance you were promised. But your parents didn't fall on their knees in gratitude when you did as you were told. After all, you were only doing what they expected you to do in the first place.

It's the same with clients. A client comes into your restaurant and orders a turkey sandwich. He gets a turkey sandwich on a clean plate. It isn't terrible, it isn't great. It's okay. Is he satisfied? If you asked, the answer would probably be an indifferent, "The sandwich? Yeah, it was okay, I guess. I've had worse meals, and I've had better. Here's your $6.95. May I have my change, please?"

Ten minutes later, he's back at work and has forgotten all about lunch, you, and your restaurant. He doesn't dream about your turkey sandwich. He isn't thinking about his next lunch at *your* place. He isn't telling his coworkers, wife, and friends all about you. The reason: You delivered only what you said you would deliver and nothing more.

Scenario 3: The Consultant Performs "Above and Beyond" the Call of Duty

This is where you can rise above your competition and score points with your clients. Remember, 80 percent of the competition in your business seeks to do only what the client requested or provide only the product the client ordered—and many times, they fail.

But not you. You can be one of the elite top 20 percent who render a superior service and give your clients *more than they have a right to expect.* By doing the unexpected, you delight and surprise the client. By giving them more than their money's worth, you elevate their level of satisfaction, build loyalty, and ensure that they'll come back to buy from you again and again.

For instance, do you remember your parents' reaction when, as a child, you did something *beyond* their expectations? Maybe it was cleaning up your room without being asked, or practicing the piano two hours instead of one, or getting straight As on a report card, or winning first prize at the science fair, or vacuuming the whole house when you were asked only to do the living room. Whatever the event, it showed you that the real way to please people and make them extraordinarily happy with you is not to do what they expect from you, but to do *more* than they expect.

Or consider our luncheonette example. You obviously aren't dazzled when you order a turkey sandwich and get "just" a turkey sandwich. But let's say it came on hot, fresh-baked rye bread, with real, home-cooked turkey instead of turkey roll or "lunch meat" turkey, with free mashed potatoes smothered in hot gravy (even though it wasn't mentioned on the menu), and a whole bowl of crisp, fresh cole slaw instead of smelly old cole slaw in one of those slinky little paper cups. When the food is superior or more than you thought it would be, you sit up and take notice of the meal and make a mental note to have lunch there again soon.

Two Easy Steps to Delivering Superior Client Satisfaction

Giving your clients more than their money's worth involves not one but two separate steps.

First, create an expectation on the client's part that is realistic, yet one you know you can not only meet but actually *exceed.*

Second, consistently exceed expectations and deliver more than promised in a way that delivers revenue to you, via increased client retention and repeat business. The revenue generated will be far greater than the cost of creating that superior level of client satisfaction.

The two steps work in conjunction and are sequential. Let's look at how to do it.

Step 1: Instead of Promising More Than You Can Give, Give More Than You Promise

As I've said, most businesses promise more than they can deliver. Instead, to achieve a superior level of satisfaction among your clients, you should deliver more than you promise.

"But," you say, "if I promise spectacular results and then have to beat even that promise, I'll either fail to deliver *or* give the client so much 'extra' that I'll lose money on the deal."

The solution is to *underpromise* rather than overpromise. Now, in today's highly competitive business environment, underpromising is a tricky thing. Underpromise too much, and you won't appear as good as other companies who are promising your clients much more. On the other hand, promising no more or less than you are capable of giving, and then giving only that, won't make any enemies but it won't turn the client into a fan for life, either. As for overpromising, you already know what happens when you overpromise and then fail to deliver.

The key is to make promises to clients that are both attractive and accommodating, yet at the same time, credible and realistic. For example, let's say you provide a certain type of service. Your service is superior, and that puts you in heavy demand. As a result, normal turnaround time is five days.

Now, a prospective client comes to you via word of mouth. She wants to know what you can do for her, and how quickly you can do it. You promise service *superior* to what the competition can provide because you know that your service *is* superior and your firm almost always does a better job. So far, so good.

Next is the issue of delivery. For this client, five days is too long. Her firm represents a big, potentially very lucrative account, and she is asking for overnight turnaround. What are you to do?

The immediate temptation is to promise your client anything to get the work and then hope she'll forgive you when you miss a deadline, because at that point you'll already have her business and she won't want to switch. Don't do it! As we've discussed, there's no faster route to losing business today than to create a dissatisfied client. And there's no surer way to create a dissatisfied client than failing to meet a deadline or live up to some other promise you've made.

So what do you do? In this case, the best thing might be a very frank, face-to-face, sit-down discussion of the situation. You explain that while you want to help and give her the benefit of your superior service, the kind of quality you provide cannot be rendered overnight. Explain the specific reasons to the client. For example, you do certain quality checks that other consultants don't, and this takes extra time that you are not willing to do without because of your reputation for doing superior work.

Also, probe the client's request. Does the work *really* have to be done overnight? What happens if it's done in two or three days instead of the one day they are requesting? The client demands may also be "artificial"—that is, the client has set a particular deadline or created a specification without any real thought to whether it's necessary. In nine out of ten cases, you find there is no real event or other concrete deadline driving the "rush" job, and that absolutely nothing would happen if it were done a day or a week later.

By having this type of discussion with clients, you get them to see that not only are there legitimate reasons why the job shouldn't be done overnight but also that it doesn't need to be, anyway.

Still, five days is too much. She says, "What can you do for us?" Here is where you put the "art of underpromising" to work. You've agreed that one day is too soon, five days too long. You know, but do not say, that you could comfortably do the work in three days but could also turn it around in two days, if need be. The client says they would really love to have it in two days but could live with three.

The right move is to *promise three-day turnaround.* The client has indicated she can accept this, and because you've already established that your service is technically superior, she'll likely go with you on a three-day basis.

Now you have created a situation where the client has come to accept and agree to a three-day turnaround. It's not ideal, but it's been proposed and accepted. So now they expect to get it in three days. This puts you in a perfect position to deliver *more than is expected* because, as we've said, you can do the work in two or three days.

What do you do? Tell her the first job will be ready in three days *and then aim to deliver in two days.* If you succeed, you will have exceeded the client's expectation, resulting in a pleasantly surprised buyer. If you fail to meet your self-imposed two-day deadline (a deadline the client is unaware of), only you will know, and the client will still get the order in three days, ensuring that no external deadlines are missed.

But let's say you do the job in only two days. What if the client, instead of being euphoric, gets a little suspicious and says, "Wait a minute. You told me that this would take three full days. So what happened? Were you playing fast and loose with me?"

In response, you simply reconfirm your original promise. Three-day delivery was realistic and what they will normally be getting, but, because you knew it was important to them on this particular project, you "pulled out all the stops" and delivered a day early. That makes you look like a hero without making you look like a fibber.

By now, you see the pattern. You promote all the superior aspects of the service you are going to deliver, while slightly *underpromising* on one small aspect. Then, when you do better than expected in this area, you exceed expectation and create the extraordinary client happiness and surprise that goes with it.

Step 2: Give Your Clients More Than They Expect

Okay. We've established that the best way to create satisfied clients is to give them *more* than their money's worth. I've also suggested a two-step formula for doing this in a way that makes the client happy while allowing you to still make a nice profit.

The first step, as just discussed, is to underpromise slightly rather than overpromise. That is, to get the client to anticipate and expect something slightly *below* the level of what you are actually capable of delivering.

The second step is to then deliver *above* that level, so that your clients now feel you are giving them *more* than they had a right to expect. This rendering of performance above the client's expectation level is what creates an extraordinary level of pleasure and satisfaction.

However, at this point you may object, saying: "All well and good. But if the client is paying for a Chevy, and I deliver a Rolls Royce, it's costing me extra money. Sure, if I deliver much more than I promised the client will be happy, but I won't make any money—and I'm in business to make a profit."

The solution is simple and straightforward. *You can create an extraordinarily high level of pleasure and satisfaction in your clients by rendering them exceedingly small and simple favors.*

The best example I know of this is the pediatrician, dentist, or barber who keeps lollipops on hand for children. The excellent checkup, dental exam, or hair cut provided is what the client, in this case the child's mother, is expecting. If that's all you deliver, she'll think you're good but not great. After all, you delivered only what she expected in the first place. But it's that little extra gesture of a free candy for her little Bobby or Suzy that puts the smile on her face and warms her heart.

Ensuring the happiness of her children is perhaps the strongest emotional drive within her. When you help achieve that by consoling a crying child with a treat, you help her make the child happy again, and in that instant, you are the hero to her. You not only rendered your service, you were kind to her child. She knows you care and will come back to you again and again. And all it took was a 3-cent lollipop.

You can create an extraordinarily high level of pleasure and satisfaction in your clients by rendering them exceedingly small and simple favors. And that's the reason why giving your clients more than their money's worth, more than they have a right to expect, doesn't cost you a lot of money, time, or effort: The "extras" you provide don t have to be big. A simple gesture, a common courtesy, a faster response, a quicker completion time, a little extra topping on the sundae, these are the small things that will make the clients' "satisfaction quotient" soar and bond you to them for a long and happy relationship.

This means we can amend the original "secret" for keeping clients happy that was presented on the first page of this chapter. *To keep your clients satisfied, don't just give them their money's worth—give them MORE than their money's worth . . . but only a LITTLE more.*

Measuring Your Clients' Satisfaction Quotient

Although you can measure levels of client satisfaction by any scale you wish to use, the Client Satisfaction Quotient provides a quick, easy way of ranking how satisfied any given client is with you at any given moment. There is no "formula" or checklist. You simply use your judgment to rank the client's satisfaction level on a scale of 1 to 10 as shown in Figure 9.1.

When I ask you to assess how satisfied a particular client would or would not be with you in certain situations, you can refer to this scale and use the rating system to quantify your answer.

Sixteen Ways to Give Your Clients More Than Their Money's Worth

We have discussed the basic premise that a business can create superior client satisfaction by giving clients a *little* more than their money's worth. But how do you do it? Here are 16 methods you can use to give your clients those "little extras" that will win their hearts and their loyalties.

1. Give Them an Unexpected Free Gift with Their Order

I recently bought several gift items in a local candy store. After packing my purchase, the clerk handed me a small box of chocolates taken from a basket on the counter. "What's this?" I asked.

"It's a free gift box of chocolates for you," she replied cheerily. "We give it as a gift to every client who buys $20 worth of candy or more."

This put a smile on my face and a "warm fuzzy" inside me. Why?

- It was a surprise. And most of us like surprises (good ones, anyway).
- It was free. I was spending a lot of money on gifts so hadn't bought any of their delicious chocolates for my own consumption. Now I could sample some without spending more money.
- It was a nice gift. We really enjoyed it.

However, from the seller's point of view, creating this unexpected surge in my client satisfaction quotient was easy and inexpensive because

- the gift was easy to offer. They make candy on the premises and probably made one large batch of this particular item just for giving away.

Figure 9.1 Client Satisfaction Quotient Rating Chart

CLIENT SATISFACTION QUOTIENT

Rank the satisfaction or dissatisfaction of your client on a scale of 1 to 10 according to the following guidelines.

10 = ULTIMATE SATISFACTION. Client is "in love" with you. Right now, you are a guru in his eyes. He loves your product or service, buys frequently, refers all his friends and colleagues to you, and sings your praises all the time. The relationship is at a near all-time high because of something you recently did for this client that he absolutely loved.

9 = HIGHLY SATISFIED CLIENT. Same as a 10 except more time has passed since you pulled off that last great feat for the client. He still loves you and all that, but that last supersuccess was a while ago, and he may soon start asking, "What have you done for me lately?"

8 = VERY SATISFIED CLIENT. Client overall is highly satisfied with you. He thinks your product or service is great and that you continually exceed expectation. He gives you lots of repeat business and referrals to friends and colleagues.

7 = SATISFIED. The client is still satisfied, but would probably give you a B or B+ at best instead of an A or A–. He likes your product or service most of the time but has an occasional dissatisfaction with some minor aspects of dealing with you. Also, you meet expectation but don't really exceed. Nothing you've done has "dazzled" him lately.

6 = SOMEWHAT SATISFIED. The client finds your product or service satisfactory but doesn't get a "warm glow" dealing with you any more. He feels he gets fair value for his money, but thinks that perhaps you are not really better than your competitors, and he may be talking to other consultants.

5 = NEUTRAL. The client is no longer fully satisfied with your product or service or his dealings with you. He finds the product quality acceptable but not special, and he would say your service is sometimes okay but other times lacking. If asked, he could come up with a list of three or four things he likes about you, but could also just as easily generate an equally long list of complaints or things he doesn't like.

4 = A LITTLE DISSATISFIED. Similar to neutral except the client is becoming more aware of and concerned with the things he doesn't like about your product or service, while becoming less conscious of those things he likes and you do right. Minor problems and slipups register more easily, stay longer in the client's memory, and annoy him more than in the past.

3 = DISSATISFIED. The client is at a point where he does not really think much of your product or service, or of the way you do business. If a friend or colleague asked what he thought of your company, the client would reply, "Not great." He feels that quality has declined, service has deteriorated, and you no longer deliver what you once did.

Figure 9.1 Client Satisfaction Quotient Rating Chart *(Continued)*

2 = EXTREMELY DISSATISFIED. Not only does the client not like your product or service, he's now fed up with you. He thinks your performance is poor and that you just do not "have it" anymore. He is already starting to buy from other consultants and is planning on doing much less (if any) business with you in the future unless things improve radically.

1 = UTTERLY DISGUSTED. Same as 2, except the latest breakdown or disappointment has made the client totally unhappy with you to the point where he won't buy from you again (at least not in the near future).

- it didn't cost them a lot of money, perhaps only $1 or $2 per box for a gift with a much higher perceived value.
- they gave it only to those clients who spent a lot of money, ensuring that each transaction was profitable. Many who saw other clients getting it went back to buy more so their totals exceeded $20 and they could qualify for the gift.

Importantly, the free gift *had not been promised.* There was no sign in the store advertising it, nor had it been featured in newspaper ads. Therefore giving it had the added impact of *surprise.* It was a totally unanticipated and unexpected pleasure.

Had I come in response to an ad offering "free gift box with any $20 purchase," I wouldn't have been excited getting the box. After all, it was what I expected to get. Perhaps I would have even been disappointed, thinking, "Gee, I came all this way for such a small box?" But the fact that it was not promised assured my satisfaction. I had expected nothing and was getting something.

In another example, a local printer I do business with printed a quantity of "Things to do" notepads. When he delivered my next print job, he gave me half a dozen of these large, attractive pads with my envelopes and cards—totally unexpected and at no extra charge. That's the kind of "little extra" clients like and appreciate far in excess of the actual value or cost of the gift.

Want to create delighted clients? Try a free gift. It can be given with purchase or just to every client who walks in or calls that week. The gift need not be elaborate. Indeed, the more unexpected it is, the less costly it need be to make the client happy. My favorite gift to consulting clients (and one they seem to appreciate) is an autographed copy of one of my books.

2. Be Accessible

In today's fast-paced electronic age, many businesspeople use modern technology to juggle their busy schedules and put up barriers between themselves and their clients so they can manage what limited time they have more effectively. The problem is, while this practice may be convenient for you, your clients hate it.

Clients want to deal with consultants who are accessible and will take their calls *when* they call. They want to feel like their calls are welcome, not an annoyance. They want to feel that their concerns and problems are your concerns and problems, not an intrusion into your already crammed schedule or busy business day.

Many of us, pressured by too much to do and not enough time, often seem agitated or distracted when we get calls from our clients. That's understandable, but not good. It annoys clients and puts them off. You may think seeming incredibly busy is a status symbol, but your client thinks you're just showing off and that you are more concerned with your other business than with their order or problem. And that's bad.

Also, most businesspeople behave hypocritically with their clients. They are always friendly, "up," and available when *making the sale,* but as soon as the contract is signed, all the client hears is "He's not at his desk right now, I'll take a message." The client senses the hypocrisy in this and is rightly offended. "I was important to you when you wanted my business," the client thinks. "Now that you've got it, you're too busy wooing other clients to return my calls, huh?"

Although they do not like this behavior, clients have come to expect it. So when you are more accessible than your client expects—friendlier, more helpful, quick to take and return calls—they become relaxed and happy. "Here's someone at last who treats me right," they think, and this elevates you head and shoulders above the other consultants they deal with.

How can you be more accessible? One possibility might be to answer your own phone, or to at least reduce the amount of "grilling" callers are subjected to before your secretary or receptionist puts them through to you.

Think about it. Are you really so important that everyone who calls your office, even valued clients, must be put through "20 questions" before you'll do them the great favor of taking or returning their calls? Come on! This kind of treatment annoys you, right? So how do you think it makes your callers feel?

And, because the people who answer your phone don't always remember the names of your clients, your clients often receive treatment equally as negative as the salespeople you want your assistant to screen.

Keep in mind that, according to a recent survey from *Communication Briefings* (reported in *Direct* magazine, April 1992, page 5), 82 percent of 564 executives surveyed said the way employees answer the phone influences their opinion of the company. So better to do less screening and let an occasional telemarketer get through than *too much* screening and risk offending a valued client with such annoyances as "Does he know you?" "What company are you with?" and "Will she know what this is in reference to?"

Train your employees to be more courteous to callers, because many of those callers are clients or potential clients. Don't, for example, allow a secretary to say, "He's not in right now; can you call back at 2 PM?" You should *never* ask the caller to call back. You should always take a name and number and promise the caller you will get back to them.

If you've installed or are thinking of installing a voice mail system, it might interest you to know that 42 percent of the executives surveyed by *Communication Briefings* said that automated business phone "menus" (e.g., "press 1 for billing, press 2 for account balances") is the phone practice that annoys them most. The second most irritating phone practice is being put on hold without first being asked.

3. Fulfill Requests Promptly and Politely

This is the equivalent of "shock therapy" in business. It jolts the client into awareness because it's so sudden and unexpected. The client has come to anticipate poor attitudes, lousy service, impolite assistance, and slow, impersonal response. When you do what the client asks promptly and politely, they're shocked and delighted.

The combination of *promptly* and *politely* is critical. An exceptional effort made on the client's behalf isn't enough to win their kudos and loyalty in the fickle, client-driven business environment of the 1990s. To create exceptional client satisfaction, you not only have to do whatever the client asks, you also have to do it quickly and with a smile on your face.

The clients will not appreciate your efforts if you are slow, because they are impatient and hate to wait. They will also be put off if there is anything in your tone, manner, or behavior that suggests you are annoyed or unhappy about their request.

4. Fulfill Requests Beyond What the Client Requested

You create a high level of client satisfaction by fulfilling requests promptly and politely. You elevate that level of client satisfaction to an all-time high by doing what the client asked of you *and more.*

For example, we hired a painter to paint several bedrooms in our home. To save money, we decided we would paint the closets ourselves. In one walk-in closet, the ceiling was chipped and flaking.

While I can paint, I'm a lousy spackler. So I asked the painter if, when spackling the ceiling for that room, he could also do the walk-in closet ceiling. Several days later, when checking his progress, I saw that not only had he spackled the ceiling, he *had painted the entire walk-in closet* at no charge. Did it cost him much extra paint, time, or effort to do it? No. Would I hire him again? You bet.

5. Correct Problems Promptly and Politely

Although you have certain policies that limit how far you'll go or how much you'll give in when dealing with clients, you should probably suspend most or all of these limitations when a problem arises.

Today's high demand clients are totally intolerant of problems, expect you to do what they ask when they ask it, and will not continue to do business with a service provider who says, "Sorry, but I can't help you."

When a problem arises, acknowledge it, apologize for it, and then move quickly to focus on the solution. Do everything you can to correct it. And do so quickly and politely.

Did you ever ask a barber, waitress, repair person, or any other service provider to fix or change something that was not quite to your liking and have them start *arguing* with you? Then you know the worst thing you can do with a client who is dissatisfied is to give them a hard time. When clients have a problem, they need to see immediately that you are "on their side" and dedicated to resolving it.

6. Correct Problems without Charge

Even better than correcting problems quickly and courteously is to do it without charging the client *even if there is just cause for you to do so.*

We have a contractor who has done three large remodeling jobs for us and will soon do a fourth. His work is excellent, and his prices are competitive but certainly not the cheapest. The main reason we will use him again, however, is that when he is in our home, he will frequently go through the house and fix minor things and never bill us for it. Even when we asked him to do a few simple repair jobs that did not involve things he had originally built for us, he did them (or had his assistant do them) and, in most instances, did not charge us.

You can imagine how delighted I was not only with this willingness to help us out but also with his invoice. The charges for the remodeling jobs were big enough as it was. It was certainly a pleasure not to have another few hundred dollars tacked on for the odd jobs he had handled. Obviously, if I had asked him to do something very time consuming, he would have billed me and I would gladly have paid it. But by giving me an extra hour of his time and labor free now and then, he has gotten repeat business from me worth more than $20,000.

7. Correct Problems and Pay the Clients for Their Trouble

You can prevent the client from becoming dissatisfied by correcting problems quickly and courteously. You can put a smile on their face by not charging them for corrections. But you'll really cement your relationship and build extraordinary loyalty by *paying them* for their time and trouble.

This, in effect, says to the client: "We believe that when you pay for our service, you have every right to be satisfied at all times. If there is a problem, and you become dissatisfied, this is our fault, and not only will we do everything in our power to correct the defect quickly and efficiently, without charge to you, but we will also *compensate* you for your 'pain and suffering.'"

You can "pay" the client through a refund or rebate on the invoice owed, but this isn't the best strategy. For one thing, it visibly reminds the client of the problems involved on this job. For another, it costs you money unnecessarily, so that you have a loss instead of a profit.

A better way to compensate the client is to offer a credit, discount, price off, fee reduction, or other cost savings on the *next* job you do for them. This is a better choice for you because

- the client will be pleased and happy with such an offer.
- it shows fairness on your part.
- you still get your fee for the current job, so you don't feel upset or angry about the incident (as you would if you didn't get paid in full).
- you have now created a strong incentive for the clients *to use you again* for their next project because they have a "credit" with you. They do not "get paid" until they actually retain you and apply the credit toward your fee on that new job.

So not only is giving a credit or discount on future service a good way to resolve today's problem in a manner that makes the client happy, but it's also a selling technique for making sure you get the next job from them.

8. Follow Up Unexpectedly One or More Times

A major mistake I have made repeatedly in dealing with my own clients (and it's an ongoing fault, I admit) is communicating with them only when necessary or only when they expect to hear from me.

Although we don't realize it, our clients are sometimes not as confident in hiring us as we may think. Perhaps they were burned in the past by a service provider whom they hired with great expectations, only to have the firm not deliver on time or not meet expectations in some other way. So, while they may be trying an outside service again by retaining you, they're a little nervous about it, a little worried that their negative past experience may be repeated.

Communication between service provider and client is the solution. We've all gotten "How's it going?" calls from clients. Maybe you don't like such calls and think of them as an annoyance. I know I used to. My feeling was: "What is the point of such a call? I am a professional and deliver a professional service reliably and on time. The client knows that or they would not have hired me. Calling me to see 'How's it going?' is an insult and means they don't trust me. And what business is it of theirs what progress I have or have not made at this time, as long as they get what they ordered on the date I promised?"

Today my attitude is different. And yours should be, too. You should respect the client's right to communicate with you to make contact or check progress from time to time. And you should treat such calls as an opportunity to build a positive relationship with the client. Act, and actually be, pleased to get and deal with such calls. Don't, as so many do, act as if clients are "bothering" you. How can they be bothering you when they are paying you and the primary reason your company exists is to serve them?

Taking it one step further, don't wait for clients to call you and ask "How's it going?" Pick up the phone and call them *before they expected to hear from you* to say hello, touch base, and give them a quick update on progress. Clients appreciate this far more than you can imagine. It shows that you are concerned not only with the job but with their personal or professional stake in having you do the job well.

Not sure whether it's time to make a "keep in touch" call to a client? Consultant Ilise Benun gives this rule, "When in doubt, reach out." It's better to overcommunicate than not be heard from enough.

For consumers, how well you perform is important because it can affect their quality of life, and the money is coming out of their own pocket. For business clients, how well you perform determines how their supervisors and superiors will judge them. If you fail to deliver, people will say they made a poor decision in hiring you. If you do well, your performance makes them look good to their management.

Therefore, hearing from you is reassuring to your clients; it makes them feel better to know that everything is going smoothly and the project is on schedule.

So don't wait for the client to call you. If you go so long without communication that the clients feel compelled to phone and ask "How's it going?" they are already experiencing mild anxiety and nervousness. You want your clients to feel relaxed and confident, not nervous and jumpy. So don't wait for them to call you—call them.

9. Pay Personal Attention to Each Client

Although you have a business relationship with your clients, you can strengthen that business relationship by establishing a personal relationship as well. This does not mean that you need to become personal friends with clients or let socializing with clients impinge on your personal life. All it requires is to "be human"—to attend to the client as a human being as well as a buyer of services.

The best way to accomplish this is by rapport achieved through small talk. Find some common ground between you and the client and use that as the icebreaker that makes them think of you as a person, and not just a "consultant," "contractor" or whatever it is you do.

You will find that, even if you and the client are very different and would not be compatible as friends, there is always some common ground that can be used to strengthen the bond between you. This might be sports, family, hobbies, likes or dislikes, similarities in lifestyle, or any one of a number of things.

For instance, I had an initial meeting with one client who had already decided to hire me but was a little difficult to deal with because he was standoffish. After we got through the business portion of our meeting, we each had a couple minutes to spare between appointments and decided to "shoot the breeze." As it turned out, we were the same age, each had one child, and our children were the same age. This resulted in a lively discussion about parenthood, which I feel established a stronger link between us and improved the working relationship.

Importantly, such bonding cannot be phony; you can't force it or fake it. Don't go looking for a shared interest or other common bond between you and the client. It will eventually come out naturally, in normal conversation. The important thing is, when you recognize it, encourage it, nurture it, and let it grow.

One important point: The area of shared interest should be a relatively safe and noncontroversial topic—gardening, for example. Avoid sex, religion, politics, money, or any other area where conflicting views often trigger passionate arguments. You don't want to state a strong political view you think the client shares, for example, only to discover he or she is diametrically opposed to your view and finds it reprehensible.

What you're looking for instead is to find out that you and the client share an interest in jazz, or model rockets, or gourmet cooking, or something similarly safe. Then, whenever you call the client, instead of getting down to business you can first ask, "How about the game last night?" or "Did you know the Dukes of Dixie are coming to town?" or something else involving the shared interest between you. This shifts the client from all business to a more friendly mode and can also make the client easier to deal with on a day he may be agitated or frazzled.

10. Offer the Client Something Special

If you're an antique dealer, for example, and you come across a piece of beautiful carnival glass that's a real find yet reasonably priced, call your client who you know collects carnival glass and offer it to her first, before you display it for your walk-in trade.

If you're an innkeeper, and you're planning special activities and fantastic meals for a particular season or holiday, send a postcard to your past lodgers inviting them for this special event and let them know it's exclusive for valued clients only.

If you sponsor public conferences or seminars, send a personal letter of invitation to past attendees of previous years' programs *before* your regular mailing goes out, and offer these past attendees a special "alumni discount."

You create extraordinary client satisfaction when you convey the impression that, even when you're not currently under contract or rendering service to that client, you're always on the lookout for things they would want or need. For instance, even if I'm just writing sales letters and not handling any other aspects of the client's marketing, I'll still send them a copy of a new magazine I come across that might be a good place for them to advertise, *even though their advertising is handled by an ad agency and I am not involved with it.* The client appreciates that I am thinking of them and doing so with no immediate profit motive in mind.

11. Give Free Seconds

Several years ago, we made a pleasant discovery: a good restaurant in New York City that gives free seconds on any dish at any time. This policy costs them very little because few patrons take advantage of it (regular portions are more than adequate). But it makes them memorable and sets them apart from their numerous competitors (there are some areas of Manhattan where there are three restaurants or more on virtually every block in the neighborhood).

This "free seconds" idea can also be applied, with a slight variation, to ensuring client satisfaction in the service business. The basic principle is this: When selling a certain service to a client, include some additional *follow-up* service which they can choose to use or not, included free with the original purchase.

For example, a friend of mine gives training seminars to corporations on business communications. He says to clients, "If any of the people you send to my seminar find they need more help or want more information, they can call my Business Communication Telephone Hotline for assistance and, because they are alumni of my program, there will be no charge to consult with them or answer their questions."

This variation of "free seconds" adds to the perceived value of my friend's training programs and also to his credibility. Not only is he giving more value for the money than seminar providers whose fees include the training session only with no follow-up privileges, but he is in effect guaranteeing that trainees will get the knowledge they need when he is hired, because he will answer their questions long after the seminar is over.

This added level of service helps differentiate him from his competitors and has accounted for part of his tremendous success in the training field. Interestingly, while many new clients comment on how much they appreciate getting the use of the hotline included with their training courses, very few attendees actually use the hotline. So it costs him very little to offer this valuable extra.

12. Give Free Product or Service

This method is extremely effective as a "sales closer," especially when selling additional services to existing clients. Let's say the client is indecisive or unconvinced the fee you are asking for the service you are providing is justified. There's probably not a huge gap between what you're asking and what they are comfortable paying. More likely, you would have to do only a "little better" to make the client feel comfortable with the value they are getting.

Instead of lowering the price, you say to the client, "Okay, I tell you what: Hire us today to do "X" and we'll also give you "Y" and "Z" at no charge." "X" is the main job; "Y" and "Z" are small related or ancillary tasks that take very little time but have a high perceived value to the client. When the client feels they are getting three services "X," "Y," and "Z" but you are charging only for "X," they grow comfortable with your fee and the level of service you are providing for that fee, which in turn helps build overall client satisfaction.

Sometimes, even if you don't absolutely have to, it's better to give the client a little extra service or, conversely, charge a bit less. Just because the client signed your contract doesn't mean she feels comfortable with it. Perhaps she signed because of imminent deadlines or other pressing needs, but feels that you are "ripping her off" and are taking advantage of her situation by charging too much for too little. You may indeed be making a high profit on that job, but are you building client satisfaction and a long-term relationship based on maintaining that satisfaction?

Any contract you get a client to sign should be a win-win situation for you and the client. Giving a little extra service or a small "freebie" is a simple way to overcome client resistance or displeasure and create a client who's comfortable with the deal and feels you are being more than fair, even generous. "The challenge is to deliver results that exceed the client's expectations," writes Paul Vaughn, chairman of Hooven Direct Mail. "Providing clients with a service they hadn't expected is an excellent client retention strategy."

13. Charge Slightly Less Than the Original Estimate

Most surprises clients get are unpleasant: a botched job, a job that was not done as ordered, a missed deadline. So it makes an enormous impression on the client when you give them a pleasant surprise.

One easy way to do this is to send an invoice that is slightly less than the original estimate. Most service providers seek to do exactly the opposite. Reason: As the job progresses, and they have to do the actual work, they realize how much effort is involved and that they probably bid too low to get the job.

So they get "revenge" on the client by charging for every little expense, for every change in client direction, for every little extra service that was provided along the way. The result is a bill 10 to 20 percent or more higher than the original estimate.

The problems? *Clients dislike receiving bills higher than they budgeted or contracted.* Everyone—the consumer and the business buyer—is on a budget today. Going over budget hurts consumers because it's money out of their pockets, and hurts business buyers because it makes them look bad to management.

A colleague of mine, who owns a small ad agency, told me that she had hired a new graphic artist to design an ad for a client. The artist bills $50 per hour. She loved his work, but when she got the bill from him, there was a $50 charge for the hour he was showing his portfolio and presenting his services and capabilities to her! This was completely unexpected. "I didn't expect to be billed for his sales presentation to me," the client said and started the relationship off on a negative tone instead of an upbeat one.

You can be different by sending the client an invoice for an amount equal to or, even better, slightly *less* than your estimate. Your invoice should show clearly the amount of the discount, both in dollars and percentage savings, as well as the *reason* for the discount (e.g., you spent fewer hours than anticipated, or the cost of materials was lower, or you didn't have to do a certain phase or step you originally thought you would have to do when you gave the original estimate).

The client will see that you were able to achieve a cost reduction and then, instead of keeping it as extra profit, passed on the savings directly through a lower charge.

Taking a few dollars off an invoice now and then won't cost you a fortune, and there are few things as effective as a slight reduction in the final bill that will pleasantly surprise your clients, making them think favorably of you. It builds your credibility and it's appreciated.

14. Complete the Job Slightly Faster Than the Original Deadline

Next to getting it done cheaper, getting it done sooner is the thing that will "knock the socks" off your client. Everybody is in a hurry nowadays. If the original deadline is tight, beating it will make your client that much happier. If the original deadline is distant, the client will appreciate the extra time to review your work or use what you provide when you get it to them a week earlier.

Be careful, though. Do not complete the work too early. The danger is giving the client the impression that you rushed their project, didn't give it your best effort, and therefore did an inadequate job. As a rule of thumb, if you are going to deliver your work or complete the job early, don't beat the deadline by more than 20 to 25 percent.

So if today is April 1 and your report is due April 20, you can please the client by beating the deadline and handing it in any time between April 15 and April 19. Hand it in earlier than that and you risk the client taking your "hasty completion" into account when evaluating the work, and so the evaluation is likely to be negative.

Speaking of being criticized for handing work in too early, Milton, a consultant friend of mine tells a wonderful story.

His first job was as assistant to the circulation director of a magazine with a large circulation. On Milton's first day on the job, the circulation director handed Milton a stack of magazines and direct mail promotions and said, "Your first assignment is to come up with at least two dozen ideas for increasing the circulation of the magazine."

Milton went to his desk, studied the material, and by lunch handed in a typed four-page memo with the heading, "24 ways to increase the circulation of XYZ Magazine." His boss became furious. "I want you to *think* about it!" he shouted as he threw Milton's memo across the desk. "Go back to work and really *think* about this problem!"

Milton went back to his desk and put the memo in his top drawer. Two weeks later, he pulled out the memo, changed the date, walked up to his boss's desk, and handed it to him. The boss scanned the four pages, turned to Milton, and smiling, said, "This is excellent! See you can do good work when you really put your mind to it." Milton said nothing. He just smiled back.

15. Keep Complete, Well-Organized Records and Have Them at Your Fingertips

Nothing annoys a client more when they call you up to ask a question and you say, "Gee, I don't know" or "I have no idea."

We live in an age of instant information, a time when people are impatient with anything less than an immediate response to their queries. For this reason, many large companies have spent hundreds of thousands of dollars on computer and communications systems designed to help client service people gain fast access to client records, track projects, respond to inquiries, and resolve problems.

For the one-person office and other small businesses, you can achieve the equivalent by keeping well organized and complete files on each job and storing those files in a place where you have quick and easy access to them.

If a client calls with a question or problem dealing with a current or past job, you should be able to access the information immediately while the client is on the phone or at least be able to find it so that you can call back with some answers or discuss the problem further within the next five minutes. Keeping a frustrated or annoyed client waiting for preliminary answers longer than that creates an impression of poor service and incompetence. Clients like to know you are in control of your information, are well organized, and have designed your office procedures to respond quickly to their needs.

In addition to keeping well organized files, you can use your personal computer to put important client information within easy reach. Some people use popular database software to maintain client information; others use personal information management or client management programs more specific to their needs. Having the proper information immediately available when clients call with a query or complaint puts them at ease and creates a professional image for your business. Being unable to "find the papers" when clients call frustrates them and creates a negative impression. And the longer you force the clients to wait for an answer to a question or a response to a problem, the more dissatisfied they will become.

16. Don't Be a Prima Donna

In the "salad days" of the 1980s, many freelancers, independents, and smaller service businesses could afford, to a degree, to indulge their egos and act like prima donnas. In those days, if you were a skilled craftsperson, carpenter, contractor, mason, photographer, graphic artist, software developer, or whatever, the demand for your services was probably greater than the supply, which meant you could call your own shots, be choosy about the clients you accepted, and be casual, even gruff, in the way you dealt with and treated your clients.

Clients would put up with prima donna service providers because they were willing to endure the less-than-exemplary treatment to gain access to the skills and services of these companies. But that doesn't mean they liked being treated poorly or indifferently.

The recession of the early l990s permanently changed the situation. When buyers stopped spending, service providers, instead of having clients lined up and waiting to buy, had to go out and ask (almost beg, in some cases) for work to keep their businesses solvent. Clients saw that they, not the consultants, were in control. The service provider needs the client's money, but the client can probably live without the service provider by going elsewhere.

As a result, a lot of service providers who were once prima donnas are prima donnas no longer. Now they are humble laborers, competing with many firms providing similar services for a shrinking number of projects as clients cut back or do it themselves.

Being a prima donna was once an effective image for service providers because it made them look busy, important, and in demand. But in today's "Age of the Customer," I am convinced this image or approach no longer works.

The bottom-line advice: *Don't be a prima donna.* Clients want to work with service providers who are friendly and accessible and have their egos in check.

Today, clients have no patience with or need for snobs. You may think you're an original and that being standoffish only makes you more desirable to the clients. In one case in a million that may be true. But for the majority, being a prima donna will bump you off the short list of consultants being considered for the job.

If you don't believe me, ask a plumber, contractor, or other home improvement specialist for a quote on a large project for your home. You'll find them happy to bid, patient, eager to please, flexible, and anxious to get the job.

If you tell clients how great and busy you are as a marketing ploy when it isn't really true, they'll see through it. They *know* what the economy is like today, and they simply won't believe your claims of glory. So be honest, accommodating, even a little humble. That's what will win you clients and their continued business in the decades to come.

C • H • A • P • T • E • R

10

Proven Strategies for

Keeping Your Clients Happy

A wise client once told me, "Subjective judgment is the death of the service business." No matter how carefully worded our agreements, how tightly written our contracts, the client's ultimate satisfaction is determined by his subjective judgment of us, our service, and our treatment of him.

Part of the problem is a combination of unrealistic expectations on the part of the client combined with overpromises or puffery on the part of the consultant to make the sale. Consultants can promise to perform services, but they cannot be sure of getting a result that meets or exceeds the client's expectations. Although we as consultants know this, the pressure of selling often motivates us to paint a picture a bit rosier or at least more optimistic than reality.

Consultant Dan Kennedy gives an honest evaluation of what consultants can and cannot, will and will not, do for clients. "All somebody like me can do is bring a lot of experience to bear, to improve your possibilities," writes Dan in his *No. B.S. Marketing Letter* (December 1992, page 1). "And we are mercenaries. Lose one war, we move on to the next." He says the client must take responsibility for getting the greatest possible value from the consultant.

Clients, unfortunately, often don't like to hear reality statements like "it can't be done," "we can't predict the response," or "there's no guarantee." If anything, they want to believe your sales pitch—that you're the great guru. They convince themselves you can do anything, which starts the relationship off on a note of high expectation, but can lead to disappointment when they discover you're only human and don't control the world.

In a Blondie cartoon strip, Blondie tells a couple hiring her to cater an affair that the price for filet is $25 per dinner, and the chicken is $17 per dinner. "Would you call yourself an excellent caterer?" the client asks. When Blondie replies positively, the client says, "Then we'll take the chicken . . . but we're counting on you to make it seem like they're having the filet." Most consulting clients are like Blondie's couple.

You can't always perform as well as you or the client would wish. You can only perform as well as you can. "Be careful not to confuse excellence with perfection," says actor Michael J. Fox (as quoted in *Reader's Digest,* February 1998, page 13). "Excellence I can reach for; perfection is God's business."

Creating Satisfied Clients

Because you do not control any individual's subjective judgment, or the mood or external circumstances affecting that judgment, you cannot totally control the client's reaction to your services. Therefore, no matter how good you are, or how hard you try, you are invariably going to run into situations where the client is not satisfied with you or your service.

Some of your peers will tell you that this *never* happens and that their clients are always satisfied. Either they're lying, or they handle so few clients that a problem hasn't happened yet. It will.

Given that clients will become dissatisfied and that client dissatisfaction can hurt your business, reduce your income, tarnish your reputation, and cause loss of accounts, you must learn strategies for coping with clients who become dissatisfied. That's what this chapter will help you do.

Early Detection of Dissatisfaction: The Best Cure

For many human illnesses, doctors tell us that early detection is the best cure. Caught early enough, the eye disease won't blind us, the cancer won't kill us. It's only when we ignore the symptoms and let the disease progress undiagnosed and untreated that it grows to a point where it can cripple us or do us in.

It's the same with the disease of client dissatisfaction. A client complaint, even one that seems serious at first, can be handled in such a way that it does no permanent harm to the client/consultant relationship, provided it is detected early and dealt with swiftly and effectively.

Client dissatisfaction can hurt us only if it goes undetected or ignored. Then the problem festers and grows to the point where it kills the healthy relationship and we lose the client and her business. According to Dun & Bradstreet, 90 percent of clients who are unhappy won't complain to you— but 96 percent of clients who are unhappy will tell others of their dissatisfaction

So the number one rule in coping with dissatisfied clients: act fast. If you suspect there's a problem, bring it out in the open where it can be dealt with. When you have a problem, acknowledge it. Be up front with the client and discuss it with them. Don't think it will go away if you ignore it. It won't.

Find a solution that not only solves the problem but also restores the client's faith and confidence in you. Don't hold back; do what it takes. Even if the solution costs you more than you want to spend, do it. You must not let dissatisfied clients remain dissatisfied. When you do, you lose their business, and they tell others, and you quickly gain a reputation that will cause others to shun you.

Avoid pushing expensive and complex consulting projects on clients when a simple solution will do just as well for a lot less money. An article in the newsletter *Words from Woody* (Fall 1997, page 2) tells the following story illustrating this point:

> A museum planned to hire a consultant to perform an expensive study to determine which exhibits were most popular with visitors. But a committee member stopped the consulting project from going through and got the information another way—by asking the janitor where he had to mop the most.

Dissatisfied Clients Tell Other Clients

Financial consultant John Cali says a dissatisfied client will tell ten to twenty or more people about their bad experience with you. You can read that and it may not sink in; you have to experience it for the statistic to have meaning.

Here's an example. I recently gave a speech at a local advertising club. Before giving my talk, people at my table—all ad agency executives and owners—were discussing which different printers, photographers, copywriters, and designers were good, bad, expensive, and so on.

The name of a copywriter friend of mine came up. To my amazement, one of the agency executives, also a friend, immediately told the others not to hire that copywriter. "He was difficult, rude, uncooperative, and his bill was much higher than his estimate," said the executive. "We agreed to pay it, but said we would have liked to make two payments over a two-month period. He screamed at us, demanded his money immediately; threatened to tell our client he would sue them unless we paid right away. We did pay him, but would never use him again. You should not, either."

I was stunned. Could you imagine how this copywriter would have felt at that moment, sitting at home, if he could somehow be transported to the table and see what was being said about him? There were people representing eight other New Jersey ad agencies sitting there. He will probably never be able to sell to any one of them.

The point is, the same has been (or will be) said about you, without you knowing it, at least once in your lifetime, by someone who for some reason doesn't like you or feels you did not treat them well.

Do dissatisfied clients *deliberately go out of their way* to slander you and besmirch your reputation? I don't think so. They don't sit at the telephone and call all their friends to get even with you or send out mailings saying you stink.

On the other hand, keep in mind that dissatisfied clients, while not "out to get you," are not hesitant to talk about you and give opinions when asked or when the subject comes up, as it did at the ad club. If asked about their experience with you, dissatisfied clients will probably give the truth as they see it, which, because they are dissatisfied, means a negative report.

For this reason, you want to work hard to prevent client dissatisfaction or minimize its negative effects when it does happen. It's not client dissatisfaction that ultimately harms your business; it's what you do to find and fix client dissatisfaction when it occurs.

A wise man once said, "It's not what happens to you in life; it's how you handle it." Screwing up with a client is bad, but it won't kill your relationship with that client. It's how you respond to the problem and what you do about it that determines whether the client's satisfaction is restored or the client's dissatisfaction is made worse.

Don't Make Excuses to Clients

Most books on customer service tell you, "No excuses. Do whatever it takes to serve the customer. People hate to hear excuses." I agree, but not totally. What I agree with is that (1) you should keep your promises and (2) you shouldn't get in the habit of making excuses.

Just as "my dog ate my homework" doesn't cut it with teachers, clients don't want to hear what so many difficult, unresponsive, unpunctual vendors tell them.

- "The materials haven't arrived yet."
- "It's not me, it's my supplier."
- "We'll come *next* Friday, I *promise*."
- "I'm sorry, but we got really busy this summer."
- "My assistant is sick."
- "My daughter wasn't feeling well."
- "I had to take my wife to the doctor."
- "Our photocopier broke down."
- "Our computer broke down."
- "We tried to call you but your line was busy."
- "I thought you said *Thursday* morning, not Tuesday morning."
- "We said *maybe* it would be ready Friday."
- "I thought my secretary sent that to you. Didn't you get it?"
- "Someone else does that; it's not my fault."
- "It's in the mail."

Get in the habit of meeting commitments, not making excuses. Think of a commitment as a promise you cannot break. Clients want to deal with vendors who are reliable and get the job done no matter what, no excuses.

On the other hand, I do not agree with those who say you should never give an excuse or a reason for the problem. We live in the real world, not the ivy covered tower of some theoretician imagining business the way it *should* be.

And in the real world, things *do* happen. Computer systems crash. Delivery trucks go off the road. Flights get canceled. People become seriously ill.

If the client's dissatisfaction is the result of a problem with your service caused by something that was unavoidable, catastrophic, or could not have reasonably been predicted or anticipated, my advice is to be honest with the client and tell him precisely what happened and why the problem occurred, rather than try to hide it.

Clients are human beings, with feelings. If you had to miss a deadline because your son was hit by a car, only the most unfeeling of clients would expect you to stay at your desk to complete a report, proposal, drawing, or design.

So do not be afraid to tell the truth. Rather than annoy clients, the truth will make them sympathetic, even helpful. When they know and understand the reason for the incident or action that caused their dissatisfaction, their anger will lessen, and it will not be a permanent blot on your record.

Those of us who are sole practitioners or the principal consultants of small businesses are particularly vulnerable to the threat of interruptions in client service caused by personal illness or other catastrophe. At a big company, for example, a technical writer whose computer stops working can simply go to the storeroom and sign out another machine. But the freelance technical writer, unable to afford a second PC, loses the ability to get work done while his machine is in the shop being repaired.

In the same way, if an employee is absent from her job due to illness or personal reasons, the corporation will still function, the department will continue to be productive. If I have a 24-hour virus and stay home in bed, however, "Bob Bly, Inc." gets no work done that day.

While in some businesses it's difficult for a substitute to step in and take over when you're unable to perform, in many other fields it may be a good idea to make an arrangement with a friendly competitor. When you are out of commission, your backup can take over and handle the work load until you return. Every doctor makes such an arrangement with another "covering doctor." Why not you too? It makes sense and can prevent service interruptions that cause lost deadlines and much client dissatisfaction and frustration.

Ten Reasons Clients May Become Unhappy with Your Service

Although there are many things that can cause clients to become unhappy or frustrated with you, here are ten of the most common.

1. The client is not pleased with you or the quality of your work.
2. Your service fails to achieve the desired or expected result.
3. You perform poorly or make a mistake.
4. You behave unprofessionally or have a conflict with the client.
5. You miss your deadline.
6. Your bill exceeds your estimate.
7. The client wants more service than you can provide.
8. The client wants a different service than you are providing.
9. The client wants more freebies and extras.
10. There is a misunderstanding, miscommunication, or poor communication between you and the client.

Let's take a brief look at each cause of client dissatisfaction, along with ideas on how to handle them and how to prevent them from occurring in the first place.

Reason 1: The Client Is Not Pleased with You or the Quality of Your Work

First, you must find out why the client is unhappy with you or your work. If you did nothing bad, inept, or incompetent, the client's displeasure is based on some subjective negative assessment of you and your service. For example, the client feels you turned in a sloppy report (even though you think it's good) or the client thinks you did not provide good service and were not attentive to her needs (even though you got the job done on time and feel you communicated with her in an efficient and service-oriented manner). If the client does not come straight out and tell you she is dissatisfied, you can usually detect it in her manner of dealing with you.

Instead of being friendly and relaxed, as usual, she becomes distant, curt, and uptight. Whenever you call or visit, you get the sense that she is angry. This is not an accident. Although the client is afraid or unwilling to tell you she is angry, she is subconsciously doing so through body language and tone of voice.

If you suspect there is a problem, say, "Rita, you seem angry and upset. Did I do something wrong?" or "I must have really done something bad to get you this angry and upset. Can you tell me what it is?" This "opens the dam" so to speak, and a flood of words, emotions, and information results, detailing what you did wrong.

So far, so good. But here's where most of us fall. When we get the client to tell us what's wrong, our immediate response is to *argue* with the client's feelings or viewpoint; that is, tell why he or she is wrong or shouldn't be angry.

We tell such clients that it's not our fault, their account of what happened is not accurate, or their perception is wrong. This doesn't work. You can't tell someone who is angry, "Don't be angry," and expect that person to say, "Okay." They'll only get angrier that you are arguing or treating their opinions and feelings as invalid.

There are two things you must do to set things right: (1) acknowledge the client's feelings and point of view, and (2) begin the process of taking corrective action. Note that it is almost irrelevant at this point whether you were wrong or right. The goal is to make the client happy again, get her in a calmer and more receptive state. Later, when she likes you again, a discussion may correct some inaccurate perceptions or get her to acknowledge that it really wasn't your fault. But for now, that doesn't matter. So when the client tells you the problem, you say, "You're right, and I'm sorry. Tell me, Rita, what can I do to set things right for you?"

Notice the two-step process. First, you acknowledge that her opinion, feelings, and perceptions are correct. After all, as the saying goes, the customer is right, even when she's wrong. Second, instead of *telling* her what should be done to solve the problem, you *ask* her how she would like you to handle it. "What can I do to set things right?"

All you need to do to correct the situation is take the corrective action she asks for and feels is appropriate. Surprisingly, what the client needs is usually *much less* than you would have imagined or offered had you not inquired.

By the way, unless her request is absolutely impossible or unreasonable, promise to do it immediately—and then do it immediately. Do not start negotiating, hemming or hawing, or modifying what she asked for because it's more convenient for you. At this point, you want to suspend your self-interest and do whatever the client wants, regardless of how difficult or time consuming it is.

Reason 2: Your Service Fails to Achieve the Desired or Expected Result

Many of us selling services sell them based on a result that is implied, predicted, or promised—but not guaranteed. A direct mail consultant, for example, will not guarantee or promise a particular response rate (doing so violates the code of ethics of the Direct Marketing Association), but will strongly imply that, by hiring him, the client is getting a pro who almost always increases direct mail response rates for other clients and will do so for this client, too. The problem, of course, is that when you overpromise to sell the job, your results are often not what you led the client to expect. What to do?

My strategy is to prevent this problem from happening by not overpromising in the first place. Instead, give the client a realistic assessment of what you can do and what results to expect.

If you have a track record of achieving record results for other clients, by all means let clients know it when selling your services to them. But at the same time, make sure they know that you cannot guarantee the same result for them. All you can guarantee is that you'll give it your best effort. You are like a mutual fund because "past performance is no guarantee of future yield."

"I can't do that!" you protest. "My competitors are all making big claims when they sell, and if I'm a milktoast about it, I won't get any projects." Actually, while this fear sounds logical, I've found the opposite is true. By being honest with potential clients and not overpromising, you stand out from the crowd because what you say sounds more honest and believable. Says stockbroker Andrew Lanyi, "The more you tell the client you are not a witch doctor or a rainmaker, the more credibility you get."

For example, a large industrial manufacturer in my area was looking for a new copywriter to write product literature. When interviewing me, the marketing director and product manager said, "Our complaint with other writers is that what they produce is not right the first time and we have to spend a lot of time rewriting it. If we give you a trial product sheet to write, can you promise that it will be right the first time?"

My answer shocked him. "That would be impossible," I replied. "Until I learn your preferences, style, and method of working, the drafts are going to have to be rewritten two or three times before they are perfect. However, I can promise that I will do all rewrites at no charge until you are satisfied, with a minimum of work on your part, although you will be required to review carefully and comment on each draft. Also, after the first three or four projects, the first drafts will be much closer to finished, as we gain more experience working with each other. But guarantee to you that the first draft on the first project will be acceptable without changes? Impossible. I can't do it, and anyone who makes such a promise doesn't know this business or is a liar."

The advertising manager later told me, "They were impressed with your honesty." Also, by setting up a realistic expectation at the start, satisfaction was far easier to achieve, because I did not have to live up to an expectation that would have been nearly impossible to satisfy. I got the trial project and soon became the firm's regular copywriter for all product literature.

Now let's consider another scenario, where you *did* overpromise and the client is complaining that the result was not achieved. What to do? You have four options.

1. *Deliver on your promise.* If you promised a specific result and did not achieve it by performing the work contracted for, you might want to consider doing additional work on the project, at no charge to the client (or at a reduced charge), until the expected result is achieved.

2. *Give a credit.* If you generated some results but fell short of the goal, you might refund part of your fee. Rather than give the money back, you might give the refund as a credit the client can apply toward purchase of more services. This has the advantage of costing you nothing out of pocket, and compels the client to try your service again.

3. *Refund money.* If you promised to generate a result, and that promise was based on a money back guarantee, or if your fee was contingent on getting that result, the client gets a refund or doesn't

pay. Of course, to avoid this, you can always offer to try again, at your expense, to get the result you promised.

4. *Give them freebies.* Another option is to give the client more service at no cost to make up for not achieving the initial result promised.

Reason 3: You Performed Poorly or Make a Mistake

This is different than Reason 1 because here the dissatisfaction is caused by your apparent and obvious error or poor performance.

The first thing you need to do to remedy this situation is analyze what caused the poor performance. Did you accept an assignment that was too big or complex for you? Was it something you'd never done before? Was the deadline too tight?

Second, take steps to ensure that the problem doesn't happen again to this client or any others in the future. Figure 10.1 lists common reasons for performance problems and how to correct them.

Third, in dealing with the current situation, the best strategy is to be up front with the client. If the job was bigger than you anticipated, say, "I made a mistake. I hadn't managed an entire project like this before, and it was much more work than I anticipated. The mistake was mine."

Always take full blame; do not attempt to share blame with clients. If they really feel that it is partially their fault, they will tell you so to make you feel better and let you off the hook. If not, you only make a bad situation worse by inferring that they are partially to blame.

Fourth, apologize and ask clients how they would like you to rectify the situation, letting them know that you will do whatever it takes to correct things and get back in their good graces. "I'm really sorry, Rita. Tell me, what can we do to set things right?"

Always expect work to take more time than you think it will, not less.

Reason 4: You Behave Unprofessionally or Have a Conflict with the Client

Whether you can fix this depends upon the severity of your transgression. If this happens frequently, you need to examine the source of your conflicts and poor treatment of clients. Perhaps you really don't like

Figure 10.1 Reasons for Poor Performance

CAUSE	CURE
Deadline is too tight.	Negotiate for longer deadlines. Do not take on projects if deadline is too short. Do not take on more assignments than you can handle. Add staff. Subcontract work to other vendors.
Project is too complex to manage (has too many tasks and activities for you keep track of).	Do not take on projects too complex for you to manage. Take a seminar in project management to improve your skills. Hire an employee to be project coordinator/manager. Acquire and learn to use a project management system or software.
You lack the expertise needed to perform project adequately.	Do not take on projects that you do not have the expertise to handle. Subcontract to other vendors with the expertise you lack. Hire employee with skills to handle this type of work.
You lack the time needed to perform work adequately.	Do not take on more work and projects than you can handle. Hire more employees. Cut back on workload. Make sure deadlines are sufficient and realistic.
Constant client contact and communication interfere with your successful performance of the work.	Hire an account representative to handle client contact. Work with clients who do not demand intensive "hand-holding." Educate clients on level of contact appropriate and necessary for successful completion of the work. Set a regular schedule of client contact to reduce unscheduled interruptions.

Figure 10.1 Reasons for Poor Performance *(Continued)*

	Use voice mail or assistant to screen phone calls. Take calls only during certain hours.
Project is more work than originally anticipated.	Make more realistic estimates of time and labor required to do job when making bid or quoting fee. Always expect work to take more time than you think it will, not less.
Client changes interfere with timely completion of the work as scheduled.	Have a policy or contract that calls for deadline extensions and fee increases when client changes job requirements midstream.
Your dislike of project interferes with quality of work.	Be selective and only take on projects that interest you. Assign boring and routine tasks to freelancers, subcontractors, or staff.
Your dislike of client interferes with quality of work.	Be selective and deal only with clients you like and with whom you work well. Have staff account coordinator be primary contact with "nonfavorite" clients.
Tiredness or lack of energy interferes with your ability to do a good job.	Take a vacation to "recharge your batteries." Take on less work. Get more sleep. Get more relaxation. Take up a hobby. Spend more time with family. Achieve better work/personal life balance. Exercise. Improve diet.
Boredom or lack of interest causes poor performance.	Take a vacation to "recharge your batteries." Take on less work. Take on more interesting projects.

Figure 10.1 Reasons for Poor Performance *(Continued)*

	Consider career change or change in business activities.
Job involves doing tasks you do not enjoy or have the skills for.	Consider cutting back on scope of work and sticking to tasks you do well and enjoy. Do not try to expand too quickly into peripheral areas.
Paperwork and administrative details bog you down and prevent you from attending to essential work.	Hire secretary or clerical support staff. Farm out secretarial work to outside word processing or office support service. Hire temps as needed for each job.
Employee, vendor, or subcontractor performed poorly on his portion of the project.	Discuss problem with employee or vendor. Look for alternative sources of services.

your clients or enjoy your job. That can cause depression and lack of self-esteem which, in turn, affects your work.

You may have to resign some accounts due to your inability to deal with that particular client in a cordial and decent way.

You might also consider a sabbatical or slowdown to reexamine your career and make sure you are in a business that brings you pleasure and satisfaction as well as financial rewards. Don't do something just for the money. You should enjoy your work, too. If you don't, this will reveal itself in your dealings with your clients.

By being happier in your work, and working with clients you like and enjoy, you are less likely to act in a rude, abrupt, or discourteous manner, and there will rarely be an incident that causes problems.

Should an incident arise, the best course of action is an immediate, direct apology: "I was curt just now, Wayne. I'm sorry. We were up all night with a sick child, I didn't get any sleep, and I'm on edge. Please accept my apology." Most clients will react in a human fashion ("I understand. I have a two-year-old myself."), and the incident will be forgiven and forgotten.

Occasional rudeness, abruptness, or less than perfect behavior, while not desirable, is only human and rarely causes permanent damage in the client/consultant relationship. What you want to avoid is major or frequent conflict or problems with clients.

If you have a short temper, you must learn to control it. A good technique is to pause and mentally count to five when you feel yourself about to let loose on a client.

The pause will give you time to gain control, calm your emotions, and formulate a rational, nonoffensive response to whatever the client said or did to set you off. Use some body language (e.g., eyes looking off to the distance, as if in concentration) or some tone of voice ("Hmmm . . .") to make the client think you are carefully contemplating your answer rather than controlling your temper. Force yourself to smile to convert from a negative to a positive mood.

Reason 5: You Miss Your Deadline

Here are my three recommendations regarding deadlines.

1. Never miss a deadline.
2. Try to complete work slightly ahead of the deadline, if possible.
3. If you are going to miss a deadline, notify the client as soon as you are sure that missing the deadline is unavoidable.

If the deadline is for an intermediate step or task, assure the client that it will not affect the final due date. Mail or fax a revised schedule to show how you will still complete the work on time, despite having missed the intermediate deadline. Then do whatever it takes to make up the lost time, with any additional expense or extra effort to be expended by you, not the client.

If the deadline you missed is the final deadline, see if you can do something so that the client does not suffer loss or hardship as a result. For instance, if you were supposed to deliver printed brochures to the client's office on October 1 so they would be ready for a trade show exhibit in Texas on October 6, and the brochures will not be printed until October 5, arrange for express overnight shipment of the appropriate number of brochures from your printing plant to the client's booth at the convention center, at your expense. Be sure to let the client know what you are doing, and show on your invoice, what you paid to have the brochures shipped via overnight express, so the client realizes the expense you incurred in taking care of the problem.

If missing the deadline cannot be avoided, and there is nothing you can do to mitigate the damage, ask the client, "What can I do to set things right?" Let them tell you, rather than you tell them.

The client will be unhappy about the missed deadline and may be seriously considering ending his relationship with you. What you should do is acknowledge the breakdown, apologize, give any legitimate reasons why the breakdown occurred (letting the client know that these factors are not excuses, and that there is no excuse), and end with this promise: "If you can trust us again, I promise that every job will be delivered by the deadline date or sooner or you don't pay us." Promising to sacrifice your payment if deadlines are not met should show the client you are sincere and serious about not repeating your mistake.

Reason 6: Your Bill Exceeds Your Estimate

Clients do not like it when your bill exceeds your estimate, and giving them such a bill risks nonpayment. Many fixed-price contracts today even call for cost overruns to be paid out of the vendor's pocket.

There are three important things you can do to prevent billing problems.

Make sure your clients understand your billing procedures and charging policies before you begin work • You, the consultant, not the client, are responsible for making these policies clear.

For example, I often hire graphic artists to work for me, as many businesses do. I will give a description of a job, and the graphic artist will come back with a quotation that says, "For design, layout, type, illustration, and camera-ready mechanicals of a four-page product brochure—$1,250."

The written estimate almost never addresses contingencies, such as "What happens if the client does not like the design?" "Is there a charge to redo it?" and " What is the cost if the client changes the text after the type is set?" The artist doesn't put these things in because he's afraid mention of these extras will make the client feel his service is too expensive and will lose him the job.

But not every client is experienced in graphic arts or knows what are typical procedures. Let's say the artist submits three designs and the client rejects them and asks for another. The artist says, "Okay, but of course, that will be extra."

The client says, "For what? Your quote says $1,250 including design. To me, that means a design I like, and I didn't like what you did." The answer is phrased in a more disagreeable tone than the client had intended, because he is taken aback by this sudden issue of paying more money for work that was, to him, no good in the first place.

The artist, feeling he is being insulted, answers stiffly, "The three designs were excellent by any standard. It was your decision not to use them, not mine. By your logic, we could do five hundred layouts and you could still say you were not satisfied. Obviously, I cannot do that for $1,250." From this point the conversation degenerates quickly from discussion to argument.

What the artist should have done is explain, in writing or verbally, the policies and procedures for making changes. For example, the contract should specify that $1,250 entitles the client to up to *three* layouts but no more, and if the client does not select one, additional designs are "X" dollars apiece. It should also state that the charge for changing the mechanical after copy has been approved is $95 an hour (or whatever the fee is). That way, when the client gets the final bill showing extra charges for "changing his mind," he may not be *happy* about it, but at least he will not find it objectionable or inappropriate.

Give the client an estimated price before you begin work • The second strategy for eliminating confrontations and problems concerning billing is to give the client a specific dollar quotation up front for any extras, changes, revisions, or add-ons to jobs.

To give you an example, when our contractor was at our home putting on various room additions, we would ask him to do small jobs around the house from time to time. I never bothered to ask him what these would cost because they were all small jobs. He never bothered to tell me, and the amounts were nominal.

One day, I asked him to put an additional electrical outlet in what was then a home office (I no longer work at home). He did, and when the bill came it was $450! When I complained, he explained that, because of the location of the room in relation to wiring, he had to spend over a day drilling and running wires, had to put in a special kind of outlet, and so on.

I was still unhappy, and said, "Mike, you should have told me that it would be that much *before you started.* If you had, there's no way I would spend nearly half a thousand dollars on a *socket.*" He apologized, but did not directly offer to reduce the charge. (I sensed he would have done so if I requested it, but was hoping and praying I would not.) I paid the bill, extremely unhappy about what had happened. In time I forgave the incident, and we hired him to do more work, but it nearly cost him all future business with me. And to be honest, for a long time I stopped referring business to him, because I was miffed about the incident.

Keep the client informed of the charges for your work • A third strategy for preventing billing problems and misunderstandings is to bill in a timely manner and send regular monthly statements that show clients what they have spent with you and what they owe you. Some clients who do a lot of business with you call you for a lot of different tasks, and they lose track of how much they're spending.

When they get a huge, unexpected bill, they become upset and unhappy. Their complaint: "Yes, I ordered all these services, but I didn't know we were spending so much with you this month. You should have told us."

For frequent users of your service, a monthly statement lets them know where they stand so they can control spending and keep the bills reasonable.

Reason 7: The Client Wants More Service Than You Can Provide

At times the client may want

- a higher level of customer service and "hand-holding" than you have time to provide.
- services that you do not currently offer and prefer not to offer.
- more services than originally contracted for (e.g., additional assignments, increased scope of the current project) in the same or even more compressed period of time.

Because clients like it when you say "yes" and dislike it when you say "no," you should comply unless

- you are unable or unequipped to offer the services they want.
- you are not experienced in offering the services they want, would probably do an inferior job, or know where they can get it better elsewhere.

Even in such cases, you want to avoid simply saying "no" and leaving the client "high and dry," with no explanation and no other options for them to pursue. The best strategy is to tell the client the truth about your limitations or preferences, but still offer to handle the work if he desires. For example, "We have never done this before, and are not experts in it. We would be happy to try it and do our best for you, if that's what you need. As an alternative, we will find a firm for you that does have this service, review their work, and make a recommendation. We can also supervise their work and manage it for you, so you don't have to spend your time worrying about it."

The idea is, if you cannot give an unconditional "yes," at least you do not want to give an unconditional "no." Rather, you want to offer clients a range of options, so they can choose how they want to proceed.

The client will be pleased that you are willing to help in any way you can. He or she will also appreciate your honesty when you admit your shortcomings and lack of ability in a specific area. It adds to your credibility and does not create an unrealistic expectation for superb performance in a discipline you've just said you know little about.

Reason 8: The Client Wants a Different Service Than You Are Providing

If the client wants you to provide a service other than what you currently provide, you have to make a decision about how important that account is to you and what business you are really in.

For instance, let's say you are in the business of booking entertainment at corporate meetings and events. An important client comes to you and says, "We want a big celebrity and a band at our next event, but our corporate meeting department has been downsized, and we have too much work. In addition to booking the entertainment, we want you to plan and coordinate the entire meeting from start to finish, from creation of a theme, to the catering and site selection, through on-site management. Can you have a proposal to me by Friday?"

Because flexibility is the ultimate skill, one positive way to approach this request is to say to yourself, "The client is very perceptive. We've always been more than just talent agents. We have always helped plan and create successful events for our clients. So yes, we'll bid on this. In fact, the client has given me an idea. Why not start a division of our firm specializing in meeting planning and management? Could be very profitable and will help us provide better service to those accounts who have wanted us to do more for them."

At the same time, however, you cannot do everything everyone asks, and there may be requests that you cannot accommodate.

There are some services you are not comfortable rendering, some you are not competent to render, and some that you just don't want to be involved in because they're not "your thing."

The strategy is to *always help clients find the solution to their problem* if you are not going to solve the problem directly through your services. This is done by forming a large network or "database" of consultants and other vendors in allied fields who can provide your clients with the services you do not provide.

For example, a meeting planner would have a network of consultants and vendors who could provide his clients with every conceivable service related to putting on meetings and special events. These would include photographers, printers, caterers, travel agents, independent meeting planners, florists, electricians, carpenters, set designers, audiovisual production houses, speakers' bureaus, hotels, resorts, convention centers, furniture rental outlets, uniform suppliers, and a host of others.

When the client calls and requests a service other than what you provide, you do not want to say "No, we don't do that." Instead you want to say, "No problem. We don't do that, but I know three of the best [set designers/caterers/videotaping services/etc.] in town. Here are their names and phone numbers. Mention my name when you call and you will get good service. If they don't work out, call me back and I will provide additional names for you to contact."

If the client has a request for a service that no firm you know of can provide, say, "I don't know the answer to that. But let me research it and I will get back to you with some names and recommendations—no charge, of course."

Then you call others within your network to see if they know of a company that can handle the request. Within two or three phone calls you'll get someone who says, "We don't do that, of course. But I know a guy. . . ." Then you call that consultant, check him out, and relay the information to your client.

It is extremely important to maintain a large network of quality, reputable consultants to which you can refer your clients. Many clients today want a turnkey, "single source" solution, and if you cannot provide it through referrals to qualified vendors, they may call your competitor instead.

In fact, for those clients who want "single source" service, you may want to hire the appropriate vendors as subcontractors, add a management fee or markup, and offer the entire meeting (or whatever it is you're providing) as a complete start-to-finish service.

Do all clients want it that way? No. Some clients want to buy the service as a "package," where one vendor handles all the details by hiring and coordinating multiple vendors. On the other hand, other clients prefer to manage the project themselves, hiring the most qualified vendor in each field on an individual basis, and paying a lower price overall by using independents rather than a larger single source consultant who adds a markup or charges more for management of the project.

You can choose to be just a specialist, offering your one service. Or you can present yourself as a full service firm, "doing it all." In either case, there are plenty of clients wanting both types of service, so you can please a wider number of clients by being flexible and going either way.

For example, if you're an independent, and the client wants a full service firm, you can provide the full service by hiring and managing other vendors to do the whole project. On the other hand, if you're a full service firm, and the client only wants you to provide service "X," you can satisfy that client by offering service "X" on an à la carte basis, instead of saying, "No, we either do the whole thing or nothing."

The more flexible you are, the greater the number of clients you can please.

Reason 9: The Client Wants More Freebies and Extras

Some clients want to squeeze every last penny of value from every vendor. It's not malicious; it's just the way they are. They feel they are paying a lot and therefore should get everything they can. This often results in clients trying to get lots of extras and freebies out of you—free copies of your books and tapes, free advice, free services.

How far should you go to accommodate such clients? My feeling is it's better to err on the side of being too generous and accommodating rather than being too limiting and restrictive.

Clients like to feel that they can go to you freely for advice and assistance on small matters on an informal basis and that you are available, willing, able, and glad to help them out.

If clients get a bill every time they spend ten minutes on the phone with you or have you do some small favor for them, they will resent it and feel you are just out to extract as much money as you can from them. Obviously there are limits, and these limits differ with each client. You give more extras and freebies to a $40,000 a year client than a $400 one- shot project client.

It's a good investment, for example, to spend an hour of your billable time (worth anywhere from $75 to $200 or more, depending on your business) to do a favor that will retain a $40,000 account. It's not a sensible investment to spend a lot of time talking to a client that spent $200 and may, if you're lucky, spend another $100 with you this year.

Interestingly, it is often the big accounts who require the least "hand holding" and make the fewest requests, while the smallest accounts expect and demand the most extras and attention.

When you do extra favors and give freebies to clients, let them know, in a polite, indirect way, the value of what they are getting from you. For example, if you give a half hour of your time to a client at no charge, send him a bill for a half hour of your time, in which you charge zero dollars ("NO CHARGE") but show the dollar value of the time.

When you communicate to clients the fact that what you are giving away for free has a dollar value attached to it, they appreciate what they are getting and the magnitude of your favor.

When you do not educate and inform the client of the real dollar value of the freebies and extras, they do not appreciate the value of what they are getting, nor are they especially appreciative of what you are giving them for free. They take it for granted, and feel it is something they are automatically entitled to, rather than a valuable bonus you are giving them as a favor.

When a small or marginal account becomes too demanding, you may decide not to give away a freebie or extend further favors. Do not directly refuse them with a "no" or "I can't do that for you," or tell them that you are tired of their taking advantage of you. Instead, simply agree to do the service and, almost as an afterthought, quote the cost of it. For example, "I'd be happy to make those calls and collect that information for you, Diane. We'll just bill you our hourly rate, and I estimate it will take one or two hours to complete. Shall I proceed?"

Clients will appreciate that you are telling them the service is not free in a polite, nonconfrontational way. After you quote the estimate, they are highly unlikely to argue and try to get the service for free, as they originally had hoped. Instead, they will either say "go ahead" if they want to pay you for it, or, "I'll think about it. Let's hold on that."

Reason 10: There Is a Misunderstanding, Miscommunication, or Poor Communication between You and the Client

For the busy consultant juggling lots of clients and projects, there is a great opportunity for miscommunication and misunderstandings with clients.

While we should take the time to clarify every point and be totally clear with clients, we often don't because of time pressures. We rush phone calls, run from meeting to meeting or job to job, fax hastily written memos rather than mail carefully considered letters, and in general, are always in a hurry, not spending as much time as we should on careful communication.

How can you help reduce and prevent client miscommunication and misunderstanding? And how can you get back on track when such misunderstandings and miscommunications do occur? Here are a few suggestions.

Call reports • After every in-person meeting write a short report or memo summarizing who said what, what was agreed to, and the actions to be taken by you and the client. Send the report to the client and keep a copy in the client's file. The purpose is not so much to inform your client of what happened in the meeting (after all, the client was there), but to make sure everyone is in agreement about what was said, eliminate any potential misunder-standings, and provide a record proving what was said and done if later a dispute arises and people have different recollections of who was supposed to do what, and when.

Phone call memos • A short memo summing up and confirming key decisions made during phone calls, or actions taken after, is also a helpful tool in preventing miscommunication and misunderstandings. For example, if the client asks you to do something during a phone call, and no purchase order or contract is to be issued, you should write and fax a memo summing up the request, confirming your go-ahead, and giving the price you quoted.

Repeat back • A useful habit for ensuring understanding is to repeat, in your own words, what the client told you, then ask if you have expressed it correctly. For example, "So, Mr. Client, what you're saying is that the system should have an automatic sensor that opens the back flow valve if the pressure exceeds the safety limit set by the process engineer. Correct?"

"You're right" • Because it is your responsibility for making sure communication is clear and that understanding is mutual, we operate on the principle that 99 percent of misunderstandings and miscommunications must primarily be the responsibility of the consultant, not the client.

Therefore, when a misunderstanding does arise, the first necessary step is to acknowledge that the client is right and you are wrong. When the client tells you, "No, we distinctly said purple, not green," you reply, "You're right. I had written 'green' in my notes, but I must have made a mistake."

The exception is when written records confirm that you are correct, not the client. Even in such cases, the goal is not to prove to the client that you are right and he or she is wrong, but to tactfully remind the client of the agreement. For example, "Well, I had thought so too, but if you look at the original call report we both signed off on, it does in fact call for a butterfly valve instead of a ball valve. What can we do to set things right?"

After acknowledging that the client is right (or gently pointing out the client's error), you immediately move to the more important issue of taking corrective action. If the action is not directly specified by the client, dictated by the situation, or obvious to you, ask the client how he or she wishes you to correct the situation.

If Everything Fails

If everything fails and the client is still dissatisfied, don't spend any more time thinking about it. You've apologized and done everything humanly possible to set things right. What else can you do? Nothing. Therefore, if there's nothing else you can do, it's now up to the client to decide to forgive and forget or refuse to reconcile with you.

Because it's up to the client, and out of your hands, do not spend further time pursuing the matter. Your efforts will be futile. Do not spend any more time thinking about it or feeling bad about it. What's the point?

Feeling bad, guilty, unhappy, or punishing yourself, isn't going to change the client's mind about you or alter the situation in any way. Because "beating yourself up" achieves no desirable result, why do it? It can only waste your time and hurt you more than you've already been hurt.

Here's a saying that seems sensible and helpful: "You can't be responsible for the client; you can only be responsible to the client." If you've done everything in your power to correct a problem situation, and the client is still unhappy, the client is *choosing* to remain unhappy and mad at you. You can't be responsible for other people's behavior, thoughts, or emotions. You can only act in a responsible manner as a professional consultant, which you have done.

So do what you can to set things right. Most clients will appreciate the effort and give you a second chance. That's wonderful. As for the others, you've done all you can. Let it go.

As honors high school student Aazim Hussain observes, "If you have a goal, you have to work hard and stay focused. Have courage and faith in God. That's all that motivates me to do well."

11

Time Management and

Organizational Skills

Today we are busier than ever. According to an article in *Reader's Digest* (October 1996, page 148A), between 1973 and 1993, the average work week increased from 41 to 50 hours.

As a consultant, the only thing you have to sell is your time. Therefore, the more efficiently you use your time, the more profitable you will be.

Successful consultants create systems, procedures, and office practices that eliminate time wasters and maximize their productivity. This chapter shows you what those systems are and how to implement them in your office.

Setting Your Daily Schedule

Productive consultants have schedules and stick with them. Yet more than 50 percent of consultants don't schedule their daily activities.

It's not enough to know the projects you're working on. You should break your day into segments—I suggest using hour increments, although quarter and half days can also work—and write down on a piece of paper the project you will work on during each of those segments.

Do this every day, at the beginning of your work day (or if you prefer, create the following day's schedule in the evening before you stop work for the night). Post your hour-by-hour schedule for the day on a wall near your desk with a piece of tape. Or pin it to a nearby bulletin board.

Although I may work on a particular consulting project for more than one hour a day, these hours are not necessarily scheduled consecutively. It's up to you.

As you go through the day, consult your schedule to keep on track. If priorities change, you can change the schedule, but do this in writing—revise the schedule, print the new version, and post the new one.

It's okay to redo the schedule as long as you don't miss deadlines. Some days I redo the daily schedule two or three times, depending on deadlines and inspiration. Why not? As long as you are organized, keep track of deadlines, and allow enough time to finish each job, you will increase your productivity by working on things you feel in the *mood* to work on.

Determining Priorities

Can you *always* work on what you want, right when you want? No. Sometimes, a pressing deadline or an insistent client can mean putting aside a more pleasurable task for something more formidable—even if you don't feel like doing it right now.

On the wall of my office near my desk I have posted a list which I update weekly. It's called "Rules of the Office," and it reminds me what I have to do to be successful in my business. Rule 1 is "First things first." This means you must set priorities and meet deadlines.

For instance, if I am burning to work on a book but have a report due the next morning, I write the report first, get it done, and fax or e-mail it to the client. Then I reward myself with a morning spent on the book. If I did the book first, I'd risk not leaving myself enough time to get my report written by the deadline.

The Three Types of To-Do Lists Every Consultant Should Keep

The key component of my personal productivity system is a series of lists I keep on the computer. In fact, I have so many lists, that I have a file called "LISTS" to keep track of them.

Every morning, I come into the office and turn on my computer. After checking my various online services (Internet, CompuServe, America Online, and AT&T Mail) for e-mail, I open the LISTS file. It tells me which lists I must read and review to start my day.

The most important lists on the "LISTS" list are my to-do lists. I keep several, but the three most critical are my daily to-do list, projects to-do list, and long-term to-do list.

1. *Daily to-do list.* Each day I type on my PC, print out, and post a list of the items I have to do that day. From this list, I create my hour by hour schedule. This list is revised daily. I enjoy work and like to work long hours, so I take on a lot of projects that interest me. But I never take on more than I can handle, so I can continue to meet all deadlines.

2. *Projects to-do list.* On a separate computer file, I keep a list of all of my projects currently under contract, along with the deadline for each. I review this list several times a week, using it to make sure the daily to-do list covers all essential items that have to be done right away.

3. *Long-term to-do list.* This is a list of projects I want to do at some point, but are not now under contract and therefore do not have any assigned deadlines. I check this list about once a week, and usually put in a few hours each week on a few of the projects from this list that interest me most.

This simple system works. Most of the techniques throughout this book are simple, yet powerful, so don't be put off by their brevity or ease of implementation. I agree with Texaco CEO Peter Bijur, who said, "As soon as you start to introduce complexity, whether it's into an organization or a set of responsibilities, the more difficult it is to operate." I also agree with Hair Club for Men CEO Sy Sperling: "Simple solutions are the best solutions."

How to Overcome Procrastination

Procrastination is the single biggest reason people fall behind in their work, miss deadlines, and turn in shoddy efforts. P.T. Barnum advised, "Never defer for a single hour that which can be done just as well now."

Having a daily to-do list—and then assigning various tasks to yourself throughout the day in one-hour increments—helps you stay on track and avoid putting things off.

As long as you have your short-term deadlines and long-term goals in mind, you can be somewhat flexible in your daily schedule, adjusting tasks and time slots to match your enthusiasm for each project.

Breaking tasks into one-hour sessions, and then juggling the schedule to work on what interests you most right now, helps overcome procrastination. When you get tired or run out of ideas on one project, just switch to another.

Give yourself rewards for accomplishing tasks. If you work for a solid hour on a budget that's slow going, reward yourself with a break to read your mail or walk around the block. If you stick with your schedule for the whole morning, treat yourself to your favorite food for lunch.

The best way to make every hour of every day productive is to have an hour by hour schedule as outlined earlier in this chapter. People who have such a schedule know what they should be doing every minute, and therefore do it. People who don't set a schedule tend to drift through the day, stopping and then starting tasks, jumping from job to job, without getting much done.

Ten Steps to Working Better and Faster

1. Use a Computer

You don't have to use a computer. But in my opinion, every consultant who wants to be productive should use a modern PC with the latest software. As Breck Speed observes in his book *Money Grows on Trees* (Cumberland House, 1996), "You can't do today's job with yesterday's tools and expect to be in business tomorrow."

Get a PC. Become computer literate. Master e-mail; the Internet; word processing, accounting, spreadsheet, and graphics programs; and anything else that can make you more productive and professional. Doing so can double, triple, or even quadruple your productivity.

2. Become a Specialist

When you specialize, the specialized knowledge you amass, the skills you master, and the expertise you build can be used over and over again on many projects related to your specialty. This allows you to "amortize" your investment in research, education, and training on a particular topic over many tasks. By concentrating on a narrow field of specialization, you maximize your efficiency and can partially escape the clutter of information overload.

Generalists, by comparison, spend an enormous amount of time gathering facts and background for projects, only to find most of this data is not applicable to their next project—because it involves a different area, market, industry, or product. What a waste!

3. Get Multiple Assignments from Repeat Clients

Marketing professionals know it is five times more costly to make a sale to a new customer than to get another order from an existing customer. Send your proposals to clients you already do business with first. They are more likely to accept your recommendations, cutting down time-consuming persuading and negotiation.

4. Create Project Templates

Whether it's a preformatted spread sheet for doing monthly sales forecasts or a " boilerplate" PowerPoint slide show into which you can quickly import new text for specific presentations, once you create a format, you can use it over and over again. This permits you to do similar jobs more quickly than if you have to start from scratch. So, create standard templates for common assignments and store them on your computer. The work will be easier, and you'll be able to do it faster.

5. Don't Be a Perfectionist

"I'm a nonperfectionist," said Isaac Asimov, author of 475 books. "I don't look back in regret or worry at what I have written." Be a careful consultant, but don't agonize over your work beyond the point where the extra effort no longer produces a proportionately worthwhile improvement in your final product.

Be excellent, but not perfect. Customers do not have the time or budget for perfection, and for most projects, being 95 percent of the way to perfection is good enough. That doesn't mean you deliberately make errors or give less than your best. It means you stop polishing and fiddling with the job when it looks good to you—and you don't agonize over the fact you're not spending another hundred hours on it. Create it, check it, then let it go.

6. Free Yourself from the Pressure to Be an Innovator

As publisher Cameron Foote observes, "Clients are looking for good, not great." Do the best you can and meet the clients' requirements. They will be happy. Do not feel pressured to reinvent the wheel or create a masterpiece on every project. Don't be held up by the false notion that you must uncover some great truth or present your client with revolutionary ideas and concepts. Most successful business solutions are just common sense packaged to meet a specific need.

Eliminate performance pressure. Don't worry about whether your work is different or better than what others have done before you. Just do the best you can. That will be enough.

7. Do Work You Enjoy

In advising people on choosing their life's work, David Ogilvy, founder of the advertising agency Ogilvy & Mather, quotes a Scottish proverb that says, "Be happy while you're living; for you're a long time dead." The Tao Te Ching says, "In work, do what you enjoy."

When you enjoy your work, it really isn't work. To me, success is being able to make a good living while spending the work day in pleasurable tasks. You won't love every project equally, of course, but try to balance mandatory tasks with things that are more fun for you. Seek assignments that are exciting, interesting, and fulfilling.

8. Switch Back and Forth between Different Tasks

Even if you consider yourself a specialist, do projects outside your specialty now and then. Inject variety into your project schedule. Arrange your daily schedule so you switch off from one assignment to another at least once or twice each day. Variety, as the saying goes, is indeed the spice of life.

Approximately 70 to 90 percent of what I am doing at any time are familiar tasks within my area of expertise. This keeps me highly productive. The other 10 to 30 percent is work in new areas, markets, industries, or disciplines outside my area of expertise. This keeps me fresh and allows me to explore things that captivate my imagination but are not in my usual schedule of assignments.

9. Don't Waste Time Working on Assignments You Don't Have

Get letters of agreement, contracts, purchase orders, and budget sign-offs before proceeding. Don't waste timing starting the work for an assignment that may not come through. An official approval or go-ahead from your client makes the assignment real and firm, so you can proceed at full speed, with the confidence and enthusiasm that come from knowing you have been given the green light.

10. Make Deadlines Firm but Adequate

Often you will collaborate with your client or even your subcontractors in determining deadlines. Set deadlines for a specific date and time, not a time period. For example, "due November 23 by 3 PM or sooner," not "in about two weeks." Having a specific date and time for completion eliminates confusion and gives you motivation to get the work done on time.

At the same time, don't make deadlines too tight. Try to build in a few extra days for the unexpected, such as a missing piece of information, a subcontractor delay, a last-minute change, or a crisis on another project.

How to Eliminate Unnecessary Activities That Slow You Down

My colleague, consultant Jeffrey Lant, has a full-time personal assistant. When I first learned this, I thought "He's crazy—why should an able-bodied man have a valet?" Now, I've come around to his point of view. The more hours you spend doing trivial activities, the fewer hours you have for important work.

Part of being a productive consultant is avoiding interruptions and putting in the necessary hours. You can't do that effectively if you are dividing your time between too many things.

Because you have multiple responsibilities, the solution is to get other people to do as many of the noncritical activities as you are willing to give up or able to afford.

My approach is to "offload" noncritical tasks, getting them off my list of responsibilities so I can concentrate on being a productive, profitable consultant. For instance, instead of picking up the kids after school each day, you can have a neighbor who has children in the same school give your kids a ride, and pay her a few dollars each week for car service. She might be thrilled to earn the extra money!

With an average life span of 75 years, we have only 27,375 days from the time we are born until the time we die. And since we're asleep for a third of that time, we have only 18,250 days that we're actually awake and active.

How you spend this finite amount of time is mostly up to you. To maximize your productivity, income, and output, meaningful work must be a priority.

Value your time. "Time is the most precious currency of life, and how we spend it reflects what we truly value," writes Richard J. Leider in his book *The Power of Purpose*. "Once we have spent it, it is gone forever. It cannot be reearned."

If you prefer to nap, watch TV, or play cards, that's perfectly fine; but don't complain that your colleague who spends those hours in front of the PC is getting more work done than you are. It's your choice.

Eliminating Bad Habits That Waste Time

First, identify any bad habits you have that waste your time. For me, it was sleeping an hour after I first woke up in the morning. Because the morning is the most productive work time for me, I forced myself to get dressed and go to the office when I awake, instead of falling back to sleep, and I increased my productivity tremendously.

For you, it may be watching a soap opera in the middle of the day, spending too much time surfing the Web, talking in chat rooms or on the phone, doing housework, or staying up too late at night to read or watch television.

After you have identified the bad habits, make a list of the ones you must avoid. Phrase each item on your list in the imperative voice. For example, if your worst time-wasting habit is procrastination, it should read "Don't procrastinate" on your list. If you take on too many ancillary responsibilities because you hate saying "no," this item should appear on your list as "Say *no.*"

Post this list in your office in a place where you will always see it, such as on the wall in front of you or on your bulletin board or door. Or place it in a desk drawer where you will see it every day. With the list of bad habits visible, you will be constantly reminded to avoid these bad habits and correct behaviors that waste time. Before long, you'll see a big improvement and you will be getting more done in less time. Try it!

Don't Procrastinate

One of the worst habits is procrastination. Procrastinators frequently miss deadlines. They complete assignments at the last minute, allowing no time to review the work before submitting it. And, they put themselves under undue stress.

Putting off unpleasant, routine, or difficult chores is human nature. But those who discipline themselves to tackle things they dislike or fear gain self-confidence and make better use of their time.

The following techniques may help you overcome procrastination:

- Think about how great you'll feel when the chore is completed. Think positively about its outcome.
- If the project is complex or overwhelming, break it down into a series of steps to be entered on your "Things To Do" list. Then set up a specific time and date to begin working on the first step, and follow through as if it was an appointment. Promise to spend 60 minutes a day on the task until it's done, and schedule these daily segments at the same time each day—preferably a quiet period when there will be no interruptions.

- Create an incentive by promising yourself a special reward for getting the job done.
- Realize the task doesn't have to be done perfectly. Some attempt is better than no attempt. Maybe you can get away with doing only part of the job and then passing it along to someone else for completion.
- Delegate or outsource segments of the work you find boring or distasteful. You can gain precious hours, energy, and enthusiasm by passing along mundane, peripheral, or partly finished work to subordinates or other consultants. The more routine jobs you can delegate, the more time you'll have for "high level" work.

Avoid Distractions

Outside distractions can be major time wasters, if you let them.

The key is to physically block out disturbances as much as possible. Shut your door, let your voice mail take your calls, post a "do not disturb" sign, work in the park with a laptop or notepad for a few hours, or ask your spouse not to disturb you. Your mind can successfully tune out a great many signals if you tell it to.

If interruptions are a real problem, try setting aside a period every day during which you will meet with people and take phone calls. The rest of the time is "private time" in which you work, uninterrupted. Most people say they accomplish more when they can work on a task uninterrupted for as long as they want.

Use the 80-20 Rule

The 80-20 rule states that 80 percent of your accomplishments come from only 20 percent of your efforts. The trick is to figure out what makes that 20 percent so productive. Then, devote more of your time to these productive activities, and reduce time spent on unproductive work. To analyze how you spend your time, keep a log of your daily activities for about two weeks. Identify those things that are inefficient and waste time. For example, going to the stationary store every time you need to make photocopies because you don't have a copier.

The next step is to find solutions to these time wasters. Can you create form letters for replying to correspondence, or have your secretary draft replies? Maybe you can create a convenient form that can be used to handle a particular type of communication, eliminating the need to draft a memo every time such an instance arises. Can you or an assistant clear up and organize the filing system? How about combining business trips, or scheduling travel during off hours? For instance, scheduling an out-of-town trip for a Monday morning meeting permits you to fly out Sunday evening, so you don't lose part of a work day in travel.

Adjust Your Schedule to Your Energy Levels

Most of us have certain times during the day when we're most alert and perform best. Once you've determined your pattern of physical and mental energy levels, try to adjust your daily schedule to mesh with it. By handling mentally demanding jobs during your peak energy periods, you can get more done in less time. Fit your schedule to your moods and energy levels, and you'll find that you'll save time and be more effective in your job.

Most of us cannot control the hours we favor. Dr. Nathaniel Kleitman, a physiologist at the University of Chicago, says body temperature varies by up to three degrees during each day. When your body temperature drops, you have maximum energy. When it rises, your energy drops. This may explain why, according to the results of a recent national survey, most people say they would rather be too cold than too hot.

So if you are a night owl, burning the midnight oil may result in maximum productivity for you. If you are an early bird, get up early and start writing while everyone else in your house is still asleep.

Other people find they can alter their biorhythm patterns deliberately, by altering when they go to bed and get up. If you have a choice of whether to be an early morning person or a late nighter, and your schedule allows you to do either, pick the one that works best for you.

If all else is equal, choose the morning. When you start early in the morning, as I do, you have the benefit of having completed a significant amount of your day's work by the time others are first stumbling into their offices. Early starters finish the day's work early, and have the rest of the time to do more work or play. Late starters are behind from the moment they get up, and feel increasing pressure to get their work done as the hours grow even later.

The easiest productivity tip in the world is to get up and start working an hour earlier than you normally do. Freelance writer Charles Flowers says whenever he has a deadline or a lot of work on a given day, he gets up as early as he has to to meet that deadline, even if it means rising at five in the morning. I have, on some days, been at the office as early as 3 or 4 AM, although this is rare.

A Surefire Technique for Maintaining Peak Energy throughout the Day

Energy is a function of many factors, one of them being enthusiasm. When you are enthusiastic, your energy can remain high, even if you are physically tired. When you are bored, your energy drains, and you become lethargic and unproductive.

To maintain peak productivity and energy, maintain peak enthusiasm and avoid boredom. The main cause of boredom is not doing what you want, when you want to do it. Therefore, you should structure your work so you are spending most of your time doing what you want, when you feel like doing it.

Obviously, you should shy away from assignments that bore you. Forcing yourself to work on things you dislike will drain your energy. But even those assignments that interest you can get boring if you work on them too long or don't feel like doing them at the time. The solution is to have many different projects, and to work on the one you want at any given time. Because you largely set your own hourly schedule each day (meetings are an exception), you can do tasks in the order that pleases you, as long as you meet your deadlines.

Of course, when a deadline is looming, you may have no choice but to put aside work you want to do and focus on what has to be done to meet that deadline. But even this is avoidable if you negotiate sufficient deadlines and then plan your time so you get started early, rather than waiting to the last minute as so many people do.

Everyone finds something that can help revitalize them throughout the day. When you find what works for you, do it. My office has a private bathroom, and when I feel my concentration and energy waning, I wash my hair. I become immediately refreshed—perhaps the wet head of hair cools my overheated brain. In the winter, I prefer a cup of homemade soup from the bagel shop across the street to coffee as a pick-me-up during the day. You can take a break and reenergize by taking a walk, running errands, meeting for coffee, or chatting on the phone.

Designing Your Work Space for Maximum Productivity

According to an Internet survey reported in *Business Marketing* (March 1997, page 48), being disorganized wastes at least an hour a day. Therefore, if you become organized, you gain an extra hour daily for billable activities. At $100 an hour times 5 hours a week times 50 weeks a year, this translates into added annual revenue of $25,000.

A key to designing your work space for maximum productivity is to have all work materials and tools at hand. A computer tech I recently hired to do some work for me commented, "I really like your computer system—everything is in easy reach." He then mentioned that in many personal computer systems, the owners put vital components, such as the CPU, disk drive, or printer, on the floor, under a desk, or otherwise out of reach.

I've seen that design and feel it wastes effort and time. My philosophy is that everything you need—computer systems, office equipment, the telephone, supplies, reference materials, files—should be reachable just by swiveling your chair and reaching out to the appropriate cabinet, shelf, or drawer, without having to get out of your seat.

Make sure your workstation has adequate lighting. According to an article in *CIO* (February 15, 1998, page 18), 88 percent of people who use a PC three hours a day or more suffer from eyestrain.

Plenty of desk space and file cabinet storage also boost productivity. There's room to organize and store work materials so they're close at hand and easy to find. Having to search for a book or folder wastes time and can cause you to lose your pace when you're in a productive groove. I have two desks and two large tables in my office, so there is plenty of surface space for various projects.

Paper Filing Systems That Work

Avoid using manila file folders stacked in file-cabinet drawers. These flimsy file folders are difficult to find and separate, and often slide under one another, making them easy to lose. Use sturdier hanging file folders and file cabinets with high-walled drawers designed to hold these folders. If your file cabinet has regular low-walled drawers, you can buy and easily install adapter brackets to hold the hanging files.

Don't get fancy with file labeling. Use a commonsense labeling scheme and file in alphabetical order. Don't cram files in drawers; this makes them difficult to find and discourages you from even looking. When space gets tight, go through your files and throw away old and obsolete material. Or buy additional file cabinets.

Handling Paperwork and Workflow Efficiently

Set up a double- or triple-decker in-basket or a separate small set of files for handling incoming paper. I plan my day so I have time every day to go through incoming papers. This way, I can take care of each piece of paper on the spot. If you let papers pile up in in-baskets or to-do files, you may find yourself missing deadlines, payments, and other commitments. Many of the papers will become too old to be meaningful by the time you get to them. And the growing stacks of papers will become depressing and disheartening.

Paperwork is a necessary evil. To gain greater control over it, decide what to do with each piece of paper as it comes into your office. Then get rid of it. Pass it along, file it, sign it, revise it, or throw it out. The key is to take action right away. Handle each piece of paper as it comes in, and you'll get things done faster, on time, and with less stress. Don't let things pile up.

When you have to store papers, use hanging files and file cabinets. Avoid stacking piles of papers and folders on the floor, desks, chairs, and other horizontal surfaces. Keep working surfaces clean. For the busy business executive or entrepreneur, better organization translates directly into getting more done in less time. Poor organization wastes time and can result in loss of important materials.

Electronic Filing Systems That Work

Electronic files are as important or more important than paper files. Your hard disk files containing your notes, memos, and research from many projects are one of your most important personal productivity resources. Here are some tips for managing these files more efficiently.

Keep a Set of "Boilerplate" Files

These are pieces of text, graphics, drawings, routine correspondence, reports, spreadsheets, timelines, and presentations you've created for one job that you can reuse in other jobs. If you write numerous sales proposals for a particular client, for example, one boilerplate file might be the company's corporate bio that appears at the end of each proposal. If you write grant proposals, much of the language might be similar or even exactly the same from grant to grant. Why reinvent the wheel each time? Name these files and keep a master list so you can find them easily when you need them.

Get a Scanner

Many times, you'll be lifting sentences and paragraphs from other documents created by other people. You will have hard copies of these documents but not the electronic files. It's a waste of time to key these documents into your computer by hand. Scanning saves a lot of time. You can buy a decent scanner today for under $500. Better still is to have an assistant who can do the scanning for you. Just tell your assistant what material you need, and she scans it and downloads the computer files onto your hard disk. Make sure you have permission to use copyrighted material you lift and scan.

Use Logical Filenames

Use "JSMEM1," for example, for memo number one to John Smith, or "OUTREP1" for a report on outsourcing. Always type the file name at the top of page one of the document, as follows: "filename: OUTREP1." Often you come across a hard copy in a file folder of something you've written and you want to find the electronic file so you don't have to rekey it. Putting the name of every file on the first page of the document makes it easy to find the electronic files. If you can't find the electronic file, you have to scan or retype the material, which is boring as well as a waste of your time.

C · H · A · P · T · E · R

12

Resolving Problems

Quickly and Efficiently

According to a survey by Gordon & Associates, approximately one in six clients is a problem account. But these 17.4 percent of your clients account for almost one-third of your job related stress.

In her booklet *Money Making Tips* (Globe Communications, 1997, page 57), L.A. Justice lists the following most common reasons why businesses fail:

- Shoddy workmanship
- Failure to deliver on time
- Pricing out of line
- Bad attitude

Some consultants have the attitude "This would be a great business—if it wasn't for the clients!" Especially in today's marketplace, where the clients are in control, and the supply of consultants outweighs the demand, you are going to encounter the occasional "difficult" client.

A difficult client is a person who seems to deliberately give you a hard time, and is interested in exerting power and control over you rather than working with you to achieve a mutually beneficial result. Although the majority of clients are not in this category, there are enough difficult people out there to warrant a chapter on how to deal with them.

Taking Action

The following are the most common situations that make client/vendor relationships difficult:

- Clients who demand perfection
- Unreasonable requests for changes and revisions
- Unreasonable demands for rush service
- Clients who take unfair advantage of your guarantee
- Uncommunicative or close-mouthed clients
- Clients who are overly controlling
- Rude, abusive clients
- Arrogant clients
- Clients who think they "know it all"
- Personality conflicts between you and the client

Let's take a brief look at each situation and one or two strategies for handling them effectively.

How to Handle the Client Who Demands Perfection

"I won't have any problem with a client who is a perfectionist," you say to me. "After all, I'm a perfectionist myself."

But watch out. What is perfect to one individual may seem severely flawed, inadequate, or inferior to another. Perfection in most things is the perception of an individual based on his subjective judgment. It's why one Olympic judge gives a diver an 8.4, while another scores the very same dive 9.2.

A good example of a perfectionist is a client who fusses over the shape, appearance, and style of every single letter in the typeset proof of his new brochure, and endlessly agonizes over color schemes, choice of paper stock and the placement of photos and drawings to the point where he's far fussier than the graphic artist doing the job.

Strategies for dealing with the perfectionist? First, don't ridicule his Felix Unger-like behavior. You don't have to agree with it, but you should at least show empathy and understanding for his preferences, habits, and way of looking at things. The wrong thing to do is to say in an impatient, condescending, or annoyed tone, "Oh, that doesn't make any difference!"

To the client, it does, and if you say otherwise, that's an indication to the client you don't share his attention to detail and commitment to quality.

Second, if the perfectionist's nitpicking is interfering with timely, cost-effective completion of projects, let him know it in a kind, gentle way. Say that you share his appreciation and concern for quality, but point out the extra expense and delay that result from being too exacting.

If the client's fussing does not visibly improve the end result to the majority of those who will evaluate your work, or does not deliver a measurable increase in benefits (e.g., sales will not increase as a result of all this agonizing), educate the client. Most perfectionists will retreat from their inflexible stand if they feel their superiors or colleagues will view them as wasting time and resources.

If the perfectionist doesn't budge, insists on an endless quest for improvement, and is not happy with a job you know is more than excellent, consider a third party opinion. Having a neutral third party review the work will most likely reinforce your stance and increase the odds of persuading your client.

Also, if you are critical of the client or in strong disagreement with him, he might get angry with you. But if the criticisms and dissenting opinions come from a neutral third party, the client will not fault you for bringing them to his attention.

Once I ghosted an article for a client who is a perfectionist when it comes to writing. I thought my draft was excellent, but he spent six hours rewriting, agonizing over every word change.

I said, "If the editor of one of the country's top business magazines read our drafts and said both serve the same purpose and are equal in quality, will you agree that the rewriting was not necessary?" We then paid a professional business editor for a neutral third party critique. As expected, it supported my argument.

How to Handle Unreasonable Requests for Changes and Revisions

What do you do with the client who changes her mind a dozen times? The most effective strategy for dealing with this problem is to address it up front when you are negotiating the terms and conditions of your work agreement.

You should spell out how many revisions or changes the client is entitled to make for the fee being paid, whether there are any restrictions on the scope or range of changes that can be requested, and what the charge is for making additional revisions not covered by the original fee.

Once that is done, revisions cease to be a problem. If the client makes an extraordinary amount of changes, and your contract calls for extra payment at your usual hourly rate, what do you care how many revisions are made? In fact, each puts money in your pocket! It is only *unpaid* revisions and changes that cost a consultant time and money and that we don't enjoy making.

Some consultants have come to me and said, "That's all well and good, but right now I am working for a client who is being totally unreasonable about changes and revisions. We did not discuss charging for revisions in advance, but what she is now asking for is unreasonable by any rational standard. What do I do?"

To a large degree, you are stuck. While you may not think doing a zillion versions is reasonable, the client's attitude may be, "I'm paying for a satisfactory job and, so far, I'm not satisfied. What's the beef?"

Because you didn't discuss the revision and change issue up front, the blame is really yours, and you should probably grin and bear it, make the necessary changes, have an unprofitable experience on this job, and not make the same mistake in the future.

If things really get bad, you can always try to explain the situation to the client and either negotiate a higher fee for the extra work, or ask for a "kill fee," a reduced payment to you for services rendered so far in exchange for ending the contract. This may be the best choice if you simply cannot abide doing more revisions on this project but the client insists on doing it over and over again.

How to Handle Unreasonable Frequent Demands for Rush Service

For many of us, tight deadlines are a fact of life, and for the most part, we have to get used to it. Especially in today's competitive, client-driven service marketplace, clients want and demand fast turnaround and immediate action. In business, the modem, computer, Internet, and fax machine have also served to "spoil" the client when it comes to expecting everything to be done right away.

For example, in the old days if a client wanted some changes to a design, he would mail you the drawing with his changes. It would take two or three days for it to arrive in the mail. You'd review it, make the changes, and mail it back. The whole thing would take about a week, and that's the turnaround time to which the client was accustomed.

Now, with the fax machine, the client faxes you the changes at 9 AM and you invariably get a call at 10 AM saying, "Have you looked at it yet? Can I have it by lunch?" The "mail float" has been eliminated and the turnaround time reduced from one week to 24 to 48 hours. This puts enormous pressure on consultants handling multiple projects for multiple clients, because for every component of almost every project, instant turnaround is fast becoming the norm instead of the exception.

What to do? The wrong solution, practiced by only a few hold-outs, is not to get a fax machine or use e-mail. Clients expect you to have one, and most will not deal with a vendor who cannot receive or return fax transmissions and e-mails.

The real cause of the problem is not only client demand, but consultant reluctance to set reasonable limits. Because we are so eager to please our clients, we are sometimes too quick to comply with demands for rush service even though it isn't good for us or, ultimately, them.

My advice? Start asking (not demanding) more time, longer deadlines, slightly more relaxed schedules. Explain that this is not for your benefit, but the good of the project. A job rushed beyond normal limits increases the probability of lower quality, more frequent and more serious errors, and additional rush charges.

Start small. Don't tell clients, "Now I need one month instead of three days." But when a client asks for it by next Tuesday, say, "How about Thursday or Friday?" Most times, the client will pick Thursday, and you've just gained two extra days to make the job that much better.

When a client sets an unreasonably tight deadline, I always ask, "Is there an event or particular milestone driving this deadline, or do you just need it as quickly as possible?" Some deadlines—such as completing the construction of a trade show exhibit in time for the show—are event driven and cannot be compromised or negotiated.

Most other deadlines, however, are usually tight simply because either the client wants it "as soon as possible" or the client was late getting the work to you and now wants you to make up for his tardiness with fast turnaround.

In a way, these are still legitimate reasons for wanting the service done quickly. The client has a right to want something as soon as possible without having a reason for it. And a consultant getting squeezed by a rush job due to the client's tardiness is just part of the job.

However, non-event–driven deadlines do have some inherent flexibility that event-driven deadlines do not. Therefore, when a client presents a tight deadline, you should ask, "Is this driven by a specific event?" For a room addition on a home, for example, that event might be the arrival of a new child. The client wants the room completed and furnished before the baby's due date.

If the deadline is not event driven, then say, "What would happen if we delivered the report to you a week from Friday instead of Friday?" The trick is not to come out and ask the client to move the date, but to ask what would happen if the deadline was a week or two longer.

When clients consider your question, it helps them realize that their deadlines are indeed "artificial" and that *nothing bad will happen* if the project is completed two or three weeks later. In many cases, they will either agree to the new deadline you suggest or pick a deadline that's halfway between yours and the original. So I suggest, if you want a one-week extension, ask for two weeks.

In some instances, however, the client will inform you the deadline is not flexible. A strategy that works here, if you are one of several vendors contributing to a project, is to request that the deadline pressure be shared equally by all the vendors involved. For example, many times when writing copy for a client, he will tell me, "I need to get it in five days, because it is due August 26th and the graphics studio needs 30 days to design, set mechanicals, print, and bind."

I reply, "I want to help you make this happen, but you have agreed that copy is a key element, and five days will not enable me to do the quality work you seek. I don't like anyone to work faster than they feel comfortable, but to meet your emergency need, both the studio and I will have to share in the burden. Ask them to do the job in 26 days instead of 30, and I will do the copy in 9 days instead of my usual two weeks. Fair enough?"

One final tip: If a client's deadline falls on a Thursday or Friday, I ask for an extension to Tuesday, explaining that this gives me an extra weekend to polish and perfect the work. Very few clients will object to a vendor who offers to work weekends on their behalf.

How to Handle the Client Who Takes Unfair Advantage of Your Guarantee

Lets face it, most of us offering strong service guarantees don't expect clients to abuse or take unfair advantage of their guarantee privileges. When they do, it's a pain in the neck, and we resent it.

I'm not talking about someone who asks for reasonable extra service according to the terms and conditions of the guarantee. I'm talking about the client who is going to hold you to the letter rather than the spirit of your guarantee and wring you for all the free service she can get. This is rare, but it does happen.

How do you handle it? First, be pleasant. Even if making the service call is a pain in the neck to you, act friendly and happy to help the client.

Second, err on the side of being too generous with your guarantee and providing extra service at no charge rather than being too strict with your guarantee and arguing with prospects who think they should be covered. For example, if you offer a 30 day guarantee on a service and the client asks for some changes to the job on the thirty 32nd, don't say "too bad, the time limit has run." Instead, make the changes or fix the problem, but do let the client know you are doing it because you care about his or her welfare, even though the guarantee has technically expired.

Third, make your guarantees as generous, lengthy, and unconditional as practical. You might think this increases the chances of clients taking unfair advantage of you. Actually, the opposite is true. The more generous your guarantee terms, the more people trust you and trust in the quality of your work. A guarantee with a short time limit and numerous restrictions and conditions creates instant distrust, suspicion, and hesitation.

For example, mail order booksellers have found that a 15 or 30 day guarantee helps increase sales more than a guarantee that offers no money back after 10 days. The reason? If the buyer has only ten days to examine the book and decide whether to keep it, she will feel rushed and pressured. If she is busy and doesn't have time to review the book immediately, she may return it unexamined simply to avoid having the guarantee period run out. With a longer guarantee period, the buyer keeps the book for later review, and the longer she keeps it, the more she forgets about returning it.

The best guarantee for service is buyer satisfaction. My wife and I recently called a toll-free service, 800-MATTRES, to order a mattress and have it delivered to our home. The advantage of this service is you can get the same brand name mattress you'd buy in a store by just dialing a toll-free number. No shopping or store visit is required.

The disadvantage is that you don't get to test out the mattress for comfort and firmness prior to purchase. The 800-MATTRES company, realizing this, offers this guarantee: "We will unpack the mattress, install it on your bed, and let you try it out right then and there. If you do not like it, tell our driver. He will pack it up, take it back, and you won't owe us a cent."

A *conditional* guarantee would have said the mattress is only guaranteed to be the right brand and model, or guaranteed to be in undamaged condition. We would not have bought a mattress under these conditions. What if we didn't like it? The *unconditional* satisfaction guarantee telling the buyer, "We guarantee your satisfaction no matter what" is what clients want today. And, increasingly, that's what consultants must offer.

How to Handle the Uncommunicative or Close-Mouthed Client

Uncommunicative or close-mouthed clients are difficult to deal with for two reasons. First, their lack of communication makes it difficult for you to extract the information needed to do a good job. Second, their unresponsiveness may be symptomatic of worse problems, such as dissatis-faction with your service, hidden anger, or resentment of something you did.

It's stressful to deal with clients that only answer your questions or respond to your comments in monosyllables. It makes you feel like you're doing something to offend them, only you don't know what. As a result, you become apologetic in your behavior without quite knowing why, and find yourself doing everything possible to carry the conversation.

How do you handle it? I have found that difficult, uncommunicative, tight-lipped people generally act that way for two reasons: (1) because they are not naturally outgoing, and this is their basic personality; and (2), because *they think they can get away with it.*

Being deliberately uncooperative and uncommunicative is a way of showing disdain for people or exercising power or control over them. It's also a way of announcing to the world "I'm antisocial," "I'm an introvert," or "I'm not a people person."

The person doing it *knows his behavior is not normal* and that the behavior is unpleasant. But as long as they think they can get away with it, the behavior continues.

The trick, then, is *not to let him get away with it.* When you let the deliberately difficult, deliberately uncommunicative person know that he is being uncommunicative, and that it's not appreciated, he realizes he's been "found out," that you're onto his game. Caught in the act, he stops this behavior or at least opens up a bit more, lets his guard down, and becomes a little more human.

For example, if someone is answering me in monosyllables, I will pause, then say, "Betty, is there a problem? Have I done something to offend you?" This is my subtle way of telling Betty (1) I know what she's doing, (2) I want her to *know* that I know she's doing it, (3) it's not appropriate or productive behavior, and (4) I would like it to stop and want her to treat me in a normal manner.

Another tactic for handling uncommunicative clients is to allow silent stretches in conversation. When you ask a question to which an appropriate response would be some conversation, and instead you get a monosyllable answer ("yes," "no," "not sure"), your natural tendency is to blab on some more to draw the person out. The result is the unpleasant pressure of trying to conduct a two way conversation in which only one person is fully participating.

Don't do this. Instead, if a longer answer is natural but the other person answers abruptly, *do not respond.* If you're on the phone, be silent. If you're there in person, smile, look pleasant, and don't say anything. Eventually, the other person will break the silence because he can't stand it—it's awkward and uncomfortable. And the only way he can break the silence is to *start talking,* which forces the client to continue the *conversation.*

By forcing the client to be the one to break the silence, you again communicate that (1) this tight-lipped, one-word answer treatment isn't cutting it with you and (2) two can play that game. The trick is to wait without talking—a five-second pause seems like an eternity. Believe me, the other person cannot handle the silence, and if you wait long enough, he will be forced to respond.

Eventually, the client will get the picture and the conversation will become less forced, more natural. In time, you'll have trained this person to conduct a normal conversation that he will learn to enjoy, which will make dealing with him more comfortable.

How to Handle Controlling Clients

All clients are in control of the client/vendor relationship because the client is the customer, the customer is always right, and the client pays the bill. But the difference is in how that control is used and to what degree. A good client realizes that the most productive client/consultant relationship is more a partnership than a master/slave relationship. True, in this partnership, the client is the senior partner; the consultant is the junior partner. But it's still a partnership. The spirit is one of mutual respect, trust, and cooperation, with both parties working toward an agreed set of mutually beneficial goals.

At the other end, the worst, least productive client/vendor relationship is that in which the client elects to exercise her power of control over her vendor to the maximum degree possible. In this type of relationship, the client consistently pushes the consultant around, taking maximum advantage of the consultant's natural desire to serve, please, and satisfy the client.

Some clients exhibit this behavior because they are pressured by circumstances (e.g., financial situation, boss, spouse) to get the maximum productivity out of the vendors they hire, and they truly believe the best way to achieve maximum performance is by being a consistently tough, stern, and demanding taskmaster.

Other clients, admittedly a minority, exert this power and control simply for the sake of doing so, and because they enjoy it. As Lord Acton said, "Power tends to corrupt, and absolute power corrupts absolutely."

The solution? Start by assuming the client's controlling, demanding behavior is driven by external factors, not by a controlling personality. This approach allows you to be empathetic rather than angry and to try to help identify the source of this external pressure.

Instead of the client becoming your enemy, you identify what's really bugging her and then make that thing your common enemy—an enemy the two of you work together to destroy or overcome. Once done, the pressure on the client is relieved, relieving the client's pressure on you. Her gratitude will make you a savior in her eyes, and saviors usually get better treatment than servants.

For example, a client was continually pressuring me into accepting tight deadlines, and then, once I agreed to them, would call halfway through the job and ask for the work to be done even sooner. Finally, I asked why every job needed to be done in two days. Was there a problem the client had that forced him to make every job a rush? Was there anything I could do to alleviate it?

The client admitted that his boss always gave him projects at the last minute and then demanded immediate turnaround, in turn forcing him to push me for faster delivery. We talked about the entire process of producing marketing materials, and I learned that his art design studio typically took three weeks for design and mechanicals of product sheets.

I introduced him to an excellent desktop publishing service that could give equivalent quality, at half the cost, with only four days turnaround! This not only solved a production problem for the client, but bought me more time on the writing end, eliminating the constant pressure to complete every job sooner than I could.

On the other hand, you may find that there is no external reason why the client is so demanding and controlling. He just *enjoys* being that way. What do you do? You might try having a heart-to-heart talk, and it might work, but frankly, I doubt it. You are the client's consultant, not his therapist, and therefore you are unlikely to achieve significant changes in his personality or behavior. The only choice is to live with it or walk away from the account.

Which option you choose depends largely on the severity of the client's behavior, how you handle it, and how much it affects you. I find I am not bothered by clients with whom others could not work. I am able to say to myself, "I'm not doing anything wrong; it's just the way they are," and move on from there.

The clients want to be controlling. My attitude is: Fine. I'm here to serve them, and if they want to be demanding, it's their right. As long as they're not abusive and my bills are paid, I don't care how they behave. Would I like it better if they were friendly and pleasant? Of course. Who wouldn't? But I simply do not allow the behavior of others to affect my attitude or my work for them in a negative way.

I agree with Dr. David Burns, director of the Institute for Cognitive and Behavioral Therapies, who says, "Your moods are created by your thoughts and, to a great extent, are caused by forces within your control—the way you are thinking about things." In other words, it's not what happens that counts most; it's how you handle it.

How to Handle Rude, Abusive Clients

Even the best people are occasionally rude, and an outburst every now and then can be forgiven. But you should not put up with clients who

- are constantly rude and abrasive.
- insult or demean you.
- sexually harass you.
- use objectionable language.
- act in a manner deliberately calculated to make you uncomfortable or attack your self-esteem.
- threaten you physically or slap or hit.
- abuse you in any way.

We are all in the business of service, but service is not a synonym for subservience or submission. Every human being has the right to expect decent, civil treatment from his or her fellow human beings. You can politely but firmly let the others know that what they are doing is unacceptable behavior and must stop for the professional relationship to continue. For example, "I'd like us to continue our association, but there is one problem that I would like to discuss with you to see if we can resolve it." Many people who have been exhibiting abusive behavior will stop when the victim explains why the behavior is wrong, damaging, and inappropriate.

Unfortunately, many others will continue despite your plea. Some view you as a "hired peon" and do not care how they treat you. Others have different values and simply cannot understand that what seems good humored and "all in fun" to them is not to you.

Once again, the choice is to stay or walk. If you find the behavior truly abusive and offensive, and damaging to your happiness and self-esteem, you really have no choice other than to end the relationship and walk away.

When you walk away, do it politely, in a calm, rational, dignified manner. If you want to avoid an unpleasant telephone confrontation, or think the person would react badly or violently face to face, a letter is fine.

Don't stoop to their level. Thank them for their business, express your regrets that it didn't work out, and wish them well. You may have the overwhelming urge to get emotions off your chest and really let the client "have it." Resist the temptation. While it might provide temporary satisfaction, there is no long-term benefit to making enemies.

How to Handle Arrogant Clients

There is one way to handle clients who have a big ego—let them. Right now, you're letting their bragging and boasting bother you. Don't. If the client wants to make himself feel big and important, even at your expense, so what? He is the client; we are the consultant. He's *supposed* to get all the glory. That's what he's paying us for.

The real reason we find arrogant clients with big egos difficult to deal with is that many of us have pretty big egos ourselves. We're specialists in our trade or skill and are proud of our ability. So when a client lords his success over us, we find it hard to take.

Consultants have an especially tough time dealing with the client who implies that he could do the job better than the consultant "if only he had the time." Arrogant people frequently build themselves up by dismissing your ability or talent and indicating it is just one of many things they can do.

The tendency in dealing with the egomaniac or arrogant client is to "call his bluff." That is, go out of your way to prove what they said isn't true, and they're not as superior as they claim. Don't do it. The only possible result of pointing out that the client is lying or exaggerating is to embarrass him, make him feel bad about himself, and possibly humiliate him in front of his peers. If you do that, do you think he will want to associate and work with you in the future? He won't.

Instead, when a client tells a whopper, *let it pass.* Don't make snide little comments or ask seemingly "innocent" questions designed to reveal the client as a phony or braggart. At the same time, you don't need to gush over a boast or claim of superiority either. Just listen, acknowledge it politely, and move on. Let the client think you are impressed. Let the client retain his dignity and inflated ego. That will make him a happy client. And clients who are happy when they are around you are clients who will continue to hire you.

How to Handle Self-Proclaimed Experts

A variation of the arrogant client is the self-proclaimed expert. For example, a client hires your interior decorating firm because she loves your work and wants the best, and then rejects every suggestion, every color scheme, and totally redesigns every room layout and plan herself.

I don't mind working with clients with strong opinions and ideas stemming from a claim of expertise in my field because many, in fact, do have good ideas. Where my copywriting, consulting, and training are concerned, I encourage client input and feedback, and I value their suggestions and ideas.

Don't assume the client is an ignoramus in your field before you know the facts; otherwise, you may embarrass yourself. Recently, I met with the vice president of engineering at a large manufacturing firm. He was interested in having me teach his employees writing skills.

During our talk, he began to suggest improvements to my presentation technique and ways to make the training better and more interesting. I was thinking, *Hey, I'm the training pro, you're the engineer. Why don't you leave it to me?* Then he casually mentioned that he had been a professional trainer and teacher for eighteen years before becoming an engineer. Actually, his suggestions were excellent, and this explains why. I am glad I did not dismiss his ideas or try to prove my superior knowledge of training to him (he had been in training longer than I had!).

Although you are the expert, many clients do have some knowledge. And nobody knows everything—you and I always have something more to learn. If you are open to client input instead of hostile toward it, you'll be amazed what your clients can teach you.

At a Boardroom Reports meeting, direct marketing consultant Sol Blumenfeld was asked, "If you could change one thing that you have done over the years, what would it be?" He replied: "I'd listen to my clients more. Some clients know more than you do. The people who are in a particular industry often have a lot to teach us before we go off to make our plans."

So rather than have the attitude that you are the guru and the client should sit still and keep quiet, be glad that the client wants to take an active role in helping you do the best job possible.

Naturally, when the client suggests something that is not practical, feasible, technically correct, or desirable, you must speak up and say so. But don't simply dismiss the client's suggestion. Show her why it doesn't work and how you propose to do it in a more effective way. Many clients like to learn, and part of our role is teaching them to do more on their own so, over time, they don't have to rely as much on outside suppliers for assistance.

What if the client *thinks* she knows it all but actually is not knowledgeable? Again, no need to dismiss her, diminish her role or value, or act as if what you're doing is beyond her comprehension. Instead, show the client what you are doing and explain why as you go along. Then suggest other resources—seminars, adult education classes, books, tapes— that can increase her knowledge of the subject.

What you should never do is tell the client that she is stupid or ignorant, that you are the expert, and that she should butt out. That's sheer arrogance on your part, and guess what? The client is paying the bill and need not put up with it—or you.

How to Handle Personality Conflicts between You and the Client

There are some difficulties in client/consultant relationships for which the precise cause or contributing factor cannot be clearly identified. Sometimes no one thing the client does makes him difficult to deal with or annoying. Sometimes it's simply a matter of personal chemistry—you and the client do not get along.

This situation can be avoided by opting to do business only with clients you like and with whom you feel you can get along. Personal chemistry is a key factor in determining whether a client/vendor relationship can work and should be initiated.

But what if you entered the relationship without much prior exposure to the client, and now you find the client difficult to get along with? Your action depends on how great the personality differences are, and the degree to which you and the client are having trouble.

You can't change the client's personality, and she cannot change yours. But you can change the way you *react* to and deal with each other. For example, if the client has a habit or mannerism that is annoying to you, you cannot get her to stop it. And you probably can't stop yourself from being annoyed by it. But you *can* control your reaction to the habit or mannerism. You can *choose* not to let the annoying habit interfere with your ability to serve the client or to treat her warmly and kindly.

The key, as sports psychologist Dr. Rob Gilbert says, is simply to change *buts* to *ands*. For example, instead of saying, "I want to be nice to Anita, but her pompous accent annoys the heck out of me," you substitute "and" for "but" and say, "I want to be nice to Anita, and her pompous accent annoys the heck out of me." That is, Anita's accent will remain pompous and annoying to you, but you will refuse to let that annoyance color your dealings with her, and you will be nice to her and treat her as if the accent did not exist.

The same technique can work for any client habit or personality quirk that makes you impatient, angry, or annoyed. For example, instead of saying, "I want to do a good job for Joe, but he is always changing his mind," you say, "I want to do a good job for Joe, and he is always changing his mind." In the first statement, the fact that Joe changes his mind is what prevents you from doing a good job for Joe.

In the second statement, you take control of your emotions, actions, and reaction to Joe's behavior. Yes, Joe is always changing his mind, but you choose not to let this interfere with your service to him. Moods—and actions dictated by mood—are within our control rather than controlled by external forces, such as what Joe or Anita do.

The One Client with Whom You Cannot Succeed

Jim Alexander, founder of Alexander Marketing Services in Grand Rapids, Michigan, once made a comment that stuck in my mind. We were talking about working with clients who are dictatorial, ignore the consultant's advice, and redo everything the consultant turns in because the client believes he can do it better.

"I can handle a client who is arrogant but knowledgeable," said Jim. "And I can handle a client who is ignorant but admits he doesn't know what he's doing. The one client that no consultant can succeed with is the one who is arrogant and ignorant, doesn't know anything, but thinks he knows it all."

Realize there are some situations in which you cannot win or salvage a good relationship because the client is simply too difficult. In those situations, the strategies suggested in this chapter may fail. If that's the case, you have two choices remaining: (1) keep the account, or (2) resign it.

How to Resign a Difficult Account without Monetary Loss

Let's say none of my techniques worked, the difficult account is still difficult, and you're thinking, *Who needs this?*

You want to resign the account, because you know it will make life easier and more pleasant. On the other hand, you don't want to lose the billings. What to do? Simple. Go out and get more accounts. Do a direct mail campaign. Run some ads. Send out a press release. Make sales calls. Pick up the telephone and call some prospects. Go on some meetings. Make sales presentations.

Do these things until the revenue from the new clients equals or exceeds the revenue from the difficult account you are resigning. That way, the emotional upset that comes with severing the relationship won't be compounded by an accompanying loss of income. And you will feel more secure about your action.

13

Boosting Your Consulting

Income with

Information Products

As discussed in Chapter 1, consultants package their expertise and information in ways other than one-on-one consulting done at a project or per diem rate.

One-on-one consultations are customized for the client, but not all clients can afford or even want customized advice. A less costly way for you to sell—and for clients to acquire—your information is to package it in standardized, noncustomized formats. This information can be sold at a lower cost than one-on-one consulting, and since it is not proprietary or customized, the same information can be sold to multiple buyers—more than you would have time to work with one-on-one by yourself. This chapter details how to create and sell information products to your clients and others.

What Are "Information Products"?

Information products are printed, recorded, or electronic files containing prewritten information sold at a per unit price. Information products is a broad term referring to everything from pamphlets, special reports, books, audio cassettes, and videos, to CD-ROMs, software, computer-based training, newsletters, and fax advisory services.

Information products present in-depth data, information, or discussion of a topic related to the consultant's area of expertise. One consultant specializing in regulatory compliance, for example, offers as an information product a "boilerplate" quality manual on a disk. The boilerplate can easily be customized to a client's operation, eliminating the time and effort of writing the quality manual entirely from scratch. Another information product produced by this consultant is a mini-directory of firms certified to perform ISO audits.

Traditionally consultants have offered booklets (because they are inexpensive and easy to produce) and books (for of the prestige and credibility). But with the growth of the Internet, many prospects like to buy information in electronic form, whether as downloads from a Web site or on a CD-ROM or computer disk.

This actually works to your advantage as an information seller. You can package essentially the same information in multiple media, and sell it many times. Not only will different people buy information in different formats, but some customers actually will pay for the same information several times to get it in different formats!

One consultant asked me, "What are the criteria for a marketable information product at a time when we are all suffering from information overload?" The answer: information products provide specific and detailed answers to questions and problems in narrow niche subjects not usually addressed by newspapers, magazines, and general media. As Richard Saul Wurman observes in his book *Information Anxiety* (Doubleday, 1989), "the information explosion has backfired, leaving us inundated with facts but starved for understanding." Information products cut through the clutter, providing clients with the precise information they want in a minimum of words.

Reasons Consultants Should Produce Information Products

Here are the main reasons consultants should produce and offer information products, and why Howard Shenson said "publishing is every consultant's second business."

- Being published builds credibility. The highest-paid consultants are typically those who have written best-selling books in their fields.

- Information products let clients "sample" your information before they hire you. The marketing director at a computer company once said to me, "I am considering several consultants for teaching direct marketing to our staff. Why should I chose you over them?" I sent him my book on direct marketing with a note that said, "If this doesn't convince you, hire someone else." I got the job and a large client I've now been working with for years on many projects.
- Information products give you an advantage over the competition. If you have written a book or produced an audio program and your competitor hasn't, you have an edge in winning contracts.
- Information products allow you to profitably serve that segment of the market that can't or won't hire you for private consultation. Instead of turning away prospects who can't afford you, you can offer them a lower-priced alternative—an information product that delivers much of the same advice you would give in a private consultation. In this way, leads you've paid to generate but that you'd otherwise have to turn down can become product buyers, generating additional income for you.
- Writing books, booklets, and articles sharpens your thinking, forces you to organize your information more logically, and builds your own expertise in your subject area. Creating information products helps you become a better one-on-one consultant.

Tips for Producing Specific Types of Information Products

Here is a quick overview of some of the more popular formats for information products, along with suggestions on producing each.

Tip Sheets

Tip sheets are short, to the point fact sheets on a particular subject. They are usually printed on one or two sides of an 8½-by-11-inch sheet of paper. Advice or information is typically (but not necessarily) presented as a series of short, numbered items or tips. You can write tip sheets as electronic files, then run them off one at a time on your laser printer as orders come in. You can also e-mail tip sheets to clients who prefer an electronic file. I typically charge $1 to $2 for a tip sheet.

Booklets and Pamphlets

These are, in essence, expanded versions of tip sheets. They contain similar information except in more detail. In a booklet, there's space to flesh out each point more fully. Booklets are generally 4 by 9 inches, so they can be mailed in a standard #10 business envelope. A booklet is constructed by printing the pages and then saddle-stitching them together (saddle-stitching is binding by stapling through the spine). Booklets typically run anywhere from 8 to 16 pages, although they can be longer. I price booklets at $5 to $12 each.

Special Reports

This format is typically longer than a booklet, and can be even more detailed. Special reports, like tip sheets, are printed on 8½-by-11-inch sheets of paper, but are multiple pages instead of one page. The larger page format allows for bigger illustrations, tables, and charts than you can put in a booklet. A special report can run anywhere from 5 pages to 100 or more, although typically they are 6 to 12 pages. I desktop publish the master pages, then run off copies of the report on my office copier, collate, and staple them. For a 10-page special report, I charge $6 to $7.

Monographs

A monograph is an essay or article on a single subject. It is similar in look and feel to a special report, but often on the lengthy side (20 to 30 pages) and written in more formal, professional language. The medical products industry frequently uses monographs written by doctors to promote a drug, material, instrument, or piece of equipment. They give monographs away free, but you can charge $5 to $14 or more for a well-written monograph on a topic of interest to your prospects.

Resource Guides

These are mini-directories of information resources in a particular field—for example, Web sites for quality control professionals. A resource guide of 5 or 6 pages might sell for $5 to $8.

Manuals

Reference manuals are long, comprehensive special reports, usually placed in a binder or notebook and organized into sections. Manuals can range from 30 to 150 pages or more. Price can range from $10 to $30 or more.

Books

As discussed in Chapter 3, many consultants write books. Not only does the book promote your consulting practice, but you can generate additional revenue from book sales. If you cannot find a publisher for a book, you can always publish it yourself. A 200-page book will sell for $10 to $30 or more. The more specialized the book, the higher the price. Costs for producing a self-published book are presented in Figure 13.1.

Figure 13.1   Sample Self-Publishing Costs

Item:	Cost:
Proofreader	$12/hour
Copyeditor	$15/hour
Indexer	$2/page
Front cover design	$800 – $1,200
Typesetting	$6 – $10/page
Printing 5,000 copies of 224-page book	$1.20 – $1.30/copy
Printing 5,000 copies of a 4-color cover	$1,200 – $2,800

Source: "What Should Things Cost?" by Curt Matthews, *PMA Newsletter,* March 1997.

Audiotapes

Audiocassettes are a popular medium for disseminating spoken-word business and how-to information. A single audiocassette is easy to produce. Just get a speaking engagement and tape your talk. Then make duplicates, put a nice label on it, and sell the tapes. A single audiocassette retails for between $10 and $15. Duplication costs for small quantities are $1 to $2 each, depending on packaging. Appendix E lists a vendor who can tape and duplicate talks for you. Some organizations routinely tape speaker presentations and sell the tapes to their members. You should make it a condition that you retain the rights to the tape and get a free master copy. This eliminates the cost of paying a professional or buying your own taping equipment.

Audio Programs

Once you have done eight, six, or even only two tapes on related topics, you can package them in a vinyl album and sell them as an audiocassette program. A six-cassette album can sell for $49 to $79. Albums are a couple of dollars each, and available from any tape duplication service.

Power Packs

A power pack is a multimedia information product. Typically, it's a combination of tapes, reports, perhaps a book or CD-ROM, all in a nice package. Power packs can sell for $50 to $150 or more.

Videotapes

You can video your presentation, duplicate it, and sell the videos. The video should be edited professionally in a video studio. Add graphics, special effects, charts, and other footage for a varied presentation that's more than just you talking at a lectern. Have a nice label or package. A single video can sell for $29 to $59 or more.

Paid-Subscription Newsletter

Some consultants produce a quarterly promotional newsletter of four to eight pages they distribute free to prospects and clients. By making your newsletter meatier (more information; no self promotion), longer (six to eight pages), and more frequent (monthly), you can charge a subscription fee ranging from $29 to $249 a year or more.

How to Design a Catalog Featuring Your Information Products

The greatest profit opportunity for selling information products is through your "bounce-back catalog." This is a mini-catalog of your entire information product line. It need not be elaborate; you can print it black ink on white or colored paper (see Appendix F for a sample mini-catalog).

A bounce-back catalog should be included in every outgoing order you ship to your clients and customers. The beauty is that it promotes your entire product line at virtually no cost—there is no postage or envelope to pay for because it is mailed with the product shipment. The only cost is the few pennies per catalog for printing.

For a small home-based information business, including a bounce-back catalog in all product shipments can double your annual gross sales or better, with no added marketing cost.

You can promote your full line of information products in other ways, of course. For instance, you can periodically mail your mini-catalog or other special offers to your list of buyers. But the cheapest, easiest way to sell information products is by enclosing bounce-back catalogs with products being shipped. If you don't do this, you are missing out on a large share of the profits your information products business can generate for you.

How to Sell Your Products Profitably to Consulting Clients and Prospects

You can get significant additional income with virtually no extra marketing cost by selling information products to clients and prospects.

Include your bounce-back catalog in the packets of information you send to potential clients. Many, even if they don't hire you, will place an order for information products. Those who do become further educated in your expertise and more likely to hire you.

Periodically remail catalogs to all leads who do not become clients. Many will place orders for your information products.

For those prospects whose business you actively seek, you can impress them by sending them some of your information products—free—as an enticement to hire you and as a demonstration of your expertise. Books, booklets, article reprints, and monographs are more interesting than sales brochures alone and more likely to make the impression you want—you are the knowledgeable authority in your field.

I give away dozens of audio cassettes, article reprints, and full-length books each year to those prospects I want to close. It pays off handsomely. What's neat is that the information product has a high perceived value—that of the price listed on its cover and in your catalog. But it costs you only a fraction of that amount to produce and give away. And while a brochure might get lost in a file folder, a book sits on the client's shelf where he can always see it, and is therefore continually reminded of you and your expertise.

How to Use Direct Marketing to Boost Your Product Sales

Is the "information explosion" a good thing for information marketers? Actually, it's a mixed blessing because

- people have too much to read and not enough time to read it.
- more and more information is competing for their attention.
- there is a proliferation of low-cost/no-cost information sources eating into the market for your expensive information products.

Fortunately, you can still succeed in selling information by mail. It's tougher than it was in yesteryear, though. So here are some rules and guidelines formulated specifically for information marketers competing in the Information Age.

Narrow the Focus

Although the most profitable product may be one with wide appeal, such as Joe Karbo's "Lazy Man's Way to Riches" or Bob Kalian's "A Few Thousand of the Best Free Things in America," "goldmine" concepts like these are difficult to come by. Today we live in an age of specialization. People have narrow, specific areas of interest and eagerly seek the best information in these niche areas. Match your own interests and consulting expertise with the information needs of an identifiable market and you're on your way.

How big must this market be? Jerry Buchanan, publisher of *Towers Club Newsletter,* a how-to newsletter for information marketers and self-publishers, says that "any group large enough that some publisher has seen fit to publish a magazine about them or for them" is large enough for your purposes.

Seize a Subject

The tendency of the typical magazine writer or book author is to wander from subject to subject to satisfy a never-ending curiosity about all things. But the consultant, an information marketer, must behave differently. He must latch onto a narrow niche or topic, make it his own, and produce a series of information products that meets the needs of information-seekers buying materials on this subject. Not only does this increase profits by giving you more products to offer your customers, it also helps establish you as a recognized expert and authority in your field.

Plan the "Back End" before You Start Marketing

Many entrepreneurial direct response advertisers dream of duplicating the one-shot success of Joe Karbo and of getting rich from a single mail order book. But it rarely happens. This "front end," or first sale, *can* be profitable, if cost-effective marketing techniques are used. But the real profits are in the back end—selling a related line of additional information products to repeat customers.

I advise you to devise and plan this back end of related products *before* launching a direct response campaign. Otherwise, precious opportunities for repeat sales will be lost if you can only offer a single product to eager, information-hungry buyers.

Test Your Concept with Classified Ads

Most information marketers want to immediately mail thousands of direct mail packages or place full-page ads.

That's fine if you can afford to risk $5,000–$25,000 on an untested idea. However, I prefer to test with small classified ads first. By doing so, I can determine the product's sales appeal and potential for under $200.

Your ad should seek inquiries, not orders. All requests for information should be immediately fulfilled with a powerful direct mail sales letter, circular, order form and reply envelope.

What should all this cost? A successful classified ad will bring in inquiries at a cost of 25 cents to $1 per lead. A good sales package will convert 10 to 35 percent of these leads to sales. I have run classified ads that pulled up to 17 times their cost in product sales.

The Importance of the Bounce-Back Catalog

A bounce-back catalog is a circular containing descriptions and order information for your complete line of related information products. When a customer orders your lead product, you insert the bounce-back in the package and ship it with the order. Ideally, he sees the catalog, scans it, orders more items—and his order "bounces back" to you.

The bounce-back catalog doesn't have to be long or elaborate. For my mail order business, the catalog is printed on four 8½-by-11-inch pages in black ink on colored paper.

Additional sales generated by bounce-backs can range from 10 to 100 percent of the front-end sales generated by your original ad or mailing. The only cost is a few cents to print each catalog sheet. There is no postage cost, because the catalog gets a "free ride" as an insert in your product shipment. (Tip: When you fulfill a bounce-back order, send out another bounce-back catalog, and then another, until the customer has bought every item in the catalog.)

Create Low-, Medium-, and High-Priced Products

Different buyers have different perceptions of what your information is worth and what they will pay. You will get more sales by testing a variety of prices for your lead item and offering a number of different products reflecting a broad range of prices.

My front-end product is a $12 book. The back-end consists of a series of $7 and $8 reports, a second book for $20 and a six-tape cassette album for $49.95. Dr. Jeffrey Lant, who sells business development products and services, has products ranging from a $4 report to a $4,800 consulting service.

Once I sent an inquiry to a well-known and successful marketer who specializes in selling information on how to make money as a speaker. I didn't buy because the only alternatives were a large cassette album or a one-year newsletter subscription—both fairly expensive—and I wasn't ready to make that kind of commitment to the subject. Most buyers prefer to sample your information with a lower-priced product, such as a book, single cassette, or inexpensive manual in the $10 to $50 range.

Let Your Buyers Tell You What Products They Want You to Create

Always put your name, address, and phone number in every information product you produce, and encourage feedback from buyers. Many become advocates and fans, calling, writing, and establishing a dialogue with you.

Welcome this. Not only can you solve their problems and answer their inquiries by telling them which current products to buy, but their questions can suggest new products. *Most of my back-end products were created to answer specific questions readers asked me repeatedly.* Instead of having the same telephone conversation over and over again, I can simply sell them a report which contains the answers they seek. It saves time and generates revenue.

Be the Quality Source

Your strongest advertisement is a good product. A clever or deceptive ad can certainly generate brisk sales, and returns may not be excessive even if your product is poor, but customers will feel cheated and will not favor you with repeat business.

A good product will have people actively seeking you out and will bring in a small but steady stream of phone calls, letters, inquiries, and orders generated by the product itself and not the advertising. You will be shocked at the enormous effort some people expend to locate the source of quality information products that are well spoken of by other buyers.

Using Small Ads to Sell Information Products

The least expensive way to start in mail order is with small classified ads. Actually, these ads generate a greater return on investment than any other medium, including full-page ads. With a winning classified ad and strong inquiry fulfillment kit, you have the foundation for making your home-based information products business profitable.

You should not ask for an order directly from a classified ad. It won't work. There is not enough copy in a classified ad to make the complete sale.

Classified advertising is two-step direct marketing. In step one, you run a small classified ad to generate an inquiry, which is a request for more information about your product.

The way to measure classified ad response for inquiry advertising is to count the inquiries, divide the cost of the ad by the number of inquiries, and thus determine the cost per inquiry. For instance, if you run a classified ad and it costs you $100, and you get 100 inquiries, your cost per inquiry is $1.

When people inquire, you implement the next step. Send them an inquiry fulfillment kit, which is a sales package promoting your product. The inquiry fulfillment kit consists of an outer envelope, sales letter, circular or brochure, order form, and reply envelope.

Bernard Lyons, editor of *KEY Newsletter,* says that classified ads must follow the AIDA principle, meaning they must get *A*ttention, generate *I*nterest, create *D*esire for the product, and ask for *A*ction. According to Lyons, sales appeals that work in classified mail order advertising include promises of obtaining love, money, health, popularity, leisure, security, entertainment, self-confidence, better appearance, prestige, pride of accomplishment, saving time, eliminating worry and fear, satisfying curiosity, success, avoiding work or risk, self-expression, pride of ownership, comfort, creativity, and self-improvement.

Lyons says effective words and phrases to use in your classified ads are: free, new, amazing, now, how to, and easy. To this list I would add: discover, method, plan, reveals, show, simple, startling, advanced, improved, and you.

One of my most successful mail order ads, run continuously for many years in *Writer's Digest,* is shown in Figure 13.2.

Figure 13.2 Sample Mail Order Ad

MAKE $85,000/YEAR writing ads, brochures, promotional
materials for local/national clients. Free details: CTC, 22 E.
Quackenbush, Dept. WD, Dumont, NJ 07628.

Here are some other examples of how to write classified mail order ads:

EXTRA CASH. 12 ways to make money at home. Free details....

MAIL ORDER MILLIONAIRE reveals money-making secrets. FREE
1-hour cassette. . . .

SELL NEW BOOK by mail! 400% profit! Free dealer information. . . .

GROW earthworms at home for profit. . . .

CARNIVOROUS AND WOODLAND terrarium plants. Send for
FREE catalog. . . .

ANCESTOR HUNTING? Trace your family roots the easy way.
Details free. . . .

The offer that will generate the most response asks for an inquiry, not
an order. This is done by putting a phrase such as "free details," "free information," "free catalog," or a similar phrase, followed by a colon and your
address (e.g., free details: Box 54, Canuga, TN 44566).

Some mail order advertisers ask the prospect to pay for the
information, either by sending a small amount of money (25 cents, 50
cents, $1, and $2 are typical), or by requiring the prospect to send a self-
addressed stamped envelope.

The theory is that asking for postage or a nominal payment brings you
a more qualified lead and therefore results in a higher percentage of leads
converted to sales. My experience is that it doesn't pay to charge for your
information kit because doing so dramatically cuts down on the number of
leads you receive.

As a rule of thumb, whenever you offer information to generate an
inquiry, make it free. The exception might be a very expensive and
elaborate catalog, for which you charge $1 to cover your costs.

"Key code" all your promotions, so you can track which ad or mailing each inquiry or order comes from. In your classified ads, put the key code in the address. For instance, in my ad "MAKE $85,000/YEAR WRITING," the key code "WD" refers to *Writer's Digest* magazine. Because the ad runs every month, I don't bother adding a code number to track the month. If you wanted to do so, you could. For example, "Dept. WD-10" would mean *Writer's Digest* magazine, October issue (the tenth month of the year). Keep track of the key code on each inquiry and record the information using the form in Appendix C.

The measure of a successful inquiry classified ad is the cost per inquiry. Therefore, if you can get your message across in fewer words, you pay less for the ad, and as a result lower your cost per inquiry.

Make your classifieds as short and pithy as possible. Here are some tips for reducing your word count.

- Be concise. Use the minimum number of words needed to communicate your idea. For example, instead of "Earn $500 a Day in Your Own Home-Based Business," write "Work at Home—$500/Day!"
- Minimize your address. You pay the publication for every word in your classified, including your address. Therefore, instead of "22 E. Quackenbush Avenue," I write "22 E. Quackenbush." The mail still gets delivered, and I save one word. This can add up to significant savings for ads run frequently in multiple publications.
- Use phrases and sentence fragments rather than full sentences.
- Remember your objective. You are only asking for an inquiry, not an order. You don't need a lot of copy, because all you are asking the reader to do is send for free information.
- Use combination words, hyphenated words, and slash constructions. For instance, instead of "GROW EARTH WORMS," which is three words, write "GROW EARTHWORMS," which counts as two words, saving you a word.

Place your classified ads in publications that run mail order classified ad sections. Send for free media kits, which include details on circulation, advertising rates, readership, and a sample issue of the publication. Ask for several issues, if the publisher will send them.

Look at the classified ad sections in the publications. Are there ads for products similar to yours? This is a good sign. See if these ads repeat from issue to issue. The advertisers would not repeat them unless they were working. If this publication is working for their offers, it can work for yours too.

Classified ad sections are divided by various headings. Place your ad in the appropriate heading. If you don't see an appropriate heading, call the magazine and ask if they will create one for you.

If you sell information by mail, avoid putting your classified under the heading "Books and Booklets." This will reduce orders. Instead, put the ad under a heading related to the subject matter. For example, if you are selling a book on how to make money cleaning chimneys, place the ad under "Business Opportunities."

We have already discussed the two key measurements of two-step classified advertising, which are the cost per inquiry and the percentage of inquiries converted to orders.

The bottom line is: Did the sales the ad generated exceed the cost of the ad space? If they did, it was profitable. If they didn't, the ad isn't working and a new ad should be tested.

Appendix C shows a form you can use to track inquiries and sales from your classified ads. Once the sheet is completed, you can, at a glance, compare the cost of the ad space with the total sales generated. My goal is to generates sales at least twice what the ad space costs. Your objectives may be different.

You can test a classified by running it just one time in a publication. The problem is, most magazines and even weekly newspapers have long lead times—several weeks or more—for placing classified ads. If you place the ad to run one time only, and the ad pulls well, you then have to wait several weeks or months until you can get it in again.

In a weekly newspaper or magazine, I test a classified ad by running it for one month—four consecutive issues. For a monthly publication, I test it for three months—three consecutive issues. If the first insertion is profitable, I will probably extend the insertion order for several months, so the ad runs continuously with no interruption.

With a full-page ad, you usually get the greatest number of orders the first time the ad runs in the magazine. Response declines with each additional insertion, and at the point where the ad is not going to be profitable in its next insertion, you pull it and try another ad.

The reason is that the first time the ad runs, it skims the cream of the prospects, getting orders from those most likely to buy. Obviously, those who buy from the first insertion of the ad will not buy when it runs again. Therefore, each time the ad runs, it reaches a smaller audience of potential new buyers.

With a classified ad, however, the total response is much less for each insertion. Therefore, it doesn't materially affect the number of potential first-time customers the ad appeals to. In fact, some people who responded once, got your sales literature, and didn't buy, may respond several times—and get your literature several times—before they eventually break down and buy. Also, each issue reaches a number of new subscribers via subscriptions and newsstand circulation, so the total audience for a classified remains fairly constant.

While response to full-page mail order ads declines with each insertion, the response to a classified ad can remain steady for many insertions. Indeed, some information marketers (myself included) have run the same classified monthly in the same magazine for years at a time, with no decline in response. In fact, response sometimes tends to increase during the first 12 months the ad is run, as people see the ad over and over again, and eventually become curious enough to respond.

14

The Lucrative Training

---

and Speaking Market

For some consultants, public speaking is a self-promotion. For others, it's a highly profitable second source of income. Others still earn all or most of their income from speaking.

Some consultants are paid "professional speakers," delivering keynotes and breakout sessions at association meetings and industry conferences. Perhaps a larger number conduct training seminars for organizations on a private basis.

What Is "Training"?

According to an article in *American Demographics* (February 1998, page 39), each year 47 percent of college-educated workers participate in skill-improvement training for their current jobs.

The American Society of Training and Development says that in 1995 American companies spent $55 billion on formal worker training (*Record,* June 23, 1997, page H-10 and December 22, 1997). About 60 percent of this money is spent on technical training, with the balance spent teaching "soft skills"—everything from leadership and assertiveness, to conflict resolution, active listening, stress management, and business writing. And an article in *Money* (December 1997) notes that 5 million adults are taking classes to keep up or catch up with skills necessary to do their jobs.

An article in *Training & Development* (November 1997, page 53) reports that respondents to a July 1997 survey of national human resources and development executives showed that the top ten training trends are:

1. Computer skills training
2. Teamwork training
3. Shift from training to performance
4. Decision-making and problem-solving training
5. Rapid development and deployment of training
6. Systems-thinking training
7. Demonstrating training outcomes
8. Measuring performance outcomes
9. Shift from training to learning
10. Making a business case for training interventions

What Can You Charge for Speaking and Training?

For an in-house corporate training seminar, companies expect to spend around $200 to $250 per employee per day. So for a typical class with 15 employees, charging $3,000 is not unreasonable. Many consultants get $1,500 a day; but some earn $4,000 a day or more. The more specialized and in-demand your program, the more you can charge.

According to an article in *Training & Development* (January 1998, page 26), the typical U.S. private sector organization with 50 or more employees spends about $504 per employee per year on training. The following training courses are the most popular:

- New employee orientation
- Management and supervisory skills
- Computer literacy and applications
- Job-specific technical skills
- Occupational safety and compliance
- Teams
- Quality, competition, and business practices
- Customer service

- Awareness
- Professional skills
- Product knowledge
- Executive development
- Sales training
- Basic skills

Overview of the Training Market

A few weeks ago I taught a writing seminar to a group of 25 logistics professionals employed by the U.S. Army. My fee: $6,000. The week before, I taught a shorter version of the seminar at a medical equipment company. For less than a day's work, I received $3,500 plus expenses.

The point: Consultants can earn significant fees teaching their knowledge and skills to others. In fact, with fees ranging from $1,000 to $4,000 a day, *teaching* a skill often pays better than performing the task or exercising the skill itself. The rest of this chapter discusses some steps you can take to get into the lucrative speaking, consulting, training, seminar, and workshop business.

Who Buys Training?

Fortune 1000 companies are the most likely candidates to hire you to train employees. Some midsize companies also buy seminars, but as a rule, the smaller the firm, the less likely they are to have a formal training program or budget.

In-house seminars are needed in such topics as business writing, technical writing, interpersonal skills, time management, quality control, diversity in the workplace, and presentation skills. Specialty subjects, such as how to write ISO 9000 documentation or comply with OSHA (Occupational Safety and Health Administration) requirements, are also in demand.

If you consult on a subject of interest to businesspeople—stress reduction, time management, leadership, success, selling, management, the Internet—you may find a ready market for in-house training seminars on these topics as well.

Contact corporations and offer your services as a trainer. Write to training managers. Or call vice presidents, supervisors, and department managers whose employees may need skills improvement. Prepare an outline of your course and a biography highlighting your credentials to send prospective clients who request more information. Design these materials so they can be faxed or e-mailed if there is immediate interest.

Training managers typically won't be interested in your program unless they've gotten a request from a manager in their company for a seminar on that topic. Most collect information for future reference. Send them your literature and follow up periodically by mail, fax, and phone. Don't call too often, or you will be perceived as a pest. Two to four times a year is just about right.

Front-line managers and supervisors may not be thinking about a training program, but if they feel lack of skills is a problem in their organization, your offer will interest them. Stress the benefits of skill improvement, especially any return on investment it can generate. If your program will help employees improve quality, productivity, customer service, sales, or profits, say so.

In corporate training, clients hire you on a per diem basis and send employees to the training sessions you conduct. They provide the bodies, room, and refreshments. You teach the seminar and supply course materials. Class sizes typically range from 10 to 25 students, although I have had as many as 35 in a session. Seminars, which take one or two days, are usually held in a conference room at the client's offices.

If the client is out of town, you'll have to travel. You don't get paid an extra fee for your travel time, but the client reimburses you for all expenses including airfare, lodging, meals, and other out-of-pocket expenses. I use the travel time to work on my program and prepare for the upcoming class. On the trip home, I tally my expenses, prepare an invoice, write the client a thank you note, and work on consulting projects I've brought with me.

Putting Your Program Together

The client does not hand you a textbook or outline and say, "Teach this course." As an independent trainer, you present a program of your own design. You must supply the complete content including handouts.

Putting together a training course is not at all difficult. Courses are organized in a similar fashion to books, except where books have chapters, courses have modules.

Therefore, if a manager at a local company asks you to present a seminar on business writing to her employees, go immediately to the bookstore and buy two or three books on the subject. You can pattern your course outline after the table of contents in these books.

Your course should be designed as a series of modules covering various subtopics related to the major topic. The outline for my "Effective Business Writing" course, aimed at corporate managers and support staff, lists the following eight modules:

1. *Overview*—elements of effective business writing; tasks of the business writer (letters, memos, proposals, reports, e-mail).
2. *Fundamentals of grammar*—grammatical rules; punctuation; abbreviation; capitalization; spelling.
3. *Principles of composition*—active vs. passive voice; simple vs. complex language; how to write concisely; tenses; style.
4. *Words and phrases*—how to eliminate sexist language, redundancy, jargon, wordiness, clichés, and other ills; correct meaning and usage for commonly misused words.
5. *Principles of organization*—organizing business documents; executive summaries; writing the lead; use of headings and subheads.
6. *Principles of communication and persuasion*—how to get your reader's attention; using facts, opinions, and statistics to prove your case; determining the level and depth of information content; how to get the reader on your side; how to get the reader to take action.
7. *Principles of tone*—informal vs. formal language; finding and using the appropriate tone; using contractions; substituting positive words for negative words.
8. *Special writing concerns of corporate employees*—how to write for a specific audience; tips for making a boring topic interesting; working with uncooperative collaborators; the editing, revision, and approval process.

Additional topics I've covered in my business writing seminars include editing, rewriting, research, outlining, and prewriting planning. In technical writing seminars, I have a module on illustrating writing with tables, graphs, charts, diagrams, and other visuals.

You can adjust the course to the customer's training objectives and class schedules by mixing and matching modules and topics within each module. Some modules of your seminar can potentially be given as complete seminars by themselves.

Most trainers include a set of handouts for each student as part of the cost, and pay the photocopying out of their own pockets. Some bind their handouts in workbook format and charge the client an additional $10 to $25 for each student receiving a workbook. If you've written a book on the topic of your seminar, give the client the option of offering copies to attendees. In the corporate world, the client will buy copies for the trainees and distribute the books to them. It is inappropriate to "pitch your products" in a training session as you might at a public lecture or association meeting.

Make your seminar entertaining as well as informative. Consider using videos, cartoons, humor, props, overheads, flip charts, games, team exercises, and other techniques to maintain attendee interest. Plan a lot of activities for the students.

Be creative in your presentation. Seminar leader Terry Smith, author of *Making Successful Presentations* (John Wiley & Sons, 1991), gets seminar attendees to participate by offering anyone who asks or answers a question a mystery prize in a sealed envelope. Terry tells the attendees that the prize may be worth one million dollars or more! Inside each envelope is a lottery ticket.

In a seminar on effective telephone selling, I had students practice conversations using toy phones. Sound effects, including dial tones and phones ringing, made the presentation fun and lively.

Remember, although you love your subject, some of the people in your seminar may not. In many instances, seminar attendees are forced by their managers to go to your course. A few may resent being sent. Others may resist your trying to teach them a skill they don't admire or care about. The more you can entertain as you train, the more enthusiastic your class will be—and the more they'll learn.

Keep in mind your trainees are busy adults with many things to do. Do not be disturbed or act annoyed if class members have to pop in and out to attend meetings, make calls, or check messages.

Show up at least an hour early. This gives you time to prepare the room and meet some of your students before class starts. Talk with students before the seminar and during breaks to get their feedback on how the day is going.

Offer some type of follow up or support service. This can be included in the fee or sold for an extra charge. Gary Blake, a writing trainer, offers free telephone support for 30 days after the seminar. He also offers an editing-by-fax service where trainees fax in their work for comment and review.

The Market for Professional Speakers

Trainers typically present intensive programs to a small group of an organization's employees. Group size ranges from 6 to 30, although it can be higher. Most training sessions are one day, though some are only half a day, and a smaller percentage are two days or longer.

Speakers address larger groups, ranging from 50 to 50,000. Their venues include rallies, sales meetings, conferences, and association events. Most talks are 60 to 90 minutes. A keynote talk means you are the main speaker of the day. A breakout talk means you are one of a number of speakers giving smaller workshops. If a client invites you to do one session, offer to do multiple sessions. You add value, amortize the cost of your travel and lodging over several talks, and can charge more for the additional sessions.

According to an article in *Sharing Ideas* (January 1998, page 5), the eight most popular speech topics for corporate and association meetings are:

1. Motivation
2. Change
3. Sales
4. Team building
5. The future
6. Humor

7. Leadership
8. Customer service

When you write and publish books and articles on a topic, you are perceived as an expert. Many authors get calls from companies, associations, and schools asking them to conduct a program on the topic of their books. If you want to generate more of these inquiries, include a description of your program, your address, and your phone number in the bios that run with your articles and books. My $6,000 Army contract came because someone in the Army had found my phone number in the back of my book *The Elements of Business Writing*.

If you write on topics that are appropriate for a business audience, there are thousands of associations that hire speakers. One good reference source is the *Directory of Association Meeting Planners & Conference/Convention Directors*. Updated annually, the directory lists more than 13,600 association meeting professionals. Listings indicate professional speaker usage as well as size and number of meetings, destinations, lengths, and schedules.

Local groups, and local chapters of national groups, typically pay no fee or a small honorarium; however, there are exceptions.

National associations pay significant fees to speakers who give talks at national meetings: $1,000 to $3,000 for a talk ranging from an hour to half a day. Sometimes the pay is even better. I know one meeting planner who paid an author $6,000 for a one-hour talk. Best-selling authors like John Naisbitt and Tom Peters can command $10,000 to $40,000 or more per talk, but they are the exception, not the rule. The top fee for noncelebrity speakers is about $5,000.

Is the seminar and workshop business for you? It depends on your personality and what you enjoy. Many consultants are excellent communicators and teachers, but some are comfortable only when there is a printed page or a telephone line between them and their audience, or when they are meeting one or two people in private. If you are introverted and dislike public speaking, you may still be able to make money training and speaking—but you simply may not want to.

On the other hand, if you are as comfortable at the podium as you are with a cell phone or spread sheet, consider giving teaching and speaking a try. It's a nice change of pace from the isolation of working at home. So are the fat paychecks—and the applause when you finish.

For more information on speaking, contact the National Speakers Association and American Seminar Leaders Association. Both are listed in Appendix D. Also, subscribe to *Sharing Ideas* magazine, listed in Appendix A.

How to Raise Your Training and Speaking Income

The best way to get paid big money as a speaker and consultant, other than becoming a celebrity or writing a best-selling book, is to be as good as you can, continually strive to get even better, and deliver to clients more than they have a right to expect.

Speaker Mikki Williams observes: "The mediocre speaker tells; the good speaker explains; the superior speaker demonstrates; the great speaker inspires."

"It's not enough to present information," says speaker Rob Gilbert. "You have to give your audience hope."

Add value to your presentations. Give the audience—and the client who hired you—something extra. Speaker Joyce Gioia gives the following suggestions for adding value to your talk:

- When speaking at a trade show, highlight exhibitors' products and services in your program.
- Get the local press to cover the event.
- Call in advance three people you know will be in the audience and weave their comments into your talk.
- Use a crossword puzzle to reinforce learning. Parsons Software has an inexpensive program, CrossWords Plus 2.0, you can use to quickly and easily create your own custom crossword puzzles.
- Find a sponsor willing to contribute money towards your fee or gifts to be used as door prizes.
- Find something from that day's news and incorporate it into your message.
- Publicly acknowledge the meeting planner or president of the organization. Find a way to relate the acknowledgment to your topic.
- Ask the meeting planner what you could do—that you're not already doing—to make her life easier and less stressful.

- Be flexible. If they need you to speak for more or less time than expected, do so graciously.
- Give away a reminder list of the highlights of your speech.

Thirty Tips for Being More Successful in Training

Madison Gross, an experienced trainer and training manager, has had a career dealing with hundreds of seminar leaders and instructors on behalf of universities, associations, and consulting firms for more than 21 years. Based on this, he has come up with 30 qualities that he looks for when hiring presenters. The better you meet these requirements, the more successful you'll be at getting training and speaking assignments.

1. Instructors should be able to "connect" with their audiences, (e.g., use eye contact and relate to each person).
2. Be prepared to come early and stay late, to meet their attendees, and answer questions.
3. Encourage real give-and-take participation with the audience (known as the Socratic technique). Avoid lecturing at people or reading your teaching material.
4. Demonstrate practical knowledge and depth of the subject matter. Clients really don't want people who are filled with one-industry war stories.
5. Be able to deal with all types of people, including the novice learner, those who possess negative attitudes, the nonparticipants, and those who are highly intelligent. Use those highly intelligent ones as "mentors" and encourage them to bring up ideas and techniques to pass on to the others.
6. Those who are poised and enjoy great personal presence always grade higher than those who don't.
7. Clients look for people who are real "leaders" or facilitators to teach short course programs.
8. Be nonoffensive in words and examples and never condescending to members of the audience.
9. *Never* sell your consulting services on the platform!
10. Demonstrate real pleasure in sharing your hard-won expertise with others.

11. Solicit questions and always answer them honestly.

12. Have a positive attitude and accept criticism constructively, especially from paying customers.

13. Be prepared and organized when arranging your material before you teach.

14. Be flexible when covering sections of the course. If the discussion on a particular subject seems to be "hot," try not to shut it off due to a strict time schedule.

15. Have a sense of humor and have some fun teaching.

16. Be articulate and keep working on your communication and presentation skills. Practice becoming a persuasive speaker.

17. Build up as much teaching experience as you can (including night school and association meetings) before attempting to teach adult seminars.

18. Use well-organized examples, tips, checklists, and forms. The workbook should always be kept up-to-date.

19. Don't bury the attendees in information. Check to make sure things are understood.

20. Never appear canned or rehearsed even if you've done the course hundreds of times.

21. Vary your presentation with judicious use of audio-visual techniques and employ a variety of training methods.

22. Keep things upbeat and remain enthusiastic from beginning to end. Remember to smile often.

23. Keep focused. Don't let the discussion roll off into tangents and side issues.

24. Have a strong opening and closing. The difference between good and excellent ratings often lies in the first and last impressions.

25. Recognize that every class group is different and it's worth varying your presentation if you feel you didn't get off to a good start.

26. Be constantly alert to breakthroughs in your field.

27. Be profit-oriented in your approach to problem-solving.

28. Always explain sophisticated material in down-to-earth terms.

29. Deliver more than is promised in the promotion piece.

30. When teaching technical programs, present identifiable and understandable "real world" company examples and case studies to illustrate your presentation.

One final tip: Some speakers develop big egos. Do not fall into the trap of thinking your training program or speech will solve all of a company's problems or challenges in a day—it won't. And don't think your seminar is the only, or even the primary, source of the attendee's education. Most learn more on the job than they do in training. In her column (*Daily News,* December 17, 1996), Ann Landers observes, "In the final analysis, the School of Experience is where most of us get our basic training for life."

Appendix A: Bibliography

Books

Bermont, Hubert. *How to Become a Successful Consultant in Your Own Field.* Rocklin, Calif.: Prima Publishing, 1995.

Bly, Robert. *The Copywriter's Handbook: A Step-by-Step Guide to Writing Copy That Sells.* New York: Henry Holt & Co., 1990. How to write effective copy.

Bly, Robert. *Getting Your Book Published.* Yonkers, N.Y.: Roblin Press, 1997. How to get a nonfiction book published. Includes sample book proposal, lists of agents and publishers, and more.

Bly, Robert. *Power-Packed Direct Mail.* New York: Henry Holt & Co., 1995. A guide to planning, writing, designing, and producing direct mail promotions.

Bly, Robert. *Selling Your Services.* New York: Henry Holt & Co., 1994. Selling skills for service providers.

Bly, Robert. *Targeted Public Relations.* New York: Henry Holt & Co., 1996. A handbook on how to do public relations.

Bly, Robert. *The Perfect Sales Piece.* New York: John Wiley & Sons, 1993. Guide to creating effective brochures, catalogs, and other sales literature.

Caples, John. *Tested Advertising Methods.* Englewood Cliffs, N.J.: Prentice Hall, 1974. Secrets of writing effective space ads.

Cates, Bill. *Unlimited Referrals.* Wheaton, Md.: Thunder Hill Press, 1996. How to get a lot of referral leads.

Cohen, William. *How to Make It Big As a Consultant.* New York: Amacom, 1993.

Floyd, Elaine. *Marketing with Newsletters.* St. Louis: Newsletter Resources, 1994. How to create effective promotional newsletters.

Garratt, Sally. *Going It Alone: How to Survive and Thrive As an Independent Consultant.* Goward Publishing, 1994.

Harris, Godfrey with Harris, J. *Generate Word of Mouth Advertising: 101 Easy and Inexpensive Ways to Promote Your Business.* Los Angeles: The Americas Group, 1995. Interesting, innovative low-cost promotions for yourself and your clients.

Holtz, Herman. *How to Succeed As an Independent Consultant.* New York: John Wiley & Sons, 1993.

Holtz, Herman. *The Complete Guide to Being an Independent Contractor.* Chicago: Dearborn Financial Publishing, 1995.

Hotz, Herman. *Proven Proposal Strategies to Win More Business.* Chicago: Dearborn Financial Publishing, 1997.

Lant, Jeffrey. *E-Mail Eldorado.* Cambridge, Mass.: JLA Publications, 1994. Best book I've seen on generating leads and sales using direct mail on the Internet.

Lant, Jeffrey. *No More Cold Calls.* Cambridge, Mass.: JLA Publications, 1994. How to generate leads for your service business.

Muldoon, Katie. *How to Profit through Catalog Marketing.* Lincolnwood, Ill.: NTC Business Books, 1996. Recommended for anyone writing catalog copy.

Ogilvy, David. *Ogilvy on Advertising.* New York: Crown, 1989. Required reading for every copywriter writing print ads.

Parker, Roger. *Roger C. Parker's Guide to Web Content and Design.* New York: MIS Press, 1997. Best book I've ever seen on creating effective Web sites.

Reeves, Rosser. *Reality in Advertising.* New York: Alfred A. Knopf, 1985. Excellent book on how to increase advertising effectiveness.

Rosenberg, Paul. *How to Be a Successful Computer Consultant.* Englewood Cliffs, N.J.: Prentice Hall, 1995.

Ruhl, Janet. *The Computer Consultant's Guide: Real-Life Strategies for Building a Successful Consulting Career.* New York: John Wiley & Sons, 1994.

Shenson, Howard. *Shenson on Consulting.* New York: John Wiley & Sons, 1990.

Simon, Alan R. *How to Be a Successful Computer Consultant.* New York: McGraw Hill Computer Books, 1993.

Smith, Terry. *Making Successful Presentations.* New York: John Wiley & Sons, 1990. Excellent guide to writing and delivering workplace, instructional, and sales and marketing presentations.

Stone, Bob. *Successful Direct Marketing Methods.* Chicago: NTC Business Books, 1996. Everything you need to know about direct marketing.

Tepper, Ron. *Become a Top Consultant.* New York: John Wiley & Sons, 1987.

Tuller, Lawrence. *Cutting Edge Consultants.* New York: Simon & Schuster, 1992.

Vitale, Joe. *CyberWriting: How to Promote Your Product or Service Online.* New York: AMACOM, 1997. How to write copy for the Internet.

Walters, Dottie and Lilly. *Speak and Grow Rich.* Englewood Cliffs, N.J.: Prentice Hall, 1989. How to make money as a professional speaker.

Periodicals

Advertising Age
740 N. Rush Street
Chicago, IL 60611
312-649-5200

Adweek
49 E. 21st Street
New York, NY 10010
212-529-5500

The Art of Self Promotion
PO Box 23
Hoboken, NJ 07030
201-653-0783

Bits & Pieces for Salespeople
Economics Press
12 Daniel Road
Fairfield, NJ 07004
800-526-2554

Burt Dubin Private Letter
1 Speaking Success Road
Kingman, AZ 86402-6543
502-753-7531

Business Marketing
740 North Rush Street
Chicago, IL 60611
312-649-5260

Commerce Business Daily
Government Printing Office
Washington, DC 20401
202-512-0000

*Computer Consultants &
Contractors Newsletter*
Corry Publishing
2840 W. 21st Street
Erie, PA 16506
814-838-0025

The Consultant's Craft
Summit Consulting Group
PO Box 1009
East Greenwich, RI 02818
800-766-7935

Contract Professional
125 Walnut Street
Watertown, MA 02172
617-926-5818

Direct Marketing Magazine
Hoke Communications
224 Seventh Street
Garden City, NY 11530
516-746-6700

DM News
Mill Hollow
19 W. 21st Street
New York, NY 10010
212-741-2095

Executive Speechwriter Newsletter
Emerson Falls Business Park
St. Johnsbury, VT 05819
802-748-4472

Industrial Marketing Practitioner
1661 Valley Forge Road, #245
Lansdale, PA 19446
215-362-7200

Journal of Management Consulting
858 Longview Road
Burlingame, CA 94010
650-342-1954

Public Relations Journal
33 Irving Place
New York, NY 10003
212-998-2230

Sales and Marketing Management
633 Third Avenue
New York, NY 10017
212-986-4800

Sharing Ideas
PO Box 1120
Glendora, CA 92711
626-335-8069

The Successful Practice
Media Publishers, Inc.
2085 Commercial Street NE
Salem, OR 97303
503-371-1390

Target Marketing Magazine
North American Publishing Co.
401 N. Broad Street
Philadelphia, PA 19108
215-238-5300

Training & Development
1640 King Street
Alexandria, VA 22314
703-683-8100

Directories

Bacon's Publicity Checker
332 S. Michigan Avenue
Chicago, IL 60604
800-621-0561
Media lists for mailing press
releases.

*Directory of Top Computer
Executives*
Applied Computer Research
PO Box 92277
Phoenix, AZ 85071-2266
800-234-2227
Good prospecting directory for
computer consultants.

The Encyclopedia of Associations
Gale Research
Book Tower
Detroit, MI 48226
313-961-2242
Associations to whose membership
lists you can target promotions.

*The Interactive Multimedia
Sourcebook*
R.R. Bowker
121 Chanlon Road
New Providence, NJ 07974
908-464-6800
Sourcebook for marketers
interested in Internet promotion.

National Directory of Mailing Lists
Oxbridge Communications
150 Fifth Avenue
New York, NY 10114-0235
800-955-0231
Directory containing descriptions
and contact information for 15,000
mailing lists.

*O'Dwyers Directory of Public
Relations Firms*
J.R. O'Dwyer & Company, Inc.
271 Madison Avenue
New York, NY 10016
212-679-2471
Directory of public relations firms.

*Standard Directory of Advertising
Agencies*
R.R. Bowker
121 Chanlon Road
New Providence, NJ 07974
908-464-6800
Directory of advertising agencies.

Standard Rate and Data Service
1700 Higgins Road
Des Plaines, IL 60018-5605
847-375-5000
Comprehensive directory of
publications that accept advertising.

Appendix B: Software

Business Planning

BizPlan Builder Interactive
Jian Co.
800-440-5426

Business Plan Pro
Palo Alto Software
800-229-7526

Plan Write
Business Resource Software
800-423-1228

MasterPlan Professional
MAUS Business Systems
509-663-9523

Lead Tracking and Contact Management

ACT!
Symantech
800-441-7234

FastTrack
Fastech and Gelco Information
  Network
400 Parkway Drive
Broomall, PA 19008
610-359-9200

LPS
Simplified Office Systems
16025 Van Aken Boulevard,
  Suite 102
Cleveland, OH 44120
216-572-1050

MailEasy
Applied Information Group
720 King Georges Road
Fords, NJ 08863
908-738-8444

GoldMine
GoldMine Software
800-654-3526

Mail Order Manager (MOM)
Dydacomp Development
  Corporation
150 River Road, Suite N-1
Montville, NJ 07045
201-335-1256

Marketing Professional's
    InfoCenter/Smart Marketing
    Suite
Group One Software
4200 Parliament Place, Suite 600
Lanham, MD 20706
301-918-0721

Maximizer 97is
Maximizer Technologies
800-804-6299

MSM
Marketing Information Services
1840 Oak Avenue, Suite 400
Evanston, IL 60201
847-491-0682

Order Power!
Computer Solutions, Inc.
6187 NW 167th Street, Unit H33
Miami, FL 33015
305-558-7000

Postalsoft
439 Mormon Coulsee Road
LaCrosse, WI 54601
608-788-8700

Pro-Mail
Software Marketing Associates
2080 Silas Deane Highway
Rocky Hill, CT 06067-2341
860-721-8929

Profit Smart
Digital Arts LLC
1551 Valley Forge Road, Suite 259
Lansdale, PA 19446-5459
215-361-2650

TeleMagic
800-835-MAGIC

Appendix C: Forms

Form for Recording Data on Sales Leads

Date _____ Source of inquiry _____ Response via _____

Name _____ Title _____

Company _____ Phone _____

Address _____ Room/Floor _____

City _____ State _____ Zip _____

Type of business:

Type of accounts (if an ad agency):

Type of projects:

For: ❒ immediate   ❒ future reference

❒ project to be started in: _____
                                        (month/year)

STATUS:

❒ Sent package on (date): _____

❒ Enclosed these samples: _____

❒ Next step is to: _____

❒ Probability of assignment: _____

❒ COMMENTS: _____

_____

_____

CONTACT RECORD:

Date: _____ Summary: _____

Date: _____ Summary: _____

Date: _____ Summary: _____

Date: _____ Summary: _____

Form for Tracking Ad Response

Month _____   Year _____

Ad or mailing _____   Key code _____

Product _____   Offer _____

Total Cost _____   Total sales _____

Day	# Inquiries	Total Inquiries To Date	Day's Sales	Total Sales To Date
31				
32				
33				
34				
35				
36				
37				
38				
39				
40				
41				
42				
43				
44				
45				
46				
47				
48				
49				
50				

Day	# Inquiries	Total Inquiries To Date	Day's Sales	Total Sales To Date
51				
52				
53				
54				
55				
56				
57				
58				
59				
60				
61				

Insertion Order

Use this insertion order form to place lead-generating classified and space ads in appropriate media. By establishing yourself as an "agency," you will often be granted the 15 percent ad agency commission. This saves you 15 percent on the cost of the ad space. When copying the form, insert your own company name and address at the top.

ADVERTISING INSERTION ORDER

From:

ABC Ad Agency
Anytown, USA
phone XXX-XXX-XXXX

Date:

Advertiser:

Product:

To:

Publication in which ad is to run: _____

Date of insertion: _____

Size of ad: _____

Instructions:

Rate: _____

Less frequency discount _____%

Less agency commission _____% on gross

Less cash discount _____% on net

Net amount on this insertion order: _____

Insertion order placed by: _____

Form for Copyright Registration

FORM TX
For a Nondramatic Literary Work
UNITED STATES COPYRIGHT OFFICE

REGISTRATION NUMBER

_____

TX _____ TXU _____
EFFECTIVE DATE OF REGISTRATION

Month _____ Day _____ Year _____

DO NOT WRITE ABOVE THIS LINE. IF YOU NEED MORE SPACE, USE A SEPARATE CONTINUATION SHEET.

1

TITLE OF THIS WORK ▼

PREVIOUS OR ALTERNATIVE TITLES ▼

PUBLICATION AS A CONTRIBUTION If this work was published as a contribution to a periodical, serial, or collection, give information about the collective work in which the contribution appeared.   **Title of Collective Work ▼**

If published in a periodical or serial give: Volume ▼   Number ▼   Issue Date ▼   On Pages ▼

2 **a**

NAME OF AUTHOR ▼

DATES OF BIRTH AND DEATH
Year Born ▼   Year Died ▼

Was this contribution to the work a "work made for hire"?
☐ Yes
☐ No

AUTHOR'S NATIONALITY OR DOMICILE
Name of Country
OR { Citizen of ▶ _____
Domiciled in ▶ _____

WAS THIS AUTHOR'S CONTRIBUTION TO THE WORK
Anonymous?   ☐ Yes ☐ No
Pseudonymous?   ☐ Yes ☐ No
If the answer to either of these questions is "Yes," see detailed instructions.

NATURE OF AUTHORSHIP Briefly describe nature of material created by this author in which copyright is claimed. ▼

NOTE

Under the law, the "author" of a "work made for hire" is generally the employer, not the employee (see instructions). For any part of this work that was "made for hire" check "Yes" in the space provided, give the employer (or other person for whom the work was prepared) as "Author" of that part, and leave the space for dates of birth and death blank.

b

NAME OF AUTHOR ▼

DATES OF BIRTH AND DEATH
Year Born ▼   Year Died ▼

Was this contribution to the work a "work made for hire"?
☐ Yes
☐ No

AUTHOR'S NATIONALITY OR DOMICILE
Name of Country
OR { Citizen of ▶ _____
Domiciled in ▶ _____

WAS THIS AUTHOR'S CONTRIBUTION TO THE WORK
Anonymous?   ☐ Yes ☐ No
Pseudonymous?   ☐ Yes ☐ No
If the answer to either of these questions is "Yes," see detailed instructions.

NATURE OF AUTHORSHIP Briefly describe nature of material created by this author in which copyright is claimed. ▼

c

NAME OF AUTHOR ▼

DATES OF BIRTH AND DEATH
Year Born ▼   Year Died ▼

Was this contribution to the work a "work made for hire"?
☐ Yes
☐ No

AUTHOR'S NATIONALITY OR DOMICILE
Name of Country
OR { Citizen of ▶ _____
Domiciled in ▶ _____

WAS THIS AUTHOR'S CONTRIBUTION TO THE WORK
Anonymous?   ☐ Yes ☐ No
Pseudonymous?   ☐ Yes ☐ No
If the answer to either of these questions is "Yes," see detailed instructions.

NATURE OF AUTHORSHIP Briefly describe nature of material created by this author in which copyright is claimed. ▼

3 **a**

YEAR IN WHICH CREATION OF THIS WORK WAS COMPLETED   This information must be given ◀Year in all cases.

b DATE AND NATION OF FIRST PUBLICATION OF THIS PARTICULAR WORK
Complete this information ONLY if this work has been published.   Month▶ _____ Day▶ _____ Year▶ _____
◀ Nation

4

See instructions before completing this space.

COPYRIGHT CLAIMANT(S) Name and address must be given even if the claimant is the same as the author given in space 2. ▼

TRANSFER If the claimant(s) named here in space 4 is (are) different from the author(s) named in space 2, give a brief statement of how the claimant(s) obtained ownership of the copyright. ▼

APPLICATION RECEIVED

ONE DEPOSIT RECEIVED

TWO DEPOSITS RECEIVED

FUNDS RECEIVED

DO NOT WRITE HERE OFFICE USE ONLY

MORE ON BACK ▶ • Complete all applicable spaces (numbers 5-9) on the reverse side of this page.
• See detailed instructions.   • Sign the form at line 8.

DO NOT WRITE HERE
Page 1 of _____ pages

EXAMINED BY	FORM TX
CHECKED BY	

| CORRESPONDENCE ☐ Yes | FOR COPYRIGHT OFFICE USE ONLY |

DO NOT WRITE ABOVE THIS LINE. IF YOU NEED MORE SPACE, USE A SEPARATE CONTINUATION SHEET.

PREVIOUS REGISTRATION Has registration for this work, or for an earlier version of this work, already been made in the Copyright Office?
☐ Yes ☐ No If your answer is "Yes," why is another registration being sought? (Check appropriate box) ▼
a. ☐ This is the first published edition of a work previously registered in unpublished form.
b. ☐ This is the first application submitted by this author as copyright claimant.
c. ☐ This is a changed version of the work, as shown by space 6 on this application.
If your answer is "Yes," give: **Previous Registration Number** ▼   **Year of Registration** ▼

5

DERIVATIVE WORK OR COMPILATION
a Preexisting Material Identify any preexisting work or works that this work is based on or incorporates . ▼

b Material Added to This Work Give a brief, general statement of the material that has been added to this work and in which copyright is claimed . ▼

6

See instructions before completing this space.

DEPOSIT ACCOUNT If the registration fee is to be charged to a Deposit Account established in the Copyright Office, give name and number of Account.
a Name ▼   Account Number ▼

7

CORRESPONDENCE Give name and address to which correspondence about this application should be sent.   Name/Address/Apt/City/State /ZIP ▼
b

Area code and daytime telephone number▶   Fax number ▶
Email ▶

CERTIFICATION* I, the undersigned, hereby certify that I am the
Check only one ▶
☐ author
☐ other copyright claimant
☐ owner of exclusive right(s)
☐ authorized agent of _____
of the work identified in this application and that the statements made by me in this application are correct to the best of my knowledge.
Name of author or other copyright claimant, or owner of exclusive right(s)▲

8

Typed or printed name and date ▼ If this application gives a date of publication in space 3, do not sign and submit it before that date.
_____ Date ▶ _____

Handwritten signature (X) ▼
X _____

Mail certificate to:	Name ▼	• Complete all necessary spaces • Sign your application in space 8
Certificate will be mailed in window envelope	Number/Street/Apt ▼	1. Application form 2. Nonrefundable filing fee in check or money order payable to *Register of Copyrights* 3. Deposit material
	City/State/ZIP ▼	Library of Congress Copyright Office 101 Independence Avenue, S.E. Washington, D.C. 20559-6000

9

*17 U.S.C. § 506(e): Any person who knowingly makes a false representation of a material fact in the application for copyright registration provided for by section 409, or in any written statement filed in connection with the application, shall be fined not more than $2,500.
September 1997—300,000   ♲ PRINTED ON RECYCLED PAPER   ☆U.S. COPYRIGHT OFFICE WWW: March 1998

Telemarketing Call Sheets

Date _____   Telemarketer Name _____

ABC Consulting Company
Prospect Data Sheet

Name _____   Title _____

Company _____

Street Address _____

City, State, Zip _____

Phone _____   Fax _____

E-Mail _____

Call Attempts:

Date _____   Time _____   Date _____   Time_____

Date _____   Time _____   Date _____   Time_____

Contact:

❏ Prospect Busy. Call Back On _____ At _____ (Day, Time)

    Best Time To Call _____ (Time of Day)

❏ Long-Term Call Back During _____ Of _____ (Month, Year)

❏ Phone Presentation Made On _____ (Month, Day, Year)

❏ Left Message To Return Call

Action:

❏ Appointment Set For _____ At _____ (Month, Day, Time)

❏ Referral Given:

    _____

    _____

❏ Not Interested. Reason:

    _____

    _____

Current Company Information:

Number of Employees _____

Types of Services Needed: _____

Date _____   Telemarketer Name _____

ABC Consulting Company Daily Activity Sheet

Outbound Calls

# of Dials _____

# of Busy Signals _____

# of Voice Mail Messages _____

# of Call Backs Scheduled _____

# of Presentations _____

# of Literature Sent _____

# of Appts. Booked _____

No Interest _____

Referrals Given _____

Inbound Calls

# of Query Calls _____

# of Presentations _____

# of Literature Sent _____

# of Appts. Booked _____

Appendix D:
Organizations and Conferences

American Consultants League
1290 Palm Avenue
Sarasota, FL 34236
813-952-9290

American Seminar Leaders
  Association
101 Providence Mine Road,
  Suite 105
Nevada City, CA 95959
800-735-0511

American Society of Training &
  Development
1640 King Street
Alexandria, VA 22314
703-683-8100

Business Marketing Association
150 North Wacker Drive,
  Suite 1760
Chicago, IL 60606
312-409-4262

The Consultants Bureau
PO Box 10057
New Brunswick, NJ 08906-0057
908-747-5786

Consultants National Resource
  Center
27-A Big Spring Road
PO Box 430
Clear Spring, MD 21722
301-791-9332

Consultants' Network
57 W. 89th Street
New York, NY 10024
212-799-5239

Direct Marketing Association
1120 Avenue of the Americas
New York, NY 10036-6700
212-768-7277

Business to Business Direct
  Marketing Conference
Box 4232
Stamford, CT 06907-0232
203-358-9900

Direct Marketing to Business
  Target Conference Corporation
90 Grove Street
Ridgefield, CT 06877
203-438-6602

Independent Computer Consultants
  Association
933 Gardenview Office Parkway
St. Louis, MO 63141
900-774-4222

Institute of Management
  Consultants
521 Fifth Avenue, 35th floor
New York, NY 10175-3598
212-697-8262

National Association of Business
  Consultants
175 Fifth Avenue, #2158
New York, NY 10010
800-571-6222

National Association of Computer
  Consultant Businesses
1250 Connecticut Avenue NW,
  Suite 700
Washington, DC 20036
202-637-6483

National Association of Personal
  Financial Advisors
355 W. Dundee Road, Suite 200
Buffalo Grove, IL 60089
888-333-6659

National Association of
  Management Consultants
4200 Wisconsin NW, #106
Washington DC 20016
202-466-1601

National Speakers Association
1500 S. Priest Drive
Tempe, AZ 85281
602-968-2552

Professional and Technical
  Consultants Association
PO Box 4143
Mountain View, CA 94040
800-286-8703

Toastmasters International
PO Box 9052
Mission Viejo, CA 92609
714-858-8255

Walters International Speakers
  Bureau
PO Box 1120
Glendora, CA 91740
818-335-8069

Appendix E:
Recommended Vendors

To accomplish some of the tasks outlined in this book, you may want to work with outside vendors. This list is by no means comprehensive—it simply lists the vendors I recommend in each category. A recommendation doesn't guarantee your satisfaction, so you should check out vendors thoroughly before hiring them.

Radio Commercials

Chuck Hengel
Marketing Architects
14550 Excelsior Boulevard
Minneapolis, MN 55345
612-936-7500

Business Plans

Lisa Hines
Business Plan Concepts
134 Oaklyn Terrace
Lawrenceville, NJ 08648
609-530-0719

Premiums and Incentives

Nelson Marketing
210 Commerce Street
PO Box 320
Oshkosh, WI 54902-0320
800-982-9159

Perrygraf Slide Charts
19365 Business Center Drive
Northridge, CA 91324-3552
800-423-5329

Translations

Harvard Translations
137 Newbury Street
Boston, MA 02116
617-424-9291

Market Research

Terrence J. Pranses
Pranses Research Services
40 Willow Terrace
Hoboken, NJ 07030-2813
201-659-2475

Peter Fondulas
Taylor Research & Consulting
6 Glenville St.
Greenwich, CT 06831
203-532-0202

Maury S. Kauffman
The Kauffman Group
324 Windsor Drive
Cherry Hill, NJ 08002-2426
609-482-8288

Media Buying

Media Planners, Inc.
Linick Building, PO Box 102
Middle Island, NY 11953-0102
516-924-8759

PowerPoint Presentations

Prime Time Staffing
1250 E. Ridgewood Avenue
Ridgewood, NJ 07450
201-612-0303

Bonnie Blake, Mary Cicitta
Design On Disk
400 River Road, 2nd Floor
New Milford, NJ 07646
516-694-1919

Telemarketing

Frank Stetz
240 E. 82nd Street, 20th floor
New York, NY 10028
212-439-1777

Grace Software Marketing
3091 Mayfield Road
Cleveland, OH 44118
216-321-2000

Mariann Weinstein
MAW Associates
115 N. 10th Street
New Hyde Park, NY 11040
516-437-0529

On-Hold Advertising Messages

Fred Guarino
Tikki
186 Glen Cove Avenue
Glen Cove, NY 11542
516-671-4555

On-Hold Marketing
4910 Urbandale Avenue
Des Moines, IA
800-259-2769

Fax Marketing

Sarah E. Stambler
Marketing with Technology
370 Central Park West, #210
New York, NY 10025-6517
212-222-1713

Web Page Design

Jason Petefish
Silver Star Productions
21 Wilwood Road
Katonah, NY 10536
914-232-5363

Kent Martin
Network Creative
104 Mountain Avenue
Gilette, NJ 07930
908-903-9090

Barry Fox
FoxTek
49 West Street
Northport, NY 11768
516-754-4304

Direct Mail Graphic Design

David Bsales
David Bsales Design
16 W. Palisade Avenue, #206
Englewood, NJ 07631
201-567-1474

Lucien Cohen
1201 Broadway, #403
New York, NY 10001
212-685-7455

Bob McCarron
MCom Communications
15 East 12th Street, 2nd Floor
New York, NY 10003
212-645-7554

Elaine Tannenbaum
Elaine Tannenbeaum Design
310 West 106th Street, Apt. 16D
New York, NY 10025
212-769-2096

Mailing Lists

Steve Roberts
Edith Roman
PO Box 1556
Pearl River, NY 10965
800-223-2194

Ralph Drybrough
Direct Media
200 Pemberwick Road
Greenwich, CT 06830
203-532-1000

Ken Morris
Morris Direct Marketing
300 West 55th Street, #19D
New York, NY 10019
212-757-7711

Letter Shop

Jerry Lake
Jerry Lake Mailing Service
Airport Industrial Park
620 Frelinghuysen Avenue
Newark, NJ 07114
201-967-5644

Mitch Hisiger
Fala Direct Marketing
70 Marcus Drive
Melville, NY 11747
516-694-1919

Don Levin
Levin Public Relations
30 Glenn Street
White Plains, NY 10603
914-993-0900

Pocket Folders and Binders

Jeff Becker
Clients First
90 Elm Street
Westfield, NJ 07090
908-232-1200

Project and Traffic Management

Grant Faurot
92 Glendale Street
Nutley, NJ 07110
201-661-5074

Graphic Design, Brochures

Paul Spadafora
Park Ridge Marketing
1776 On The Green
67 Park Place
Morristown, NJ 07960
201-984-2622

Steve Brown
Brown & Company
138 Joralemon Street, #4R
Brooklyn, NY 11201
718-875-0674

Library Research

John Maddux
2665 Leda Court
Cincinnati, OH 45211
513-662-9176

Bob Concoby
PO Box 754
Kent, OH 44240
330-494-5504 ext. 814
330-677-8085

Custom Calendars

Judith Roth
Judith Roth Studios
3 Stone House Road
Mendham, NJ 07945
201-543-4455

Public Relations Agencies

Mark Bruce
GHB Marketing Communications
1177 High Ridge Road
Stamford, CT 06905
203-321-1242

Photographers

Jonathan Clymer
Jonathan Clymer Photography
180-F Central Avenue
Englewood, NJ 07631
201-568-1760

Phil Degginger
Degginger Photography
9 Evans Farm Road
Morristown, NJ 07960
201-455-1733

Bruce Goldsmith
Bruce Goldsmith Photography
1 Clayton Court
Park Ridge, NJ 07656
201-391-4946

Audiotaping

Mike Moe
Moe Company
133 Deerfield Road
Sayreville, NJ 08872
908-257-3760

Digital Printing

Paul Lukas, Account Executive
Regent Group
20 West 20th Street
New York, NY 10011
212-691-9791

Trademark Searches

Thomson & Thomson
800-692-8833

Direct Mail Printers

KoBel, Inc.
115 Catamount Drive, #102
Milton, VT 05468
800-893-6000

Proofreading

Debra Godfrey
Godfrey Editorial Services
3 Rush Court
Plainsboro, NJ 08536
609-936-0753
dgodfrey@prodigy.net

Infomercials

Robert A. Klayman
Beverly Hills, CA 90210
213-937-0915

Literary Agents

B. K. Nelson
84 Woodland
Pleasantville, NY 10570
914-741-1323

Tony Seidl
TD Media
515 East 79th Street, #16C
New York, NY 10021
212-734-3807

Appendix F:
Sample Documents

Sample Virus Protection Policy

Send a memo to new and existing clients explaining the steps you take to ensure that files you send them are not contaminated by viruses.

TO: All clients and potential clients

FROM: Bob Bly
Center for Technical Communication
22 E. Quackenbush Avenue
Dumont, NJ 07628
201-385-1220

RE: Our anti-virus policy

LAST UPDATED: 10-13-97

filename: VPOL

1. We make every effort to ensure that files sent to our clients via e-mail or disk are virus-free—but we CANNOT guarantee it.
2. We run McAfee 3.5 VirusScan, which is the most widely used anti-virus program worldwide. It is used by 25 million people, 80 percent of the Fortune 1000, and 40,000 organizations.
3. According to McAfee, VirusScan technology has been shown in lab tests to detect virtually every virus. These include boot, file, multi-parties, stealth, mutating, encrypted, and polymorphic viruses.
4. Because new viruses crop up all the time, we routinely upgrade our VirusScan program by downloading the latest versions from the McAfee BBS (bulletin board). We recommend that clients running VirusScan do likewise.

---

5. Even running the latest anti-virus software cannot guarantee a virus-free file, because new viruses are launched constantly. Clients should run the most recent version of their anti-virus software before downloading or receiving e-mail.

6. If you open a file we sent you via e-mail and it contains a virus, that does NOT mean the virus came from our end. Files sent via the Internet can pick up viruses in transit.

7. The only 100 percent foolproof protection against receiving a virus is to request that documents be faxed instead of e-mailed. You can't pick up a virus from a hard copy.

8. If you have any problems with a virus in a file we send you, please notify us immediately: 201-385-1220. If you are having a virus problem in general, we can refer you to computer consultants who may be able to help.

Thanks,

BOB BLY

One-Page Course Description for an In-House Corporate Training Seminar

Persuasive Presentations Skills for Technical Professionals

Making technical sales presentations is a difficult task. Often the audience is diverse, consisting of listeners at many different levels of technical competence with different interests and objectives. Your challenge is to deliver the technical "meat" to the hardcore techies while giving less technical listeners the bottom-line information they need to make a decision in your favor. On top of that, many technical professionals are uncomfortable speaking before groups, making the task even tougher.

This seminar shows technical professionals how to make team and customer presentations that get their message across, build their credibility as an authority in the topic, and get the audience to trust them and want to do business with them. You'll discover how to make even the most seemingly boring subjects come alive for listeners by finding and focusing on the "kernel of interest" that connects their needs with the subject matter.

Contents:

- Determining the exact topic of your talk
- Researching your subject matter beyond your own knowledge
- Organizing your material for maximum audience interest and appeal
- Grabbing and keeping your audience's attention
- Determining—in advance—what the audience needs and wants to hear from you
- Getting the audience to "buy into" your approach, technology, system, or solution
- Creating, finding, and using visual aids that enhance rather than detract from your talk
- Determining what materials you should hand out—and when
- Positioning the audience to take the next step
- Answering questions—especially when you don't know the answer
- Overcoming stage fright and gaining comfort and confidence when speaking to groups
- Communicating one-on-one with your audience
- Offering advanced tips to boost your presentation quality to the next level—quickly and easily

Length of Program: 1 or 2 days

CTC, 22 E. Quackenbush Avenue, Dumont, NJ 07628, 201-385-1220

Sample Client Satisfaction Survey (Post-Assignment)

TO: Clients

FROM: Bob Bly

RE: Performance evaluation

filename: Survey1

Dear Valued Client:

Would you please take a minute to complete and return this brief questionnaire to me? (Doing so is optional, of course.) It would help me serve you better—and ensure that you get the level of quality and service you want on every job. Thanks!

1. How would you rate the quality of the final draft of the copy I wrote for you?

   ❏ Excellent ❏ Very good ❏ Good ❏ Fair ❏ Poor

2. What overall rating would you give my copywriting services?

   ❏ Excellent ❏ Very good ❏ Good ❏ Fair ❏ Poor

3. How would you rate the value received compared with the fee you paid?

   ❏ Excellent ❏ Very good ❏ Good ❏ Fair ❏ Poor

4. What did you like best about my service? _____

5. What would you like to see improved?_____

Your name (optional): _____

Company _____

Please return this form to:

Bob Bly
22 E. Quackenbush Avenue
Dumont, NJ 07628
fax: 201-385-1138
phone: 201-385-1220
e-mail: rwbly@bly.com

Memo to Clients Advising Them That You Are Going on Vacation

TO: Clients and prospects

FROM: Carolyn Mazza, assistant to Bob Bly

RE: April schedule

filename: 3-20-98

Bob Bly will be out of the office traveling April 21–25. He will be in touch with the office via voice mail. The office will be open during this period, and if you need anything, you can leave a voice mail for Bob at 201-385-1220, or call me directly at 201-703-8860. Let me know if you have any questions or need additional information.

Sample Lead-Generating Letter: In-house Corporate Training Seminar

Important News for Every Systems Professional Who Has Ever Felt Like Telling an End-User, "Go to Hell. . . ."

Dear IS Manager:

It's ironic.

Today's users demand to be treated as *customers* of IS.

Yet many systems professionals don't have the customer service skills to make the relationship work.

Our training program, "Interpersonal Skills for IS Professionals," solves that problem—by giving IS staff the skills they need to deal effectively with end-users and top management in today's service-oriented corporate environment.

Presented jointly by The Center for Technical Communication and The Communication Workshop—two leaders in teaching "soft skills" to technical professionals—"Interpersonal Skills for IS Professionals" quickly brings your team to a new level in listening, negotiating, teamwork, customer service, and other vital skills for communicating complex systems ideas and technical processes to managers and end-users.

Many leading companies—including IBM, AT&T, Symbol Technologies, Price Waterhouse, Cigna, American Airlines, Lever Brothers, Barnett Technologies, First Union, and Turner Broadcasting—count on us to help their technical professionals communicate more effectively and work more productively. You can too.

For more information, including an outline of our "Interpersonal Skills for IS Professionals" program, just complete and mail the enclosed reply card. Or call (516) 767-9590. You'll be glad you did.

Sincerely,

Gary Blake, Ph.D., Director

P.S. Reply now and we'll also send you a FREE copy of our new tip sheet, "The IS Professional's Guide to Improving Listening Skills." It will help everyone in your department gain a quicker, more accurate understanding of what users want, while helping to transform your customers from uninitiated "end-users" into "educated consumers" who are easier and more reasonable to deal with.

(reply card)

YES, I'm interested in learning more about your on-site seminars in:

❐ "Interpersonal Skills for IS Professionals"

❐ "Technical Writing for Systems Professionals"

Name _____ Title _____

Company _____ Phone _____

Address _____

City _____ State _____ Zip _____

❐ Call me now. *Number of people requiring training:* _____

❐ Call me in _____
(month/year)

For immediate information, call 516-767-9590

Or fax this card to 516-883-4006

Sample Lead-Generating Letter: Selling Training Seminar to a Niche Market

Dear «Title» «LastName»:

Your claims professionals are always on the firing line. They write important letters to the insured, attorneys, doctors, and other insurance companies. If those letters are ambiguous, vague, disorganized, or don't get to the point, your company could be in jeopardy. Customers may be lost—and so may court cases.

Last month, I ran four seminars in "Effective Business Writing for Claims Professionals" at Farm Bureau Insurance in Lansing, Michigan. According to Susan Earley, Claims Training Analyst, "Because of our sessions with you . . . we are going to conduct a review of our form letters. Also, as our claims adjusters compose letters, their words will be friendlier and more clear to the person they're intended for—the reader!"

Couldn't your claims professionals benefit from writing better denial letters? Reservation-of-rights letters? Letters to insurance companies, doctors, and attorneys in which gaining specific information is vital?

I'm Gary Blake, and I'd like to help your claims professionals write better and faster. You may have seen my articles and ads in *Claims Magazine*. Over the past 15 years, I've run writing seminars at more than 50 insurance companies, including Blue Cross/Blue Shield of Florida, Equitable, Maryland Casualty, and Liberty Mutual. By booking a one-day seminar, you'd be going a long way toward helping every claims adjuster, examiner, and representative in your department write better, be more productive, and keep more customers.

Sound interesting? If you'd like to learn more about how your department can benefit from this seminar, please call me at 516-767-9590, or return the enclosed card.

Sincerely,

Gary Blake, Director

This seminar is *completely customized* to claims professionals. Call me now and I'll send you my FREE "Eight Tips on Writing Better Claims Letters."

Sample Lead-Generating Letter: Consulting Services

Dear Marketing Professional:

"It's hard to find a copywriter who can handle industrial and high-tech accounts," a prospect told me over the phone today. "Especially for brochures, direct mail, and other long-copy assignments."

Do you have that same problem?

If so, please complete and mail the enclosed reply card, and I'll send you a free information kit describing a service that can help.

As a freelance copywriter specializing in business-to-business marketing, I've written hundreds of successful ads, sales letters, direct mail packages, brochures, data sheets, annual reports, feature articles, press releases, newsletters, and audio-visual scripts for clients all over the country.

But my information kit will give you the full story.

You'll receive a comprehensive "WELCOME" letter that tells all about my copywriting service—who I work for, what I can do for you, how we can work together.

You'll also get my client list (I've written copy for more than 100 corporations and agencies); client testimonials; biographical background; samples of work I've done in your field; a fee schedule listing what I charge for ads, brochures, and other assignments; helpful article reprints on copywriting and advertising; even an order form you can use to put me to work for you.

Whether you have an immediate project, a future need, or are just curious, I urge you to send for this information kit. It's free—there's no obligation— and you'll like having a proven copywriting resource on file—someone you can call on whenever you need him.

From experience, I've learned that the best time to evaluate a copywriter and take a look at his work is *before* you need him, not when a project deadline comes crashing around the corner. You want to feel comfortable about a writer and his capabilities in advance, so when a project does come up, you know who to call.

Why not mail back the reply card TODAY, while it is still handy? I'll rush your free information kit as soon as I hear from you.

Regards,

Bob Bly

P.S. Need an immediate quote on a copywriting project? Call me at 201-385-1220. There is no charge for a cost estimate. And no obligation to buy.

Sample Memo Outlining Monthly Retainer Arrangement for Consulting Services

TO: Victoria Glickman, Alpha Software

via e-mail

cc. Richard Rosen, Doug Ross, Ilise Benun

RE: A possible arrangement for handling Alpha's ongoing
         copywriting and consulting requirements

FROM: Bob Bly, phone 201-385-1220

DATE: 10-10-97

filename: VGMEM2

Dear Victoria:

Ilise mentioned that you folks perceive an ongoing need for copywriting, rewriting, editing, and consulting on numerous smaller projects with quick turnarounds.

Our typical arrangement is a monthly retainer for one day's time at our current rate of $1,600. We find that's a sufficient amount of time to handle requirements of this type. Larger, stand-alone projects (such as our two upcoming mailings) are quoted separately.

Retainer clients get 24 to 48 hour turnaround with no rush charges and priority in handling their retainer assignments. If I spend more than a full day in a month on your work, you do NOT get charged extra, as long as my time on your account *averages* one day a month. If you regularly require more or less service, we can talk about adjusting the monthly fee upward or downward accordingly.

There is no advance payment required. At the end of each month, you're billed the month's fee net 30 days. You can cancel at any time, and just have to pay for the time spent to date that month.

Does this work for you? We look forward to continuing this conversation.

Sample Press Release

FROM: Bob Bly, 174 Holland Avenue, New Milford, NJ 07646

CONTACT: Bob Bly 201-385-1220

For immediate release

NEW BOOKLET REVEALS 14 PROVEN STRATEGIES FOR KEEPING BUSINESSES BOOMING IN A BUST ECONOMY

New Milford, NJ—While some companies struggle to survive in today's sluggish business environment, many are doing better than ever largely because they have mastered the proven but little known strategies of "recession marketing."

That's the opinion of Bob Bly, an independent marketing consultant and author of the just published booklet, "Recession Proof Business Strategies: 14 Winning Methods to Sell Any Product or Service in a Down Economy."

"Many business people fear a recession or soft economy, because when the economy is weak, their clients and customers cut back on spending," says Bly. "To survive in such a marketplace, you need to develop recession marketing strategies that help you retain your current accounts and keep those customers buying. You also need to master marketing techniques that will win you new clients or customers to replace any business you may have lost because of the increased competition that is typical of a recession."

Among the recession-fighting business strategies Bly outlines in his new booklet:

- *Reactivate dormant accounts.* An easy way to get more business is to simply call past clients or customers—people you served at one time but are not actively working for now—to remind them of your existence. According to Bly, a properly scripted telephone call to a list of past buyers will generate approximately one order for every ten calls.
- *Quote reasonable affordable fees and prices in competitive bid situations.* While you need not reduce your rates or prices, in competitive bid situations you will win by bidding toward the low end or middle of your price range rather than at the high end. Bly says that during a recession, your bids should be 15 to 20 percent lower than you would normally charge in a healthy economy.

- *Give your existing clients and customers a superior level of service.* In a recession, Bly advises businesses to do everything they can to hold onto their existing clients or customers—their "bread-and-butter" accounts. "The best way to hold onto your clients or customers is to please them," says Bly, "and the best way to please them is through better customer service. Now is an ideal time to provide that little bit of extra service or courtesy that can mean the difference between dazzling the client or customer and merely satisfying them."
- *Reactivate old leads.* Most businesses give up on sales leads too early, says Bly. He cites a study from Thomas Publishing which found that although 80 percent of sales to businesses are made on the fifth call, only one out of ten salespeople calls beyond three times. Concludes Bly: "You have probably not followed up on leads diligently enough, and the new business you need may already be right in your prospect files." He says repeated follow-up should convert 10 percent of prospects to buyers.

To receive a copy of Bly's booklet, "Recession Proof Business Strategies," send $8 ($7 plus $1 shipping and handling) to: Bob Bly, Dept. 109, 174 Holland Avenue, New Milford, NJ 07646. Cash, money orders, and checks (payable to "Bob Bly") accepted. (Add $1 for Canadian orders.)

Bob Bly, an independent copywriter and consultant based in New Milford, NJ, specializes in business-to-business, hi-tech, and direct response marketing. He is the author of 18 books, including *How to Promote Your Own Business* (New American Library) and *The Copywriter's Handbook* (Henry Holt). A frequent speaker and seminar leader, Mr. Bly speaks nationwide on the topic of how to market successfully in a recession or soft economy.

Sample Article Query Letter

You can promote yourself by publishing how-to and informational articles related to commercial writing in trade and business magazines read by your potential clients. To propose an article to an editor, use a query letter. The sample query below got me an assignment to write an article on letter-writing for Amtrak Express magazine—they even paid me $400!

Mr. James A. Frank, Editor
Amtrak Express
34 East 51st St.
New York, NY 10022

Dear Mr. Frank:

Is this letter a waste of paper?

Yes—*if* it fails to get the desired result.

In business, most letters and memos are written to generate a specific response: close a sale, set up a meeting, get a job interview, make a contact. Many of these letters fail to do their job.

Part of the problem is that business executives and support staff don't know how to write persuasively. The solution is a formula first discovered by advertising copywriters—a formula called AIDA. AIDA stands for Attention, Interest, Desire, Action.

First, the letter gets attention with a hard hitting lead paragraph that goes straight to the point, or offers an element of intrigue.

Then, the letter hooks the reader's interest. The hook is often a clear statement of the reader's problems, his needs, his concerns. If you are writing to a customer who received damaged goods, state the problem. And then promise a solution.

Next, create desire. You are offering something—a service, a product, an agreement, a contract, a compromise, a consultation. Tell the reader the benefit he'll receive from your offering. Create a desire for your product.

Finally, call for action. Ask for the order, the signature, the check, the assignment.

I'd like to write a 1,500 word article on "How to Write Letters That Get Results." The piece will illustrate the AIDA formula with a variety of actual letters and memos from insurance companies, banks, manufacturers, and other organizations.

This letter, too, was written to get a specific result—an article assignment from the editor of Amtrak Express.

Did it succeed?

Regards,

Bob Bly

P.S. By way of introduction, I'm an advertising consultant and the author of five books including *Technical Writing: Structure, Standards, and Style* (McGraw-Hill).

Sample Pitch Letter to Get Speaking Engagements

Another excellent way to market yourself is by giving talks and speeches to groups of advertising and marketing professionals. Here's a model query letter you can use to generate such engagements.

Ms. Jane Smiley
Program Director
Women in Engineering
Big City, USA

Dear Ms. Smiley:

Did you know that, according to a recent survey in *Engineering Today,* the ability to write clearly and concisely can mean $100,000 extra in earnings over the lifetime of an engineer's career?

For this reason, I think your members might enjoy a presentation I have given to several business organizations around town "10 Ways to Improve Your Technical Writing."

As the director of Plain Language, Inc., a company that specializes in technical documentation, I have worked with hundreds of engineers to help them improve their writing. My presentation highlights the 10 most common writing mistakes engineers make, and gives strategies for self-improvement.

Does this sound like the type of presentation that might fit well into your winter program schedule? I'd be delighted to speak before your group. Please phone or write so we can set a date.

Regards,

Blake Garibaldi, Director
Plain Language, Inc.

Letter to Answer Queries from Nonprospects

As you spend time in this field, you will get inquiries from other consultants, wanna-be consultants, small businesses asking for free advice, and other nonprospects. I use this letter to respond to all these inquiries without having to make a phone call or write a personal letter.

I REALLY HATE SENDING YOU THIS LETTER, BUT . . .

Dear Colleague:

I like sending form letters even less than you like getting them. But sometimes, it's necessary.

For example, I get enough calls and letters requiring a response that, if I were to personally answer them all, I'd have no time to get my work done. So rather than not answer at all, I've prepared this form response. Let's see if I can help you this way.

If you're like most of the people getting this letter, you're one of the following:

- A businessperson with questions about marketing and selling your products and services
- A writer seeking help getting published or getting clients

If this describes you, the information you need is available in one of three ways.

1. *Publications.* Chances are the information you want is already in one of my books, reprints, or audio tapes. A publications catalog with order form is enclosed.
2. *Quick phone chats.* I charge $200 an hour for my time. I'll gladly give you 5 minutes on the phone at no charge—but I can't set appointments for these chats. Call me at 201-385-1220—and if I'm there, we'll talk. If I'm not, leave a number where I can call you back collect.
3. *Paid consultations.* If your problem requires more in-depth consultation, it's available on a limited basis for $200 an hour. However, I'm often booked to capacity, so my preference would be to have a quick no-charge chat or guide you to the appropriate book or report.

Thanks so much for writing. Let me know how else I can help you.

Sincerely,

Bob Bly

P.S. If there is any material enclosed with this letter in addition to my publications catalog, I sent it to you—at no cost—because I thought, based on your letter or call to me, that the information would be helpful to you. Enjoy!

Sample Ads

You can run ads promoting your consulting services in local business magazines, association newsletters, advertising trade publications, and other media. Classified or small display ads (1- or 2-inch) work best. Here are some of the more successful ads I have run over the years.

I Write Ads!

Over 75 corporations and ad agencies count on my crisp, accurate, hard sell copy for ads, brochures, direct mail, PR, and A/V scripts. High-tech, industrial, and business-to-business advertising my specialty. Call or write for free information kit: Bob Bly, 22 E. Quackenbush Avenue, Dumont, NJ 07628, 201-385-1220.

Call the High-Tech Copy Pro

I specialize in industrial and high-tech copy: computers, electronics, chemicals, software, telecommunications, heavy equipment, banking, health care, corporate, and many other products and services. To receive full details by mail, call today. Bob Bly 201-385-1220.

Improve Your Direct Marketing Results!
Send for Free Report . . .

I specialize in writing lead-getting sales letters, DM packages, and ads for high-tech and business-to-business clients and agencies. For FREE report, "23 Tips for Creating Business-to-Business Mailings That Work," phone or write: Bob Bly, 22 E. Quackenbush Avenue, Dumont, NJ 07628, 201-385-1220. Also ask for a free information kit on my copywriting services.

Sample Generic Agreement

Agreement

This agreement is entered into this _____ day of _____,
year _____ between _____ of _____
and _____
of _____

The parties agree as follows:

This is the entire agreement between the parties and may be amended or
altered only in writing, signed by both parties. This agreement is governed
by the laws of the State of _____

By _____   By _____
                name   name

_____   _____
            signature   signature

Sample Letter of Agreement

Letter of Agreement

Robert Gallo, President
Latitude Media Enterprises, Ltd.
P.O. Box 224
Calverton, NY 11933

Dear Robert,

This letter will confirm our agreement in regards to you and Latitude Media Enterprises, Ltd., becoming a client. As we discussed, these are the terms.

1. Andrew S. Linick will provide Latitude Media Enterprises, Ltd. with advertising mail order copy which can be used for a $7'' \times 10''$ space advertisement, to promote a video product presently named "Relight the Flame."
2. Andrew S. Linick can also provide marketing expertise and consulting services for all aspects of this particular promotion at my retainer fee of $400/hour or, at my discretion, barter partial payment for gross profits on ancillary products.
3. All copy, copywriter's layout & design provided will be able to fit a $7'' \times 10''$ space ad. Camera-ready mechanicals—type, specing, copy-editing, proofing, plus two AAs. Estimated $500–$750.
4. If both of us agree the initial test is not sufficiently successful to warrant a roll out in large volume, I will revise the copy up to two additional times at retainer time at $400/hour or any part thereof.
5. The fee for my services is $15,000 in advance plus a royalty of 10 percent of gross sales generated by said mail order promotion. This royalty is to be paid monthly on or before the 15th. If the promotion is a lead generator, the royalty will be in the form of a mailing fee of 10 cents ($.10) per piece mailed.
6. It is hereby understood and acknowledged by you that I, Andrew S. Linick, am relying on the accuracy of the information provided by you, the client, in order to develop the mail order direct response advertising. Furthermore, it shall be your responsibility to carefully examine any and all facts, representations, and information in the ad copy, and to delete any inaccuracies or untrue statements. You, as the client, are solely responsible for the contents of any advertising. Nothing in this agreement shall be construed to create or imply a joint venture between you and me and if anything occurs regarding this advertising which may require the services of an attorney, you are solely responsible for any and all legal fees.

If you are in agreement with everything as set forth in items 1 through 6, please sign where indicated. If there are any changes you wish to discuss, please call me right away.

AGREED TO AND
SINCERELY,   ACCEPTED THIS 22
                                             DAY OF APRIL, 199x

The Linick Group, Inc.   Latitude Media Enterprises, Ltd.

_____   _____
Andrew S. Linick   Robert Gallo
President   President

Sample Sheet Listing Terms and Conditions of Fee Structure

Statement of General Terms & Conditions

1. Fee Structure

All time, including travel hours, spent on the project by professional, technical, and clerical personnel will be billed. (Travel time billed at half hourly fees, portal to portal.) The following approximate ranges of hourly rates for various categories of personnel are currently in effect:

HOURLY RATE	CATEGORY
$400	Principal in Charge
$100–$200	Senior Consultants
$40–$75	Marketing Analysts
$30–$50	Research Technicians
$15	Computer Typists

Hourly rates will be adjusted semiannually to reflect changes in the cost of living index as published. If overtime for nonprofessional personnel is required, the premium differential figured at time-and-one-half of their regular hourly rate is charged at direct cost to the project. *Unless otherwise stated, any cost estimate presented in a proposal is for budgetary purposes only, and is not a fixed price.* The client will be notified when 75 percent of any budget figure is reached, and the budget figure will not be exceeded without prior authorization from the client.

2. Reimbursable Expenses

a) Travel expenses necessary for the execution of the project, including rail, taxi, bus, air, rental vehicles, and highway mileage in company or personal vehicles, which will be charged at 20 cents per mile. Air travel will be by tourist class, except when tourist class service is not regularly available. Accommodations, all meals at cost.

The following expenses will be billed at direct cost:

b) Telephone charges/fax
c) Postage & shipping/courier services
d) In-house printing and reproduction
e) Computer services, including word processing
f) Other expenses directly attributable to the project: photocopying, laser printing

3. Art Production (typed layouts, type specs, mechanical assembly)

Artist's time charged at $50/hour or estimated on project fee basis; supervisory time by Dr. Linick at $400/hour; by Gaylen Andrews at $75/hour.

Sample Purchase Order

| Excelsior Electronics, Inc.
1724 Industrial Avenue
Voltage, Ohio 45333
555-675-6657

Issued to: _____

Telephone Number: _____ | Purchase Order

Date: _____

Authorized by: _____

Ship via: _____

Ship to attn.: _____

By (date): _____ |

Description	Price	

Purchase order number must appear on all invoices and correspondence. Please sign and return second and third copies.

Signed: _____ Date: _____

Sample Contract

Some consultants use simple contracts to confirm job assignments from clients. Here's one I have developed.

CONTRACT FOR CONSULTING SERVICES

From: Bob Bly   Phone: 201-385-1220
        22 E. Quackenbush Avenue   Fax: 201-385-1138
        Dumont, NJ 07628

Date:

Client:

Job:

Fee:

Advance retainer required:

Balance due upon completion:

Notes:

Your signature below authorizes me to perform consulting services for the project described above, for the fee listed. Payment due net 30 days upon receipt of invoice.

Signed _____

Title _____   Date _____

Please sign and return this form with your check for the amount listed under "Advance retainer required." This will give me the go-ahead I need to proceed with the assignment.

NOTE: If no retainer is required, you can save time by signing above and faxing the form back to me at 201-385-1138.

Sample Letter of Agreement: Short Form

If you find a contract too formal and intimidating, you can confirm assignments in writing with a simple letter of agreement, such as this one.

Mr. Joe Jones   Date
President
Big Corporation
Anytown, USA

Dear Mr. Jones:

Thanks for choosing XYZ Ad Agency to handle your Job #3333.

Job 3333 is a series of three capability brochures. I will write these brochures for you and provide such marketing and editorial consulting services as may be required to implement the project.

My base fee for the services I described above is $10,000. That fee estimate is based on 100 hours of working time at my hourly rate of $100, and includes time for copywriting, editing, teleconferencing, meeting, consulting, travel, and research.

Copy revisions are included in my base fee, provided that at such time as the total time devoted by me shall exceed 100 hours, I shall bill you for additional working time at the rate of $100 per hour.

Out-of-pocket expenses, such as toll telephone calls, photocopies and computer printouts, fax charges, messengers, local and out of town travel incurred in connection with the project will be billed to you in an itemized fashion.

Payment of the base fee will be made as follows: one-third of the above mentioned base fee is due upon my commencement of work; one-third upon delivery of first draft copy; one-third due upon completion. Payment for expenses will be made within ten days following receipt of invoice.

Sincerely,

John Jones

ACCEPTED AND AGREED:

By: _____   Date _____

Confidentiality Agreement

Some clients may ask you to sign a confidentiality agreement saying you won't share the client's proprietary information with other people. If the client wants you to make such a promise but doesn't have his own confidentiality agreement, you can use this simple confidentiality memo.

TO: Sue Simon, ABC Systems

FROM: Bob Bly, 201-385-1220

DATE: 12-11-96

RE: Nondisclosure agreement

1. "Confidential information" means any information given to me by ABC Systems.

2. I agree not to use, disseminate, or share any confidential information with my employees, vendors, clients, or anyone else.

3. I will use reasonable care to protect your confidential information, treating it as securely as if it were my own.

4. I won't publish, copy, or disclose any of your confidential information to any third party and will use my best efforts to prevent inadvertent disclosure of such information to any third party.

5. The copy I do for you shall be considered "work for hire." ABC Systems will own all rights to everything I produce for you, including the copyright. I will execute any additional documents needed to verify your ownership of these rights.

Sincerely,

Bob Bly

Letter Requesting Referrals

One of the best sources of sales leads is referrals from existing clients. If your clients aren't giving you as many referrals as you want, here's a letter you can use to ask for more.

Ms. Joan Zipkin
Acme Retail Outlets
Anytown, USA

Dear Joan:

I'm glad you liked the Spring catalog I recently completed for you. Like you, I'm always on the lookout for new business. So I have a favor to ask. Could you jot down, on the back of this letter, the names, addresses, and phone numbers of a few of your colleagues who might benefit from knowing more about my services?

(Naturally, I don't want anyone whose product line competes with your own.)

Then, just mail the letter back to me in the enclosed reply envelope.

I may want to mention your name when contacting these people. Let me know if there's any problem with that.

And thanks for the favor!

Regards,

Sam Tate

Letter for Soliciting Testimonials from Clients

After completing a job successfully, you can use this letter to solicit a testimonial from the client. A sheet of paper filled with testimonials is a very powerful addition to a promotional package and convinces prospects you are good at what you do (see my promotional package later in this section). I always send a self-addressed stamped envelope and two copies of the letter. This way the recipient doesn't have to make a copy of the letter or address and stamp his own envelope.

Mr. Andrew Specher, President
Hazardous Waste Management, Inc.
Anywhere, USA

Dear Andrew:

I have a favor to ask of you.

I'm in the process of putting together a list of testimonials, a collection of comments about my services from satisfied clients like yourself.

Would you take a few minutes to give me your opinion of my writing services? No need to dictate a letter—just jot your comments on the back of this letter, sign below, and return to me in the enclosed envelope. (The second copy is for your files.) I look forward to learning what you like about my service—but I also welcome any suggestions or criticisms, too.

Many thanks, Andrew.

Regards,

Bob Bly

YOU HAVE MY PERMISSION TO QUOTE FROM MY COMMENTS, AND USE THESE QUOTATIONS IN ADS, BROCHURES, MAIL, AND OTHER PROMOTIONS USED TO MARKET YOUR FREELANCE WRITING SERVICES.

Signature _____ Date _____

Letter for Getting Permission to Use Existing Testimonial

Some clients will send you letters of testimonial unsolicited. Before you use them in your promotions, get their permission in writing, using this form letter.

Mr. Mike Hernandez
Advertising Manager
Technilogic, Inc.
Anytown, USA

Dear Mike:

I never did get around to thanking you for your letter of 2/15/87 (copy attached). So, thanks!

I'd like to quote from this letter in the ads, brochures, direct mail packages, and other promotions I use to market my writing services (with your permission, of course). If this is okay with you, would you please sign the bottom of this letter and send it back to me in the enclosed envelope. (The second copy is for your files.)

Many thanks, Mike.

Regards,

Bob Bly

YOU HAVE MY PERMISSION TO QUOTE FROM THE ATTACHED
LETTER IN ADS, BROCHURES, MAIL, AND OTHER PROMOTIONS
USED TO MARKET YOUR FREELANCE WRITING SERVICES.

Signature _____ Date _____

Follow-Up Fax to Reactivate Inactive Client

From: Ilise Benun for Bob Bly

Phone: 201-653-0783

Dear

We try to practice what we preach and we know that it's good marketing practice to keep in touch with the clients we enjoy and want to work more closely with—in a word, clients like you.

Because we think there's a good fit between your needs and our skills, would you take a moment to tell us about your current or future copywriting needs.

❒ We have an upcoming project. Give me a call.

❒ May have something within   ❒ next 6 months

    ❒ 6–12 months   ❒ next year

❒ We're not using copywriting services right now, but we'll keep you on our vendor file.

❒ No longer interested because _____

                                   (please give reason—thanks)

P.S. As a thank you for responding, we'll send you a free copy of Bob's new book, "Quick Tips for Better Business-to-Business Marketing Communications," recently published by the Business Marketing Association.

FAX BACK TO: 201-222-2494
OR CALL 201-653-0783

Sample Invoice

Here is a typical invoice to send a client upon completion of a job.

Invoice for Services Rendered July 15,1997

From: David Willis
15 Sunnyville Drive
Anyplace, USA
201-XXX-XXXX
social security #XXX-XX-XXXX

To: XYZ Corporation
Anytown, USA
ATT: June Chapman, Advertising Manager

For: Copy for MAXI-MIX equipment brochure

Reference: Purchase order #1745

Amount: $2,200

Terms: net 30 days

THANK YOU.

Sample Collection Letter Series

Letter 1

Dear Jim:

Just a reminder . . .

. . . that payment for the brochure I wrote for you (see copy of invoice attached) is now past due.

Would you please send me a check today? A self-addressed stamped reply envelope is enclosed for your convenience.

Regards,

Sam Smith

Letter 2

Dear Jim:

I haven't gotten payment for this invoice yet. Did you receive my original bill and follow-up letter?

If there is any problem, please let me know. Otherwise, please send me a check for the amount due within the next few days.

Thanks,

Sam Smith

Letter 3

Dear Jim:

This is the third notice I've sent about the enclosed invoice, which is now many weeks past due.

Was there a problem with this job I don't know about? When may I expect payment?

Sincerely,

Sam Smith

Letter 4

Dear Jim:

What do you think I should do?

Despite three previous notices about this invoice, it remains unpaid. I haven't heard from you, and you haven't responded to my letters.

Please remit payment within 10 days of receipt of this letter. I dislike sending you these annoying notices, nor do I like turning accounts over to my attorney for collections. But you are leaving me little choice.

Sincerely,

Sam Smith

P.S. Please be aware that the copyright on the copy I wrote for you for this assignment does not transfer to your company until my invoice has been paid in full.

Sample Fact Sheet: Consulting Services

Bob Bly

Copywriter/Consultant/Seminar Leader

22 East Quackenbush Avenue, 3rd floor
Dumont, NJ 07628
Phone (201) 385-1220 • Fax (201) 385-1138

Marketing Communications Planning, Strategy, Consultation, and Copy

In today's economy, it pays to make every marketing communication count. But do yours?

From time to time, you've probably felt the need for help in planning, creating, and implementing effective direct mail, advertising, and public relations programs. For example, maybe you need advice and assistance in:

- Converting more leads to sales
- Generating more inquiries from print advertising
- Determining which vertical industries or narrow target markets to pursue
- Producing effective sales brochures, catalogs, case histories, and other marketing literature
- Writing and placing press releases, feature stories, and other publicity materials
- Creating response-getting direct mail offers, packages, and campaigns
- Designing, writing, and producing a company newsletter
- Or any of dozens of other marketing problems.

Maybe you've felt that the usual sources of assistance—freelancers, advertising agencies, and PR firms—were not focused on solving your particular problems, lacked the specific knowledge you require, didn't understand your product or service, charged unreasonable prices, or were not interested in your project because they wanted all your business.

Or maybe you just want some occasional guidance and assistance, and prefer to handle most of your marketing communications in-house.

> *Now there's a service designed especially to help you—*
> **Marketing Communications Planning, Strategy, and Consultation**
> *From Bob Bly—Copywriter/Consultant/Seminar Leader*

Here are some questions prospective clients typically ask me—and the answers:

What is the Marketing Communications Planning, Strategy, and Consultation Service? This is a service which assists small and medium-size firms in planning, creating, and implementing effective advertising, marketing, direct mail, publicity, and promotional programs. I act as your ongoing adviser, answering your questions, making recommendations, and providing whatever help you need to market and promote your product or service successfully.

How does it work? My service is flexible and available to you on whatever basis meets your needs. You can hire me by the project, by the day, by the hour, or on a flexible retainer basis. While I am happy to use our time in any way you like, I will always advise you on how I think you will get the best results for your money.

What is discussed between us? The topics range from the general to the specific. You can ask me basic information about direct mail or any other topic you want to know more about; or we can deal with the nuts-and-bolts specifics of any project you have in mind.

How is the service rendered? Most of my clients prefer to work by mail, phone, and fax. However, I am available to meet with you at your office or mine, and a number of my clients use a combination of face-to-face meetings and telephone conferences.

What aspects of marketing communications are you expert in? About 50 percent of my business is planning and writing direct mail campaigns. The rest involves planning and creating a wide assortment of marketing materials and programs including ads, brochures, feature articles, slide presentations, film and videotape scripts, press releases, newsletters, catalogs, case histories, annual reports, product guides, manuals, and speeches—in short, whatever you need to help you sell more of your products and services.

- over -

Sample Fact Sheet: Consulting Services *(Continued)*

What industries do you specialize in? My specialties include business-to-business, industrial, high-tech, direct marketing, and financial services. Within these broad categories, I've worked with over a hundred clients in dozens of fields including computers, chemicals, pulp and paper, construction, electronics, engineering, industrial equipment, marine products, software, banking, health care, publishing, mail order, seminars, training, telecommunications, consulting, corporate, and many other areas. But that's just a sampling. If you want to know whether I have experience in your specific field, call me and I'll tell you.

What are some of the specific services you provide for clients? Clients have hired me to create marketing and advertising plans; review and discuss ongoing marketing activities; make recommendations on new ways to effectively market existing products and services; review and critique ads, mailings, and other marketing documents; plan and write direct mail campaigns; train in-house staff in copywriting and marketing; and simply be available to provide input, answer questions, or bounce around ideas.

What size companies do you work with? I work with small firms, medium-size companies, and divisions of large corporations. My service can be tailored to the complexity of your program and the size of your budget.

Do you actually implement recommendations? I am a copywriter and consultant, not an ad agency or design studio. I create marketing strategies and write copy, but I do not design, print, or produce the piece. If you need art or production services, I will refer you to qualified vendors in my network with whom you can work directly. This gives you greater control, faster delivery, and eliminates costly mark-ups on their services. I will be happy to review any work done for you by these or any other vendors you use (for example, many clients mail or fax rough layouts to me for comment before mechanicals are created).

Who will handle my account? All services are provided directly by Bob Bly. Mr. Bly is a well-known copywriter and consultant specializing in business-to-business and direct marketing. He has consulted with—and written copy for—more than 100 organizations including On-Line Software, Timeplex, Convergent Solutions, JMW Consultants, Associated Air Freight, Sony Corporation, Yourdon Inc., American Medical Collection Agency, Grumman, GE Solid State, and Philadelphia National Bank. He is the author of 20 books including *How to Promote Your Own Business* (New American Library), *Ads That Sell* (Asher Gallant), *The Copywriter's Handbook* (Henry Holt), *Create the Perfect Sales Piece* (John Wiley), *Direct Mail Profits* (Asher Gallant), and *Selling Your Services* (Henry Holt). A client list and publications catalog are available upon request.

What is the cost of Bob Bly's marketing consultation services? Clients can choose to be billed on an hourly, daily, retainer, or project basis. The base fee is $200 per hour.

What's the typical fee for new clients? I offer an introductory consultation for $600 which includes a review of your materials and questions, a 1-2 hour consultation (by phone, mail, or in-person), and a follow-up report outlining my recommendations. You get approximately 4 hours of consultation (an $800 value) for a package price of $600, so this is my best value.

Is all time billable? No. To see whether my service is right for you, I offer a free initial consultation by phone for 20 minutes. Thereafter, however, time is billable at $200 per hour.

Why would an organization choose Bob Bly's Marketing Communications Planning, Strategy, and Consultation Service over hiring a full-service agency? For at least three good reasons:

1) *Cost.* Most agencies won't help you unless they get your whole account and you spend at least $50,000 to $75,000 a year with them. I will help you solve your marketing problems within whatever budget constraints you set. Significant results can be achieved for as little as $600.

2) *Results.* Because my orientation is toward results, not aesthetics, many clients report an immediate increase in leads and sales after using my services. (Client testimonials available upon request.)

3) *Education.* As we work together, I teach you my techniques and strategies for boosting marketing communications effectiveness—so, over time, you learn to do more and more on your own.

What's the next step? Please call me at (201) 385-1220 and tell me how I can be of service. You may even want to schedule your free 20-minute telephone consultation to discuss how we can solve your most pressing marketing problems. Be sure to request your free Marketing Communications Audit, too.

Bob Bly • Copywriter/Consultant/Seminar Leader
22 East Quackenbush Avenue, 3rd floor • Dumont, NJ 07628
Phone (201) 385-1220 • Fax (201) 385-1138

Sample Promotional Brochure for an Independent Consultant

THE CENTER
FOR TECHNICAL
COMMUNICATION

Technical and business writing
seminars for corporations

In-house training programs

Public seminars

Conferences

Publications

The Technical Writing Hotline™

Fax Critique service

Train-the-trainer programs

Contract technical writing services

CTC Trainers Bureau

The Center for Technical Marketing

**Everything you need
to train your employees to write
better and faster, boost productivity,
and enhance the quality
of your organization's
written communications.**

Sample Promotional Brochure for an Independent Consultant *(Continued)*

WHAT IS THE CENTER FOR TECHNICAL COMMUNICATION?

The Center for Technical Communication (CTC) is a company that specializes in improving the writing skills of corporate employees and the quality of written communications within your organization.

CTC's primary service is conducting in-house workshops in technical and business writing for corporate clients nationwide. Our on-site writing seminars give your employees the skills and confidence to write better, faster, and more productively.

CTC also offers public seminars, conferences, and publications covering all aspects of technical and business communication. Other services designed to improve the quality of communication in your organization include our telephone hotline, fax critique service, contract technical writing services, and more.

IN-HOUSE WRITING WORKSHOPS

CTC offers the following in-house training seminars for corporations and associations:

Effective Technical Writing

A 1 or 2-day workshop on how to write clear, correct, technically accurate reports, manuals, documentation, specs, proposals, papers, and other technical documents. This program is designed to improve the writing skills of engineers, scientists, systems analysts, technicians, technical writers, technical editors, and others whose writing deals with technical or semi-technical subject matter.

Effective Business Writing

A 1 or 2-day workshop on how to write clear, concise, persuasive letters, memos, reports, proposals, and other business documents. This program's focus is on improving the writing skills of executives, managers, professionals, and support staff.

Our instructors know technical writing because they are technicians and technical writers.

What sets CTC apart from other training firms is that our instructors are not only skilled and entertaining trainers but are also *recognized authorities* in their fields. Our technical writing seminars, for example, are taught by instructors who hold technical degrees, have worked as full-time professional technical writers for large corporations, and have taught technical writing at the university level. In-depth experience and technical background not only improve the quality of instruction but also break down barriers between the instructor and the audience: Your technical trainees become more receptive when they realize the instructor is a "techie" like them.

PUBLIC SEMINARS AND CONFERENCES

Although CTC gives priority to meeting the in-house training needs of our corporate clients, we occasionally sponsor public seminars and conferences on technical and business writing. Companies with six or more people requiring training, however, will probably find an in-house program more cost-effective.

TRAIN-THE-TRAINER PROGRAM

Some companies do not have the budget to send as many of their employees as they'd like through our technical writing workshops. As a cost-effective alternative to on-site training, we offer a train-the-trainer program in which CTC licenses its course materials, including outlines and hand-outs, to you for use within your organization. We also coach your trainers in how to present our program effectively.

PUBLICATIONS

CTC offers books, special reports, monographs, and audio cassettes on a variety of topics including technical writing, marketing communications, and business communications.

THE TECHNICAL WRITING HOTLINE ™

This unique telephone hotline gives you instant access to technical writing experts who can provide immediate answers to questions concerning grammar, punctuation, spelling, usage, word choice, format, and style.

Sample Promotional Brochure for an Independent Consultant *(Continued)*

FAX CRITIQUE SERVICE

Clients can fax drafts to CTC for immediate review and editing. A qualified CTC technical editor reads the document, edits, provides further suggestions for improvement, and returns the original with corrections and comments to the client via fax.

CONTRACT TECHNICAL WRITING SERVICES

CTC maintains a large database of qualified technical writers with varied backgrounds and hourly rates. If your staff is overloaded and you need a technical writer, call CTC. We'll provide technical writers to work at your place or theirs on a project, hourly, or per diem basis. Should you wish to hire the writer full-time, CTC can arrange this through our Executive Search and Placement Division.

CTC TRAINERS BUREAU

In addition to staff instructors specializing in technical and business writing, CTC operates a trainers bureau providing trainers who fit your budget and can speak on such topics as:

- Business writing
- Technical writing
- Copywriting
- Persuasive writing for salespeople
- English as a second language
- Presentation skills
- Selling
- Direct mail/direct marketing
- Client service
- And many others.

THE CENTER FOR TECHNICAL MARKETING

The Center for Technical Marketing (CTM) is a division of CTC specializing in business-to-business, industrial, high-tech, and direct response marketing.

CTM creates award-winning, result-getting direct mail, packages, sales letters, brochures, ads, press releases, newsletters, data sheets, and other marketing documents for more than 100 clients nationwide.

CLIENTS (A PARTIAL LIST) *

Airco
Associated Distribution Logistics
Atech Software
Brooklyn Union Gas
Cambridge Scientific Abstracts
Chemical Bank
The Conference Board
Convergent Solutions
CoreStates Financial Corporation
Creative Group, Inc.
Crest Ultrasonics
Dow Chemical
Drake Beam Morin
EBI Medical Systems
Executive Enterprises
Fala Direct Marketing
Fielder's Choice
Grey Advertising
Howard Lanin Productions
IBM
IEEE
ITT
International Tile Exposition
The Institute of Management Accountants
JMW Consultants
J. Walter Thompson
Leviton Manufacturing
Metrum Instruments
Midlantic
M & T Chemicals
On-Line Software
Optical Data Corporation
Prentice Hall
PSE&G
Reed Travel Group
Sony
Siemens
Specialty Steel & Forge
Thompson Professional Publishing
Timeplex
Union Camp
Value Rent-a-Car
Wallace & Tiernan
Wolfram Research
And many, many others...

* The firms and associations listed have retained the seminar, training, writing, or consulting services of CTC, Bob Bly, or The Center for Technical Marketing.

Sample Promotional Brochure for an Independent Consultant *(Continued)*

WHAT CLIENTS AND ATTENDEES SAY ABOUT CTC SEMINARS AND SERVICES...

" Thanks for the seminar. Besides clarifying technical points, you gave me insight into my position, and my abilities, as a writer. And observing you in action was excellent training. "

— Mike Goldscheitter, technical writer
Loveland Controls

" Thanks again for joining us in Atlantic City. I, and the entire group, found your thoughts insightful and right on target."

— Edward H. Moore, editor
communication briefings

" Your presentation for our seminar was sparkling, enthusiastic, and informative. The audience response was wonderful to see and hear. Our group benefited greatly and were quite vocal in their praise of you."

— Wendy Ward, program chair
Women in Communications

" The first issue of the spinal newsletter is enclosed. The sales force was very receptive to the newsletter and its contents. Thank you for helping us launch this important project. "

— Mary Ellen Coleman, product manager
EBI Medical Systems

" I just wanted to thank you personally for the energy and effort you put into your two days with us. We are now far better equipped to do direct mail for our clients and ourselves that will have a greater impact and get measurable results. "

— Greta Bolger, account executive
Sefton Associates Inc.

" I just finished reading the copy for our CERTIN-COAT system brochure and I was very happy with it. You did an excellent job of editing a large amount of information, much of it extraneous, into a strong, cohesive selling message."

— Len Lavenda, advertising manager
M&T Chemicals Inc.

" I found the seminar helpful and noticed a definite greater awareness of style afterwards. Your presentation was lively, and kept the participants' attention well into the afternoon and longer than I had expected beforehand."

— J.E. Koschei, editorial director
Thompson Professional Publishing

ABOUT CTC'S DIRECTOR

Bob Bly, director of the Center for Technical Communication, has been a technical writer and technical writing instructor full-time since 1979.

He taught technical writing at New York University and has presented training sessions to such groups as the American Chemical Society, the American Marketing Association, and the American Institute of Chemical Engineers.

Mr. Bly is the author of 25 books including *Technical Writing: Structure, Standards, and Style* (McGraw-Hill), *The Copywriter's Handbook* (Henry Holt), and *The Elements of Business Writing* (Macmillan).

Bob Bly has worked as a staff technical writer for the Westinghouse Electric Corporation and also as an independent technical writer handling projects for dozens of firms including Brooklyn Union Gas, Crest Ultrasonics, On-Line Software, and M&T Chemicals.

Mr. Bly holds a B.S. in engineering from the University of Rochester. He is a member of the Society for Technical Communication, American Institute of Chemical Engineers, and the American Society for Training and Development.

THE NEXT STEP

For more information on any of the services described in this brochure, or to discuss scheduling a technical writing or business writing seminar for your organization, call CTC at (201) 385-1220. Or write us today.

THE CENTER FOR TECHNICAL COMMUNICATION
22 E. Quackenbush Avenue
Dumont, NJ 07628
phone (201) 385-1220
fax (201) 385-1138

Sample Mini-Catalog of Information Products (Related to Consulting Specialty)

Bob Bly's
Sales and Marketing Resource Guide™

Books, special reports, audio tapes, and other resources to help you communicate more effectively, improve marketing results, and sell more of your products and services.

Cassette programs (800-Series)

803   How to Boost Your Direct Mail Response Rates
Proven techniques for dramatically increasing your direct mail response rates. Includes rules for testing, target marketing strategies, offers, list selection, copy, mistakes to avoid...and much, much more.
Single cassette $12

**804   Sixteen Secrets of Successful
          Small Business Promotion**
How to use low-cost/no-cost advertising, marketing, sales promotion, and public relations techniques to build your business. Learn how to: Gain credibility through public speaking. Generate thousands of leads using simple press releases. The "Busy Doctor" Success Strategy. Resource boxes. Big results from tiny ads. Telephone hotlines. Client newsletters. And more.
Single cassette $12

805   Selling Your Services in a Soft Economy
How to successfully sell and market your service or product in a recession or soft economy.
Single cassette $12

806   How to Write Copy That Sells
Tips on writing result-getting copy for ads, direct mail, and other marketing communications.
Single cassette $12

**807   The 7 Fundamental Shifts in Your Customer's Buying
          Habits in the 1990's**
Corporate and consumer customers buy differently today than when the economy was stronger. You need to adjust your marketing and selling to meet the buyer's new shopping habits. This tape shows how.
Single cassette $12

**808   Twelve Things You Can Do to Sell More of Your
          Products and Services—NOW!**
Tips on prospecting, qualifying, closing, and improving overall sales results.
Single cassette $12

809   How to Become a Published Author
Why writing a book can enhance your career—and how to get your book published. Covers literary agents, advances, royalties, book contracts, and more.
Single cassette $12

810   How to Create Effective Seminar Brochures
Guidelines for writing and designing brochures to sell public and in-house seminars.
Single cassette $12

812   The Motivating Sequence
A proven, easy-to-follow 5-step formula for writing more persuasive sales letters, billing series, ads, mailers, and more.
Single cassette $12

813   Secrets of Successful Lead Generation
How to make your ads, sales letters, and mailers generate more leads.
Single cassette $12

814   Conversations on Getting and Keeping Customers
Two in-depth radio interviews with Bob Bly on the topics of selling and customer service.
Single cassette $12

815   How to Create Great Promotional Literature
12 tips on how you can create and use sales literature and other promotional materials more effectively.
Single cassette $12

Full-length books (300-Series)

300   Get Paid to Write Your Book
The definitive work on how to write a nonfiction book and sell it—for a nice advance—to a major New York publishing company. Topics include: coming up with book ideas, evaluating the market potential of your book, how to write a successful book proposal, how to get a literary agent to represent you, selling your book to publishers, and negotiating your advance and royalties.
Oversize paperback, 100 pages $22

301   The Copywriter's Handbook
The Copywriter's Handbook tells you how to write, commission, review, edit, and approve effective copy for ads, brochures, catalogs, direct mail, press releases, TV and radio commercials, newsletters, speeches, and other projects—with the emphasis clearly on business-to-business, industrial, hi-tech, and direct response. "I don't know a single copywriter whose work would not be improved by reading this book," says David Ogilvy, founder of Ogilvy & Mather. "And that includes me." Also recommended by The Los Angeles Times and Ad Day.
Updated trade paperback edition, 353 pages $15

305   The Elements of Technical Writing
A fully revised, completely updated edition of our 1982 bestseller, *Technical Writing: Structure, Standards, and Style.* Presents the guidelines and rules of technical writing in a concise, clear, easy-to-follow handbook, organized for quick and easy reference.
Hardcover, 144 pages $21

306   Creative Careers: Real Jobs in Glamour Fields
A job-hunter's guide to ten of today's most exciting industries including advertising, television, gourmet foods, finance, music, publishing, film, photography, theater, and travel.
Trade paperback, 334 pages $12

**307   Create the Perfect Sales Piece:
          A Do-It-Yourself Guide to Producing Brochures,
          Catalogs, Fliers, and Pamphlets**
Provides step-by-step instructions on how to successfully outline, plan, write, design, and produce sales brochures, booklets, fliers, pamphlets, annual reports, catalogs, and other collateral materials. Also contains model outlines for product, service, and corporate capabilities brochures.
Trade paperback, 242 pages $20

313   How To Promote Your Own Business
A practical, do-it-yourself guide to advertising, publicity, and promotion for the small-business manager or owner. Written especially for the small and medium-size firm (or division of a larger company) with a limited budget for advertising and marketing.
Trade paperback, 241 pages $13

**315   Selling Your Services: Proven Strategies for Getting
          Clients to Hire You (or Your Firm)**
If you sell professional, personal, consulting, trade, technical, support, or any other kind of service, this book will give you the information you need to get large numbers of prospects to call you, convince those prospects to hire you at the fees you want, and dramatically increase the sales of your services.
Hardcover, 349 pages $27

Sample Mini-Catalog of Information Products (Related to Consulting Specialty) *(Continued)*

Full-length books (300-Series), cont'd

316 The Elements of Business Writing
The Elements of Business Writing presents the basic rules of business writing in a concise, easy-to-use handbook organized along the lines of Strunk and White's classic book, *The Elements of Style.*
Hardcover, 140 pages $20

317 Business-to-Business Direct Marketing
This book is for business-to-business marketers who want to improve results from all their marketing communications including **ads**, direct mail, PR, brochures, catalogs, postcard decks, and more. Also identifies and explains the 7 key differences between b-to-b and consumer marketing.
Hardcover, 267 pages $42

318 Targeted Public Relations
A no-nonsense guide to achieving maximum visibility, press coverage, leads, and sales from public relations done on a limited budget.
Hardcover, 330 pages $25

319 Keeping Clients Satisfied
In today's economy, clients and customers are more demanding than ever: They want it better, they want it cheaper, and they want it *yesterday!* This book shows you the customer service techniques necessary to satisfying and retaining clients in this new competitive mar·etplace where the client reigns supreme.
Hardcover, 275 pages $27

323 The Advertising Manager's Handbook
A comprehensive instruction manual on how to plan, implement, and manage an advertising and marketing communications program. Written from the advertising manager's point of view, the *Handbook* is recommended for *anyone* involved in producing, managing or evaluating marketing communication.
Hardcover, 800 pages $80

324 How to Sell Your House, Co-op, or Condo
Selling your house or apartment? Want to get it sold quickly at a good price? This book tells how.
Trade paperback, 242 pages $17

325 The Ultimate Unauthorized Star Trek Quiz Book
More than 750 trivia questions to test your "Trekpertise." covers the Star Trek movies, TV shows, and novels.
Trade paperback, 162 pages $11

326 Power-Packed Direct Mail
Complete, easy-to-follow instructions on how to increase direct mail response rates. Covers planning, offers, mailing lists, testing, copy, design, formats, personalizations, and more.
Hardcover, 349 pages $27

Reprints, monographs, booklets, and special reports (100-Series)

101 Thirty-One Ways to Get More Inquiries From Your Ads
Proven, easy, inexpensive strategies for increasing your ad's pulling power and getting more leads from each insertion.
1-page reprint $1

**102 Using Testimonials To Improve Your
Marketing Communications**
Using testimonials is one of the easiest and most effective ways to add interest and credibility to marketing documents and make them more persuasive. This reprint tells how to get testimonials, how to use them, and provides model letters for soliciting testimonials and getting approval for publication.
2-page reprint $2

103 How To Prepare For a Copywriting Assignment
A four-step procedure for gathering the information you or your agency will need to write persuasive, meaningful copy. Includes

a checklist of 20 questions to ask before you write your ad or brochure.
1-page reprint $1

104 Marketing To Engineers
What works in advertising aimed at engineers—and what doesn't—is concisely spelled out in this report. Should industrial advertising mimic consumer advertising—or should it be more technical?·Send for this tip sheet and find out....
1-page reprint $1

105 How To Sell Software By Mail
How to sell software using direct response space ads, direct mail packages, and sales brochures. Tells: How to select your offer based on the list price of the software. Proper use of demo diskettes. One-step vs. two-step promotions. And more.
2-page reprint $2

**106 Creating Effective Sales Brochures For Technical
Products**
Five industry experts—including Terry Smith of Westinghouse and Dick Hill of Alexander Marketing—reveal their secrets for creating effective technical sales literature.
6-page reprint $4

**107 In Search of Ink: How To Write a Feature Article or
Case History and Get It Published**
A step-by-step, proven procedure for writing business and technical articles and getting them published in trade journals. Includes interviews with top trade journal editors who tell what they like (and don't like) about PR agencies, PR managers, outlines, query letters, sloppy manuscripts, authors, and more.
4-page reprint $3

**108 The Twelve Most Common Direct Mail Mistakes—and
How To Avoid Them**
How many of the 12 most common direct mail mistakes are you making right now? Even one could kill the response to your next mailing. Learn how to avoid these costly mistakes and create effective direct mail that generates lots of leads and orders!
4-page reprint $3

109 Recession-Fighting Business Strategies That Work
14 proven techniques for successfully selling and marketing your product or service in a recession, soft economy, or when business is slow.
16-page booklet $7

110 Twenty-Five Japanese Business Secrets
Most of what you need to know about doing business with the Japanese is covered in this insightful insider's briefing by Milt Pierce.
8-page report $6

111 Ten Ways to Improve Your Technical Writing
Ten tips for more effective technical communication. How to overcome Writer's Block. Nine ways to organize your writing. And more.
4-page reprint $3

112 Tips for Marketing High-Tech Products
Eight useful ideas for getting more response from marketing communications designed to promote high-tech products and services.
2-page reprint $2

113 The Key to Great Inquiry Fulfillment
How to put together a winning inquiry fulfillment package that gives the prospects the information they need and convinces them to take the next step in the buying process.
4-page reprint $3

114 Adventures in the Seminar Trade
How to make money in the public seminar business. How to promote your product or service using free seminars.
2-page reprint $2

BBL-520.11

Sample Mini-Catalog of Information Products (Related to Consulting Specialty) *(Continued)*

Reprints, monographs, booklets, and special reports (100-Series), cont'd

115 How to Write and Sell Your Nonfiction Book
How to write and organize your book...write a winning book proposal...get a literary agent...sell your book to a publisher...book contracts...royalties and advances...and more.
2-page reprint $2

116 How to Set (and Get) Your Fees
Presents a simple formula for setting your fees. Helps you avoid charging too little (which can hurt your image and limit income) or too much (which can blow potential clients away and cost you sales).
2-page reprint $1

117 Writing Catalog Copy That Sells
Proven techniques for organizing and writing catalog copy that sells. A collection of my best columns from the Sroge newsletter on catalog marketing.
10-page report $6

118 Fifty Lead-Generating Tips
50 proven techniques for increasing response to lead-generating direct mail.
1-page reprint $1

119 Twenty-two Rules for Successful Self-Promotion
22 marketing tips for freelancers, consultants, and other self-employed professionals who market their services, plus 5 techniques for generating new business leads using direct mail.
2-page reprint $2

120 How to Give a Successful Speech or Presentation
More than 40 sensible suggestions on how to organize, write, and deliver an effective, memorable lecture, talk, speech, or presentation.
3-page reprint $2

121 The 29 Types of Article You Can Include in Your Company Newsletter
Wondering what to put in a company newsletter? Here are 29 types of stories you can use.
1-page reprint $1

122 How to Write a Good Advertisement
The 8 characteristics of a successful print ad. Plus: 7 ways to create business publication ads that get results.
2-page reprint $1

123 How to Sell "Information Products" By Mail
Tips on how to sell books, newsletters, special reports, audio cassettes, videos, monographs, and other "information products" successfully by mail.
1-page reprint $1

124 Videos and Audio Cassettes as a Marketing Tool
How to use audio cassettes and videotapes as a marketing tool to increase response to direct mail, ads, inquiry fulfillment, etc.
2-page reprint $2

125 How to Hire a Freelance Copywriter
7 key questions to ask before you hire a freelance copywriter.
1-page reprint $1

126 How to Present Your Product's or Service's Features and Benefits
Should you stress features? benefits? both? how? This reprint shows how to achieve the right balance when describing features and their benefits in your copy.
2-page reprint $2

127 Designing an Effective Outer Envelope
Answers "Should I use a teaser?", "First-class or third-class?", "Stamp, meter, or indicia?", "Label, window, or inkjet?" and other commonly asked questions about designing outer envelopes so that the direct mail package will be opened instead of thrown away.
1-page reprint $1

128 Creating a Successful Corporate Capabilities Brochure
4 main functions of corporate literature. 4 questions to ask before you create your company brochure. 10 tips for creating more effective capabilities brochures.
4-page reprint $3

129 Ten Ways to *Stretch* Your Advertising Budget
Proven money-saving techniques from a master miser for stretching your marketing communications budget in today's economy.
2-page reprint $2

130 Taking the Mystery Out of High-Tech Direct Mail
How to increase response rates to direct mail packages designed to sell software, computers, and other high-tech products and services.
4-page reprint $3

131 Ten Ways to Improve Your Trade Show Direct Mail
How to create mailings that get more qualified prospects to visit your booth
3-page reprint $2

132 Twenty-Three Tips for Improving Your Business-to-Business Direct Mail
The title says is all. First published in Who's Mailing What.
4-page reprint $2

133 Premiums for Subscription Promotions
Five experienced circulation directors discuss how to select and test premiums for subscription promotion.
7-page reprint $3

134 Using Direct Mail to Promote Consulting and Professional Services
5 tips on generating leads for consulting and professional services using direct mail.
1-page reprint $1

135 The Seven Key Differences Between Business-to-Business and Consumer Marketing
At last, an authoritative answer to the long-standing debate, "Are business-to-business and consumer marketing the same, or different?"
3-page reprint $2

136 How to Write Business Letters that Get Results
Tips for writing more effective letters and memos.
4-page reprint $2

137 Ten Direct Mail Copywriting Tips
How to write potent copy that generates more leads and sales by mail.
4-page reprint $2

138 Ten Ways to Improve Your Copywriting
10 controversial suggestions on how to improve your copy by breaking the conventions.
3-page reprint $2

139 How to Review, Approve, and Critique Copy from Your Freelancer or Agency
Outlines the proper way to review, approve, and make changes to copy written by others.
2-page reprint $1

140 Ten Tips for Writing Better User Manuals
Ideas for creating software documentation that's easy to use.
2-page reprint $2

141 Practical Techniques for Producing Profitable Ideas
9 steps toward enhancing your creative thinking and coming up with better ideas.
2-page reprint $2

142 Eight Ways to Improve Your Managerial Skills
Tips for becoming a more effective manager.
2-page reprint $1

Sample Mini-Catalog of Information Products (Related to Consulting Specialty) *(Continued)*

Reprints, monographs, booklets, and special reports (100-Series), cont'd

143 Improving Your Listening Skills
Tells how to become a better listener.
2-page reprint $1

144 Improving Your Time Management Skills
Common-sense (but often ignored) ways to gain control of your
schedule and make more productive use of your time.
1-page reprint $1

145 Improving Your Telephone Skills
Guidelines on telephone etiquette to help you make the right
impression with customers, prospects, colleagues, and other
callers.
2-page reprint $1

146 Improving Your Technical Writing Skills
How to overcome anxiety and write more effectively using the
TAP and SPP formulas.
2-page reprint $1

147 Improving Your "People Skills"
Tips on getting along with others and coping with difficult people.
2-page reprint $1

148 Improving Your Negotiating Skills
How to be less afraid, more assertive, ask for what you want,
and get it a lot of the time.
2-page reprint $1

149 Ten Ways to Reduce Stress
Ten proven techniques for coping with work-related pressure.
1-page reprint $1

150 Twelve Ways to Improve Your Reading Efficiency
Strategies for reading faster while increasing comprehension
and retaining more of what you've read.
1-page reprint $1

151 Negotiate Your Way to a Better Salary
9 strategies to help you ask for and get a raise.
1-page reprint $1

152 Job Burnout
The causes and cures. How to enjoy work again.
3-page reprint $2

153 On-Target Advertising
10 steps to creating ads that work.
5-page reprint $1

154 Out On Your Own: From Corporate to Self-Employment
What to do if you want to quit your job (or are fired) and start
your own business.
2-page reprint $1

155 Ten Tips for Writing More Effective Industrial Copy
Copywriting tips for industrial trade ads, brochures, data sheets,
and catalogs.
2-page reprint $2

156 Marketing Chemicals and Chemical Equipment
How to use advertising and publicity to market chemicals and
process equipment. Contains sample press releases, sales
letters, and a list of chemical publications.
30-page reprint $12

Dear Business Professional:

If you want affordable solutions to your sales and marketing
problems, here's a valuable resource for you.

The **Sales and Marketing Resource Guide** gives you
access to virtually everything I've written on sales, marketing, management, and business communication, including all
of my books and articles, plus tapes of my seminars and
speeches. Specific, relevant, practical information on key
issues of interest to you is available in a variety of formats,
for as little as $1. That's a bargain you can't beat anywhere.

Have a question? Call me at (201) 385-1220. As always,
there's no charge for me to answer brief questions about
something you've read in my books or articles. If your need
is more complex and requires more extensive attention, I'll
tell you what's involved and what it would cost for me to work
with you. No obligation, of course.

–Bob Bly

Clip this coupon and mail it with your payment. (You may photocopy it, if you wish.)

Items you wish to order (indicate item #'s): _____ _____ _____ _____

_____ _____ _____ _____ _____

_____ _____ _____ _____ _____

_____ _____ _____ _____ _____

Name _____ Title _____

Company _____ Phone _____

Address _____

City _____ State _____ Zip _____

❑ Check here if you would like to receive free, no-obligation information on my copywriting and consulting services. (If
you have an immediate need, call Bob Bly at 201-385-1220.)

Enclose money order, cash, or check (payable to "Bob Bly") for appropriate amount. NJ residents add 6% sales tax.
Canadian residents add $2 (U.S. dollars) per order. 30-day money-back guarantee on all books and cassettes. All
items guaranteed to please. We require payment with order and do not accept purchase orders.

Mail to: **Bob Bly, 22 East Quackenbush Avenue, 3rd floor, Dumont, NJ 07628**   BBL-520.11

Sample Pre-Program Questionnaire for In-House Training Program

THE CENTER FOR TECHNICAL COMMUNICATION
22 EAST QUACKENBUSH AVENUE, DUMONT, NJ 07628 · (201) 385-1220 · FAX (201) 385-1138

Pre-Program Questionnaire

This questionnaire is designed to help us tailor our seminar to the specific needs, interests, and background of the audience.

Please answer each question as best you can and return this form to our office. Thanks!

1. Program you would like us to present for you:
   [ ] Effective technical writing
   [ ] Effective business writing
   [ ] How to write copy that sells
   [ ] How to use direct mail to generate more leads and sales
   [ ] Selling your services
   [ ] Successful selling
   [ ] Keeping clients and customers satisfied
   [ ] 14 ways to sell any product or service in a recession
   [ ] Other: _____

2. Tell us a little more about the group.
   Number of people who will be in the audience: _____
   Average age: _____
   Male/female ratio: _____
   Annual personal income (if relevant): _____
   Educational level: _____
   Average number of years with company or organization:_____
   Job titles/functions of people in the audience:
   (1)_____
   (2)_____
   (3)_____

3. Which of the following best describes the attitude of the majority of your audience toward our upcoming training session?
   [ ] Very eager and enthusiastic—really looking forward to it
   [ ] Somewhat eager and enthusiastic—if perhaps a tad skeptical about our ability to deliver something they can use
   [ ] Neutral—neither enthusiastic nor skeptical—their attitude is "show-me"
   [ ] Not terribly interested but not unhappy about going
   [ ] Hostile, bored, or both—don't want to go and are being forced to by supervisor or manager
   [ ] Smug—think they already "know it all"
   [ ] Other: _____

(over, please)

Sample Pre-Program Questionnaire for In-House Training Program *(Continued)*

4. How well educated is the audience in the topic of the seminar?
   [ ] They're all experts—the presentation should be advanced and on a high level
   [ ] They're fairly knowledgeable but recognize there's always more to learn and room for improvement
   [ ] They have some knowledge of the topic but haven't been exposed to it that much
   [ ] They're novices and require a strong education in the fundamentals
   [ ] Other: _____

5. What are the three most pressing challenges or problems faced by the members of your group?
   (1) _____
   (2) _____
   (3) _____

6. Which professional seminar leaders have you previously used to present programs on my topic?
   (1) _____
   (2) _____
   (3) _____

7. What are your specific objectives for our program? (e.g., what skills do you want your people to gain, what topics do you want to make sure we cover, etc.?)
   (1) _____
   (2) _____
   (3) _____
   (4) _____
   (5) _____

8. Are there any issues or topics that you want me to avoid during the program?
   (1) _____
   (2) _____
   (3) _____

9. Have you any other suggestions or advice to help me make this program your best ever?
   (1) _____
   (2) _____
   (3) _____

Instructions:
Please complete this form and mail it back to us at the address below:

Return to:
Bob Bly
CTC
22 E. Quackenbush Avenue
Dumont, NJ 07628
phone (201) 385-1220 • fax (201) 385-1138

BBL-523.101

Sample Needs Assessment Form

**Bob Bly's
Business-to-Business
Marketing Communications Audit**

In today's economy, it pays to make every marketing communication count.

This simple audit is designed to help you identify your most pressing marketing communications challenges—and to find ways to solve problems, communicate with your target markets more effectively, and get better results from every dollar spent on advertising and promotion.

Step One: Identify Your Areas of Need

Check all items that are of concern to you right now:

❏ Creating a marketing or advertising plan

❏ Generating more inquiries from my print advertising

❏ Improving overall effectiveness and persuasiveness of print ads

❏ Determining which vertical industries or narrow target markets to pursue

❏ How to effectively market and promote our product or service on a limited advertising budget to these target audiences

❏ Producing effective sales brochures, catalogs, and other marketing literature

❏ How to get good case histories and user stories written and published

❏ Getting articles by company personnel written and published in industry trade journals

❏ Getting editors to write about our company, product, or activities

❏ Getting more editors to run our press releases

❏ Planning and implementing a direct mail campaign or program

❏ Increasing direct mail response rates

❏ Generating low-cost but qualified leads using postcard decks

❏ How to make all our marketing communications more responsive and accountable

❏ Designing, writing, and producing a company newsletter

❏ Creating an effective company or capabilities brochure

❏ Developing strategies for responding to and following up on inquiries

❏ Creating effective inquiry fulfillment packages

❏ Producing and using a video or audio tape to promote our product or service

❏ Writing and publishing a book, booklet, or special report that can be used to promote our company or product

❏ Choosing an appropriate premium or advertising specialty as a customer giveaway

❏ Getting reviews and critiques of existing or in-progress copy for ads, mailings, brochures, and other promotions

❏ How to promote our product or service using free or paid seminars

❏ How to market our product or organization by having our people speak or present papers at conventions, trade shows, meetings, and other industry events

❏ Training our staff with an in-house seminar in:

_____
(indicate topic)

❏ Learning proven strategies for marketing our product or service in a recession or soft economy

❏ Other (describe): _____

_____

_____

– over –

Sample Needs Assessment Form *(Continued)*

Marketing Communications Audit

Step Two: Provide a Rough Indication of Your Budget

Amount of money you are prepared to commit to the solution of the problems checked off on page one of this form:

❑ under $500   ❑ under $1,000   ❑ under $2,500

❑ under $5,000   ❑ other: _____

Step Three: Fill in Your Name, Address, and Phone Number Below

Name _____ Title _____

Company _____ Phone _____

Address _____

City _____ State _____ Zip _____

Step Four: Mail or Fax Your Completed Form Today

Mail: Bob Bly, 174 Holland Avenue, New Milford, NJ 07646
FAX: (201) 599-2276
Phone: (201) 599-2277

If you wish, send me your current ads, brochures, mailing pieces, press releases, and any other material that will give me a good idea of the products or services you are responsible for promoting. I will review your audit and materials and provide a free 20-minute consultation by telephone with specific recommendations on how to solve your marketing problems, implement programs, and effectively address your key areas of concern. To schedule a specific date and time for your free, no-obligation phone consultation, indicate your preferred date and time below:

Preferred date and time_____

Alternate date and time_____

Mail your audit form today. There's no cost. And no obligation.

Bob Bly • Copywriter/Consultant • 174 Holland Avenue • New Milford, NJ 07646

Appendix G: Web Sites of Interest to Consultants

Association of Consulting
  Engineers
www.acenet.co.uk
U.K.-based association for
consulting engineers.

Copywriting Web Site
www.bly.com
How-to articles, books, resources
on copywriting.

Management Consultant Network
www.mcninet.com
Professional resources for
management consultants.

Roger C. Parker
www.rcparker.com
How to create your own successful
Web site.

Western New York Consultants
  Association
www.mmaweb.com/wnyca
A regional association of
independent consultants.

Working Relationships
www.customerrelations.com
Information on customer service,
customer care, and customer
relationships.

World Profit
www.worldprofit.com
Dr. Jeffrey Lant's Web site of
resources for entrepreneurs.

Appendix H:
Consulting Code of Ethics

Code of Ethics

Clients

1. We will serve our clients with integrity, competence, and objectivity.
2. We will keep client information and records of client engagements confidential and will use proprietary client information only with the client's permission.
3. We will not take advantage of confidential client information for ourselves or our firms.
4. We will not allow conflicts of interest which provide a competitive advantage to one client through our use of confidential information from another client who is a direct competitor without that competitor's permission.

Engagements

5. We will accept only engagements for which we are qualified by our experience and competence.
6. We will assign staff to client engagements in accord with their experience, knowledge, and expertise.
7. We will immediately acknowledge any influences on our objectivity to our clients and will offer to withdraw from a consulting engagement when our objectivity or integrity may be impaired.

Fees

8. We will agree independently and in advance on the basis of our fees and expenses and will charge fees and expenses that are reasonable, legitimate, and commensurate with the services we deliver and the responsibility we accept.

9. We will disclose to our clients in advance any fees or commissions that we will receive for equipment, supplies, or services we recommend to our clients.

Profession

10. We will respect the intellectual property rights of our clients, other consulting firms, and sole practitioners and will not use propriety information or methodologies without permission.
11. We will not advertise our services in a deceptive manner and will not misrepresent the consulting profession, consulting firms, or sole practitioners.
12. We will report violations of this Code of Ethics.

The Council of Consulting Organizations, Inc. Board of Directors approved this Code of Ethics on January 8, 1991. The Institute of Management Consultants (IMC) is a division of the Council of Consulting Organizations, Inc.

Appendix I: Consulting Specialties (A Partial List)

By specialty

- Accounting
- Acoustics
- Actuary
- Administration
- Advertising-Consumer
- Advertising-Industrial
- Affirmative Action
- Appraisal
- Arbitration
- Architecture
- Association Management
- Audit
- Bankruptcy
- Barter
- Benefits
- Call Centers
- Cash Management
- Collections
- Communications
- Compensation
- Computer Aided Design
- Computer Aided Engineering
- Computer Aided Manufacturing
- Computer Hardware
- Computer Software
- Computer Training
- Construction
- Corporate Culture
- Cost Analysis
- Customer Service
- Data Collection
- Data Processing
- Design
- Direct Mail
- Disaster Recovery
- Distribution
- Downsizing
- Ecology
- Economics
- Empowerment
- Energy
- Engineering—Electrical
- Engineering—Industrial
- Engineering—Mechanical
- Environment
- Executive Search
- Facilitation
- Facilities
- Factory Automation
- Finance
- Fire Prevention
- Flood Control
- Forecasting
- Foreign Trade
- Franchising
- Fund Raising
- Heating/Air Conditioning
- Human Resources
- Image
- Import/Export
- Industrial Development
- Inspection
- Insurance
- Interim Personnel
- Interior Design
- Inventory
- Investments
- ISO 9000
- Job Costing
- Labor Relations
- Leadership
- Leasing
- Lighting
- Management
- Management Information Systems
- Manufacturing
- Manufacturing Information Systems
- Market Research
- Marketing—Industrial
- Marketing—Consumer
- Marketing—International
- Materials Handling
- Materials Management
- Media
- Meetings

❏ Merchandising
❏ Mergers/
   Acquisitions
❏ Metallurgy
❏ Minority Affairs
❏ Motivation
❏ New Product
   Development
❏ Office Automation
❏ Organization
❏ Outplacement
❏ Packaging
❏ Patents/Trade Marks
❏ Personnel
❏ Planning
❏ Politics
❏ Polling
❏ Pricing
❏ Productivity
❏ Project Management
❏ Pubic Relations
❏ Public Opinion

❏ Public Policy
❏ Publishing
❏ Quality Assurance
❏ Quality Control
❏ Quantitative Analysis
❏ Raw Materials
❏ Recreation
❏ Rehabilitation
❏ Relocation
❏ Renovation
❏ Reorganization
❏ Risk Management
❏ Roofing
❏ Safety
❏ Sales Promotion
❏ Sales Training
❏ Sanitation
❏ Scheduling
❏ SEC Filings
❏ Security
❏ Simulation
❏ Special Events

❏ Statistics
❏ Storage
❏ Strategic Planning
❏ Structural Design
❏ Succession
❏ System Design
❏ Systems Analysis
❏ Taxes
❏ Team Building
❏ Telemarketing
❏ Telephone Systems
❏ Testing
❏ Total Quality
   Management
❏ Trade Shows
❏ Training (other than
   computer or sales)
❏ Turnaround
❏ Value Engineering
❏ Workout
❏ Writing

By industry

❏ Aerospace
❏ Agriculture
❏ Automotive
❏ Aviation
❏ Banking
❏ Brokerage
❏ Charities
❏ Chemicals
❏ Commodities
❏ Communications
❏ Computers
❏ Construction
❏ Consumer
   Electronics
❏ Consumer Products
❏ Data Processing
❏ Distribution
❏ Education
❏ Electronics

❏ Energy
❏ Entertainment
❏ Financial Services
❏ Food and Beverage
❏ Forestry
❏ Government
❏ Health and Beauty
   Aids
❏ Health Care
❏ Heating/Ventilation/
   Air Conditioning
❏ Import/Export
❏ Insurance
❏ Law
❏ Leasing
❏ Manufacturing
❏ Media
❏ Metals
❏ Mining

❏ Not-for-Profit
❏ Packaging
❏ Petroleum
❏ Pharmaceuticals
❏ Plastics
❏ Raw Materials
❏ Real Estate
❏ Religion
❏ Retailing
❏ Services
❏ Telecommunications
❏ Textiles
❏ Trade Associations
❏ Transportation
❏ Travel and Leisure
❏ Utilities
❏ Ventilation
❏ Warehousing
❏ Wholesaling

Index

About the Author

Robert W. Bly is director of The Center for Technical Communication (CTC), a consulting firm providing on-site seminars in business and technical writing, marketing, selling, customer service, and personal productivity for corporate clients. CTC also provides a number of related services including marketing consultation and copywriting.

CTC has served more than 100 clients including AT&T, Lucent Technologies, Associated Global Systems, CoreStates, The Conference Board, BOC Gases, Wallace & Tiernan, Leviton Manufacturing, EBI Medical Systems, Optical Data Corporation, Value Rent-a-Car, Fielder's Choice, Grumman, Sony Corporation, Reed Travel Group, PSE&G, ADP, Agora Publishing, Medical Economics, Norwest Mortgage, and Ascom Timeplex.

Mr. Bly is the author of 40 books including *Selling Your Services* (Henry Holt & Co.), *The Elements of Business Writing* (Macmillan), and *Business-to-Business Direct Marketing* (NTC). His articles have appeared in such publications as *Cosmopolitan, Writer's Digest, Business Marketing, Computer Decisions, Chemical Engineering, Science Books & Films, Direct Marketing, New Jersey Monthly,* and *Amtrak Express.* He is editor of the monthly magazine, *Bits & Pieces for Salespeople,* published by Economics Press.

Bob holds a B.S. in chemical engineering from the University of Rochester. He has taught business communication at New York University and held marketing positions with Koch Engineering and Westinghouse Electric Corporation. He is a member of the American Institute of

Chemical Engineers, the Business Marketing Association, and the Institute of Management Consultants.

For the past several years, Bob's consulting practice has grossed between $200,000 and $300,000 annually. Since 1982, clients have paid Bob well over $2 million in consulting fees and royalties.

Questions and comments on this book may be sent to:

Bob Bly
Center for Technical Communication
22 E. Quackenbush Avenue
Dumont, NJ 07628
phone: 201-385-1220
fax: 201-385-1138
e-mail: rwbly@bly.com
Web site: www.bly.com